The Tanks

THE
TANKS

The History of the Royal Tank Regiment, 1945-1975

Major Kenneth Macksey,
M.C., R.T.R. (Retd.)

Foreword by
Field Marshal Lord Carver,
G.C.B., C.B.E., D.S.O., M.C.

ARMS AND ARMOUR PRESS
London—Melbourne

Published in Great Britain by
Arms and Armour Press, Lionel Leventhal Limited,
2-6 Hampstead High Street, London NW3 1QQ;
and in Australasia at
4-12 Tattersalls Lane, Melbourne, Victoria 3000.

British Library Cataloguing in Publication Data:
Macksey, Kenneth
The tanks.
1. Great Britain. Army. Royal Tank Regiment—History
I. Title
358'.18   UA656.R/
ISBN 0-85368-293-3

Contents

CONTENTS

Foreword

BY FIELD MARSHAL LORD CARVER,

G.C.B., C.B.E., D.S.O., M.C.

All those who are serving and who have served in the Regiment, as well as those who serve in it in the future, will be grateful to Major Kenneth Macksey for having written this account of the Regiment's activities since 1945. It is difficult to realize that the period which this volume covers is greater than that surveyed by Basil Liddell Hart's masterly two volumes from the birth of the tanks to the end of the Second World War. The experiences of the different units of the Regiment since then, and of its members, have been varied and have covered the globe. The Regiment has every reason to be as proud of its record in that time as it has rightly been of that of its earlier history.

Field Marshal

Preface

It is unusual for a Regiment of the British Army to commission a history about its activities in times of so-called peace. The two previous volumes of the History of the Royal Tank Regiment, covering, as they did in some detail, what went on between 1918 and 1939, dealt for the most part with the events of the two World Wars. And yet the years between 1945 and 1975 have been anything but tranquil, and there has been scarcely a moment when one element or another of the R.T.R.'s units have not been either in action or confronted by the expectation of it. The Regiment, along with the rest of the Army, has been exposed to challenge, not only along the contracting frontiers of the old British Empire, but in the forefront of the technological, institutional and sociological revolutions which have left practically nothing unchanged. In all these fields, members of the R.T.R. have played a notable part.

As a member of the Royal Armoured Corps from 1941 until 1968, and of the R.T.R. since 1946, I have found it both difficult and easy to write this history – difficult because of having lived at close quarters to the events under discussion and being emotionally involved as part of the Regimental family; easy – or made easier – because, knowing the Regiment and so many of its members as I do, the unstinted help I have been given has made the collection of material relatively simple. So I can only repeat the cautionary words of my predecessor, Captain B. H. Liddell Hart, in his Preface to Volumes I and II of *The Tanks*: 'Any reader who questions the facts or conclusions in it will find me very ready to agree that I may be wrong – though not necessarily with their alternative views.' In so far as it is possible, within the space of a single volume, I have tried to cover the major episodes which occurred between 1945 and 1975 and, at the same time, present a picture of life within the R.T.R. during that testing period.

Many members of the Regiment, both past and present, have contributed to this history. All have my thanks and, in most cases, will find themselves mentioned within the text. Several more have scrutinized and criticized the draft at various stages

10

of its preparation and, as a result, have made fresh contributions not only in establishing accuracy, but also in adding to content. With the deepest sense of gratitude I would like to thank them and record their names:

Field Marshal Lord Carver; General Sir Richard Ward; Major-Generals N. W. Duncan, L. W. A. Gingell, J. R. Holden, G. C. Hopkinson, H. A. Lascelles, R. G. Lawson, H. M. Liardet; Brigadiers H. J. B. Cracroft, J. K. Greenwood, J. P. Maxwell, D. J. O'Flynn, R. E. Simpkin, R. B. P. Wood, A. K. F. Walker, H. B. C. Watkins; Colonels A. R. Bissett, A. Cooper, J. A. Cowgill, J. G. R. Dixon, G. L. D. Duckworth, M. J. Evans, G. Fitz-Talbot, P. R. Hordern, R. R. Moss, E. F. Offord, G. Read; Lieutenant-Colonels J. J. Dingwall, K. Ecclestone, T. H. Gibbon, P. Hammond, S. I. Howard-Jones, J. F. Miller, J. Prichard, J. A. T. Slade, M. G. Tweed; Majors B. H. S. Clarke, A. J. Cornwell, I. J. B. Galloway, M. N. S. Moriarty, A. L. P. Weeks, C. J. Wieland.

In addition, the following officers from other Regiments kindly made important contributions besides giving permission to quote their remarks: Field Marshal Sir Richard Hull, late 17th/21st Lancers; Colonel J. D. Lunt, late 16th/5th Lancers; Lieutenant-Colonels A. C. Ansell, 13th/18th Hussars and J. S. F. Murray, 15th/19th Hussars; Colonel P. H. Hordern (Director of the Tank Museum), Colonel R. R. Moss (Armour School), Major B. H. S. Clarke and Sergeant W. Watling (both of R.H.Q., R.T.R.) – besides the Librarian and staff of the Ministry of Defence (Army) Library – also helped with the production of the book. Mr. R. Bonner very kindly drew the maps, and each unit of the Regiment sent in a great many photographs from which the final selection was made.

In addition, I wish to add my especial thanks to my closest colleague in the project, Lieutenant-Colonel W. F. Woodhouse, who carried out a great deal of painstaking research, who read the draft at two stages and who encouraged me by his forthright and entirely constructive criticism at all times.

In the final analysis, a Regiment writes its own History. So if I have managed to transmit to the reader the sensation of what it was like to belong to the R.T.R. during the years from 1945 to 1975, then it is principally due to the strength of purpose projected to me by the officers and men. Their sense of professionalism and their dedication to whatever job they had in hand, cannot but impress themselves upon anyone charged with the task of writing their story. It is to the human beings of this organization, dedicated to the service of machines, that the credit must go. — K.J.M.

List of
Abbreviations

A.A.	Anti-aircraft
A.A.C.	Army Air Corps
A.A.G.	Assistant Adjutant-General
A.B.T.U.	Army Basic Training Unit
A.D.C.	Aide-de-Camp
A.E.P.	Army Equipment Policy
A.E.R.	Army Emergency Reserve
A.F.V.	Armoured Fighting Vehicle
A.P.	Armour Piercing
A.P.C.	Armoured Personnel Carrier
A.P.C.B.C.	Armour-Piercing Cap, Ballistic, Capped
A.P.D.S.	Armour-Piercing Discarding Sabot
A.R.D.E.	Armament Research and Development Establishment
A.R.V.	Armoured Recovery Vehicle
A.T.G.W.	Anti-Tank Guided Weapon
A.T.O.	Ammunition Technical Officer
A.V.R.	Armoured Vehicle, Reconnaissance
B.A.O.R.	British Army of the Rhine
B.A.T.	Battalion Anti-Tank
B.T.E.	British Troops, Egypt
C.C.F.	Chinese Communist Forces
C.C.O.	Clandestine Communist Organization (Borneo)
C.D.B.	Combat Development Board
C.-in-C.	Commander-in-Chief
C.I.G.S.	Chief of the Imperial General Staff
C.I.V.	Central Inspectorate of Vehicles
C.O.	Commanding Officer
C.S.E.	Combined Services Entertainment
C.V.R.(T.)	Combat Vehicle, Reconnaissance, Tracked
C.V.R.(W.)	Combat Vehicle, Reconnaissance, Wheeled
D.A.A.	Deputy Assistant Adjutant
D.A.S.D.	Director of Army Staff Duties
D.C.I.G.S.	Deputy Chief of the Imperial General Staff
D.D.	Duplex Drive (swimming tank)
D.E.R.R.	Duke of Edinburgh's Royal Regiment
D.F.	Defensive Fire
D.G.	Dragoon Guards
D.G.F.V.	Director General of Fighting Vehicles
D.G.M.T.	Director General of Military Training
D.G.W.	Director General of Weapons
D.O.A.E.	Defence Operational Analysis Establishment
D.R.A.	Director of the Royal Artillery

LIST OF ABBREVIATIONS

D.R.A.C.	Director of the Royal Armoured Corps
D.W.R.	Duke of Wellington's Regiment
E.O.D.	Explosive Ordnance Disposal
E.R.E.	Extra-Regimentally Employed
E.S.B.A.	Eastern Sovereign Base Area (Cyprus)
E.T.W.	Equipment Trials Wing
F.L.O.S.Y.	Front for the Liberation of South Yemen
F.R.A.	Federal Regular Army (Aden Protectorate)
F.V.R.D.E.	Fighting Vehicles Research and Development Establishment
G.H.Q.	General Headquarters
G.M.C.	General Motors Company
G.O.C.	General Officer, Commanding
G.O.C.-in-C.	General Officer, Commanding, in Chief
G.S.	General Staff
G.S.O.	General Staff Officer
H.E.	High Explosive
H.E.A.T.	High Explosive Anti-Tank
H.E.S.H.	High Explosive Squash Head
H.M.S.O.	Her Majesty's Stationery Office
H.Q.	Headquarters
I.D.G.	Inniskilling Dragoon Guards
I.R.A.	Irish Republican Army
I.S.	Internal Security
K.A.P.E.	Keeping the Army in the Public Eye (slogan)
K.D.	Khaki Drill
K.R.R.C.	King's Royal Rifle Corps
L.A.D.	Light Aid Detachment
L.C.T.	Landing Craft, Tank
L.M.G.	Light Machine-Gun
L.S.T.	Landing Ship, Tank
L.V.T.	Landing Vehicle, Tracked
M.B.S.	Muzzle Bore Sight
M.Co.S.	Military College of Science
M.G.	Machine-gun
M.G.O.	Master General of the Ordnance
M.O.D.	Ministry of Defence
M.T.	Motor Transport
M.V.E.E.	Military Vehicles Engineering Establishment
N.A.A.F.I.	Navy Army and Air Force Institutes
N.A.T.O.	North Atlantic Treaty Organization
N.L.F.	National Liberation Front (Aden)
N.S.	National Service
N.S.Y.	North Somerset Yeomanry
O.B.	Ordnance Board
O.C.T.U.	Officer Cadet Training Unit
O. Group	Orders Group
O.L.O.S.	Organization for Liberation of Occupied South (Aden)
Op.	Operation
O.R.	Other Rank(s) or Operational Research

LIST OF ABBREVIATIONS

P.I.R.A.	Provisional Irish Republican Army
P.O.W.	Prisoner-of-War
P.S.P.	People's Socialist Party (Aden)
Q.D.G.	Queen's Dragoon Guards
Q.M.G.	Quartermaster General
Q.R.I.H.	Queen's Royal Irish Hussars
R.A.C.	Royal Armoured Corps
R.A.F.	Royal Air Force
R.A.O.C.	Royal Army Ordnance Corps
R.A.P.C.	Royal Army Pay Corps
R.A.R.D.E.	Royal Armament Research and Development Establishment
R.A.S.C.	Royal Army Service Corps
R. & D.	Research and Development
R. & R.	Rest and Recuperation (leave)
R.C.A.F.	Royal Canadian Air Force
R.C.L.	Recoilless
R.C.P.	Reflector-cum-Periscope (sight)
R.E.M.E.	Royal Electrical and Mechanical Engineers
R.G.	Ranging Gun
R.H.A.	Royal Horse Artillery
R.H.Q.	Regimental Headquarters
R.N.F.	Royal Northumberland Fusiliers
R.O.K.	Republic of Korea
R.S.M.	Regimental Sergeant-Major
R.T.R.	Royal Tank Regiment
R.U.C.	Royal Ulster Constabulary
R.U.R.	Royal Ulster Rifles
S.A.D.E.	Specialized Armoured Development Establishment
S.A.E.	Specialized Armoured Establishment
S.A.L.	South Arabian League
S.A.S.	Special Air Service
S.E.A.T.O.	South-East Asia Treaty Organization
S.L.R.	Self-Loading Rifle
S.P.	Self-propelled
S.Q.M.S.	Squadron Quarter-Master Sergeant
S.R.D.E.	Signals Research And Development Establishment
S.T.T.	School of Tank Technology
T.A.	Territorial Army
T.Q.M.S.	Technical Quarter-Master Sergeant
T.S.M.G.	Thompson Submachine-Gun
U.D.R.	Ulster Defence Regiment
U.N.F.I.C.Y.P.	United Nations Forces in Cyprus
V.C.P.	Vehicle Check Point
V.H.F.	Very High Frequency
W.D.	War Department
W.R.A.C.	Women's Royal Army Corps

CHAPTER I

Restoring the Frontiers
1945-1946

On the evening of 5 July 1945, a troop of Cromwell tanks, crewed equally by men of the 1st and 5th Royal Tank Regiment and led by Lieutenant B. H. S. Clarke of 5th R.T.R., entered Berlin. Travelling with them were the 11th Hussars, another famous unit of the Royal Armoured Corps which the R.T.R. had helped to mechanize in 1927, and with whom they were proud to share the honour of reaching the end of a long road which had started in Britain in 1939 and in Egypt in 1940. This was a supreme moment, fraught with symbolism. Clarke's command, the Defence Troop of H.Q. 131st Lorried Infantry Brigade, comprised men who had served in units which, at the outbreak of the Second World War, had been members of the original British armoured divisions – the 1st and the 7th Armoured Divisions. They represented two famous formations whose divisional signs, the rhinoceros and the jerboa (the celebrated desert rat), had been painted boldly along the route to victory, from El Alamein to Tunisia, through Sicily, Italy, France, Belgium, and Holland. At last they had reached the capital of Germany, the nation they had done so much to defeat. But of far greater significance was the immense pride these men of the Royal Tank Regiment could take in the magnitude of their achievement since 1916 when tanks first went into action. Now it had been demonstrated beyond dispute that the 'tank idea' which, prior to 1939, the R.T.C. had promoted against bigoted opposition, was a dominant factor in modern war. As a result of this triumphant vindication its officers and men enjoyed a reputation for determination and efficiency such as few regiments of the British Army could lay claim. For, confronted with immense difficulties and frustrated by failures, they had made miracles happen. And now, already, they were being confronted by the next set of problems.

Of intense interest to Clarke and his soldiers was the Russian Army. For the first time they were seeing elements of the huge organization which had played the major rôle in defeating the Germans on land, and which some believed might be the next enemy. Already, the ally of to-day was displaying an intransigence and bellicosity which could soon sour the ostensible comradeship of wartime. Certainly, the British column's sporadic progress through the Russian zone of occupation, to a destination and a task which had been agreed at the highest level, gave little cause for confidence in the quality of collaboration that might be expected in the future. Clarke recalls '. . . frequent and long delays whilst every sort of difficulty was placed in the way. Such delays meant little to the gun and tank crews who were self-supporting as ever and thus able to brew up whenever the opportunity occurred; but it was tiresome in the extreme for those travelling in personnel-carrying vehicles. The journey was not difficult . . . and at times interesting when passing leaguers of Russian tanks in nearby trees . . . However, it was somewhat *infra dig* to be overtaken by the occasional Russian cantering his horse along the road.' In Magdeburg there was a further halt caused by obdurate Russians – solved, so it was rumoured, by the Brigade Commander presenting a sentry with a packet of cigarettes – and an opportunity to see the Russian Army at closer quarters, with transport which '. . . seemed to consist so often of four or five "Lease-Lend" jeeps joined together by tow ropes and being pulled by a despondent horse'. Yet here was a force which had motored right across Europe, but which, at this moment, seemed to be approaching, as was the Soviet Union, total exhaustion.

So when at last all barriers were removed, an opportunity was given to the British to show off. Speeds of 40mph were reached, with some of the Cromwells' road tyres catching fire prior to entering the ruined city where they were cheered on their way by joyful West Berliners, emerging in relief from the cellars and shelters to watch the reception by Major-General 'Lou' Lyne, the Divisional Commander.

Throughout Europe, behind this spearhead troop, stood a regiment which had played a leading part in a war dominated by tanks, and in its contribution to the culminating triumph. From Flensburg, throughout Western Germany, Austria, Italy and Greece, units of the R.T.R. now performed unaccustomed duties – those of an occupying force. In Britain they provided a large proportion of the training and reinforcement elements which centred upon the Royal Armoured Corps A.F.V. School and Officer Cadet Training Unit at Bovington Camp, and in the six Royal Armoured Corps training regiments located at Carlisle, Barnard Castle and Catterick Camp, where the Royal Armoured Corps Depot was also to be found. In Britain, too, the 43rd Battalion was in the process of training and equipping with Grant Canal Defence Light (C.D.L.) tanks in readiness for transfer to the Far East where it was scheduled to take part in the forthcoming invasion of Malaya.[1] For in July, the war against Japan seemed likely to continue for at least another year. Parts of the British Empire, lost in 1941 and 1942, had yet to be recovered and there remained a duty to fight alongside the Americans in the conquest of the Japanese homeland – until, that is, the first atom bomb hit Hiroshima on 6 August.

It would be misleading, however, to claim that, in the summer of 1945, the attitude of the R.T.R. was so very different from that of the rest of the British Army, or that its attention was exclusively fixed upon prosecution of the war in the East, on administering the occupied countries or of cheerfully returning to the task of maintaining the security of the Empire and mandated territories. These tasks were obligatory, within the limitations imposed by post-war conditions. But inevitably, the resources available would be governed by the political and economic state of the nation, and conditioned by the anxiety of a majority of officers and men to return as quickly as possible to take up again the threads of their pre-war careers. A rapid, but controlled reduction in the size of the armed forces was important in order to restore, in an orderly manner, the nation's well-being. The release of men with special skills to fill key positions in industry was essential while, at the same time, no question of unfairness by queue jumping should be engendered in the remainder. A system of demobilization on the basis of age and length of wartime service was introduced and received general approval. As a result, there was nothing like the discontent and mutinous behaviour which had attended demobilization after the First World War. At the same time, a system known as PYTHON had been introduced to repatriate men who had served overseas for excessive periods. There were also two supplementary schemes, one known as LILOP (leave in lieu of PYTHON) and the other, LIAP (leave in addition to PYTHON). And, had someone in 2nd R.T.R. had his way, there might have been a third called LOLLIPOP (lots of little leaves in place of PYTHON).

The effects of these measures were unavoidably disruptive and often catastrophic for certain units. Almost overnight, crews which had lived and worked together as teams over months, and in some cases, years, were dispersed, leaving a

[1] Until 1946, units of the R.T.R. were designated as Battalions (although in some units the word was abandoned in 1940). Thereafter, the term was eventually abandoned by order of the King, and each unit was known officially by its number, as it is throughout this History – 1st Royal Tank Regiment, etc.

gap to be filled by the arrival of, often, uninterested officers and men from other units which had been disbanded. Once the war against Japan had ended on 2 September, the reduction of the regular army to its peace-time size gathered pace, a programme which was to hit the infantry far harder than it did the Royal Armoured Corps. For while the former would lose their second battalions when, in 1946, the old Cardwell System was abandoned in favour of a system of regimental grouping (and thus see their strength of 138 battalions in 1939 reduced to 73 by 1947), the armoured units would merely return to their pre-war strength of two regiments of Household Cavalry, 20 of Cavalry and 8 of R.T.R. But it would take two years to implement the initial changes, shrinkage being governed by random variations due to fluctuations in operational commitments. For example, it was easier to discard wartime units in areas such as Germany and Italy, where the army's rôle could be fairly easily foreseen, than it would be in the Middle and Far East where the political situation was in a state of flux. As a result, in 1945 the R.T.R. immediately lost its 9th, 11th, 12th, 48th and 51st battalions of those still remaining at the beginning of the year, while units then being employed on essential peace-keeping rôles in Greece and India survived. For that reason, the ex Territorial Army, 40th (Lieutenant-Colonel R. A. Maclaren), 46th (Lieutenant-Colonel R. A. H. Walker) and the 50th (Lieutenant-Colonel J. R. D. Carlton) stayed in Greece in 23rd Armoured Brigade (Brigadier R. H. B. Arkwright, late 12th Lancers) and the 43rd (Lieutenant-Colonel E. H. Gibbon) found plenty to do in India, as will be described later. Cross-postings were frequent as disbanded units sent men with a sufficient length of time to serve alongside the volunteers (who opted to extend their service) in the remaining units. There they met comrades from the abandoned wartime cavalry units, the Reconnaissance Corps, and the mechanized infantry units who had been formed into Regiments, Royal Armoured Corps. The scene was one of constant movement and not infrequent turmoil at a time when the R.T.R. was trying to re-establish itself on a firm peace-time footing. It is all the more creditable that, far from breaking under the strain, a quite remarkable strength was forged – and all the more interesting that it was achieved with remarkably little assistance or guidance from a central regimental agency.

When, with the formation of the R.A.C., the R.T.C. Depot gave way to the R.A.C. Depot in April 1939, the R.T.R. was deprived of its official home. For the next six years, with its roots deeply embedded in Bovington, it had maintained in that camp an office for the administration of the Regimental Association and Benevolent Fund. In 1944, this had been expanded when an office for the Representative Commandant was set up, run by the Association's secretary, and staffed by two misemployed clerks provided, unofficially, by R.A.C. Records. The Representative Colonel Commandant, Lieutenant-General Sir Charles Broad, also maintained an office at his home, but this presented difficulties in 1945 when 'home' for him became Ireland, and contact therefore was mainly by post or on his occasional visits to England. This lack of a properly established central regimental agency at a crucial time in the regiment's development, could have caused disaster. But if some things did go wrong, it was clearly the system which was at fault and not the man at the helm. Broad is renowned for his leading rôle between the wars in creating modern armoured formations controlled by radio, but his part afterwards in re-establishing the regiment is no less remarkable when all the handicaps are taken into account.

In a series of meetings held at Bovington between June and November 1945, a policy was thrashed out and action commenced on a variety of projects. Lieutenant-Colonel D. J. McLeod, who ran the R.T.R. Association and Benevolent Fund, also acted as secretary to the Representative Colonel Commandant, and the commanding officers of regiments were asked if they would staff the Colonel Commandant's office with clerks on loan – an improvisation of the sort that would be employed until the day an established Regimental Headquarters was approved by the War Office more than ten years later. Important among the list of objectives was the establishment of a system for the selection of prospective officers, a task which up to then had been left to a variety of agencies from commanding officers to AG 17 Branch at the War Office. Yet, at this stage, insufficient thought seems to have been given to achieving balance within the total regimental establishment and, in consequence, some of the older age groups became over-stocked and some of the younger ones were allowed to fall below the desired number. In due course a moment would arrive when certain younger officers with highly satisfactory qualifications would have to be either diverted to other regiments or be lost to the army for ever. As for the selection of officers for promotion, hardly any attention seems to have been given to this at the time, while the administration of warrant officers and non-commissioned officers was left entirely in the hands of the Officer in Command R.A.C. Records.

Attempts were made to obtain the views of commanding

officers on a variety of subjects. A letter was circulated in July 1945 and the answers to its inquiries were sifted in October. But the decisions of the October meeting were distributed through selected senior officers in the theatres where units of the Regiment were located – leaving some COs, it appears, unaware of the decisions reached. This promoted a sense of isolation and, with it, a tendency by frustrated commanding officers to strike out on their own. In September, for example, 1st R.T.R. had sent a signal of Greeting to H.M. the King, as Colonel-in-Chief, on its own behalf and not that of the R.T.R. Nevertheless, solid foundations had been laid by placing the administration of regimental funds on a firm footing, by appointing officers to make visits to schools in search of officer candidates and recruits, with special emphasis on 'the more brainy types who show aptitude for the technical side'. At the same time, interviews at the Colonel Commandant's office were initiated.

Besides this, the publication of *The Tank* was placed under the control of a committee and a more attractive format for the magazine was agreed. Measures were taken to strengthen the Band and, by the end of 1946, the Regimental March, 'My Boy Willie', would be rewritten by the Bandmaster, Mr. D. J. Plater, to include a folk-song from Cambrai called 'Cadet Roussel' (a popular hero of the French Revolution). Some projects met with opposition, the one for an Officers' Club in London being high in this category – the objectors predicting that, like another such club called 'The Goat', it would be insufficiently used – a forecast which proved all too correct as the years went by. As for the Tank Museum, which had survived the war with the loss of a few prize specimens, the chances of its continuance were rated poor. Accommodation was hard to come by, it would be difficult to find a curator, and the fund stood at precisely £85. So far, all its curators have come from the Regiment, but no one at that time foresaw the day when the Royal Armoured Corps Tank Museum would stand among the most successful military museums in the world. Nor did anyone foresee that it would take the combined labour of Captain B. H. Liddell Hart and others, 13 years to write and publish the Regimental History – *The Tanks*. Yet so it was to prove after the decision to commission it had been taken in 1946. It is to the credit of Major-General Sir Percy Hobart (Hobo), who later persuaded several hard-working senior officers to write various sections, that Volume 2 was saved from disaster.

Knowing little of what their country and the colonels commandant had in store for them, the officers and men of the

Regiment set about adjusting themselves to a changing world, in various stations where the dissimilarity of service was considerable. To the victors were given the spoils of war. This meant that, so far as the Regiment in Germany and Austria was concerned, it occupied buildings far superior, for the most part, to those occupied by the indigenous and deprived local populace. Armoured units found themselves quartered on airfields, and in the good barracks previously occupied by the tank regiments of the defeated enemy. Likewise, the food and recreational facilities they enjoyed were among the best in Europe, living as they were off what little fat was left in the land. In the autumn of 1945, the Germans were on the threshold of starvation and, particularly in the damaged urban areas, were living in squalor. Their country, too, was swarming with hundreds of thousands of displaced persons (D.P.s) from all over Europe, whose depredations had to be controlled, and for whom camps had to be found if they could not be repatriated to their country of origin – as was all too frequently the case for many people from the Communist occupied East. D.P. administration was one initial task: in due course, 1st R.T.R., for example, found itself training Yugoslavs for the Civil Mixed Watchmen's Service, later known as the Military Service Organization. In Austria, conditions were slightly better and in Italy, better still, but how each regiment spent its time was decided very largely by the nature of greatly varying tasks.

While Japan remained in the war, units not condemned to instant disbandment could be divided into two clear categories – those which would remain in Europe and those destined for the Near or Far East. The R.T.R. was to provide three regiments for the Far East, each assembling in a different theatre, to become the collecting-points for officers and men who volunteered for the duty, or whose eligibility for service was unaffected by PYTHON or early demobilization. The 43rd (Lieutenant-Colonel E. H. Gibbon) assembled in England, the 4th (Lieutenant-Colonel A. Jolly) in Germany and the 8th (Lieutenant-Colonel S. D. W. Seaver) in Italy, on the shores of Lake Bracciano. For the 8th, the experience was, perhaps, the most traumatic because it had served overseas for much longer than the other two and so contained a very small proportion of members who could remain. Almost overnight, the old and tried 8th died, and a new regiment was born, composed mostly of officers and men posted in. But then the Japanese surrendered and the reconstituted unit was flown back to England at the end of August to make ready for overseas service elsewhere.

The 43rd, on the other hand, sailed to India and a peace-keeping rôle, while the 4th remained in Kreis Tecklenburg, the latter, according to its report to *The Tank* (whose pages reflect so well the attitudes and multifarious tasks undertaken by the R.T.R. throughout the post-war years) '. . . carrying out what is known as battlefield clearance, and the result has been the reporting of the location of heavy bombs which no one is prepared to move'. Assisting, too, in hampering the Black Market '. . . which is rampant throughout Germany. Patrols have helped minimize the traffic in food, and though arrests have been made, it is thought that only a change in policy will stop the gamble against hunger.' Precautions to deal with civil disturbances, should they occur, were taken, for after the threatened sabotage by Nazi 'Werewolves' failed to materialize, something more spontaneous was expected from a people whose living conditions were bad and whose spirit was unbroken. But in Germany very little happened, although 2nd R.T.R. in Austria helped round up some former members of the S.S. in September, and had the job of guarding a power-station as well as explosives at various coal-mines and at Austria's only explosives factory.

As a result of such duties, the R.T.R. in Europe spent but a small part of its time training with tanks, and its standards suffered. Only rarely in 1945, and for the better part of 1946, did they undertake serious exercises. A relaxed atmosphere replaced wartime tension, as people tried to indulge in the delights of peace-time pursuits. The delayed arrival of families until August 1946, caused by the shortage of accommodation, affected morale. From the end of July 1945, the first of many permanent, as well as temporary, liaisons with German girls were formed, after fraternization (which had been banned between members of the occupation forces and the Germans) was allowed. Higher training was subordinated to occupation duties (often on foot), individual training, educational courses, pre-release courses, sport and relaxation. Under these circumstances, commanding officers were hard put to maintain high standards.

Ceremonial also played its part and with it the sort of celebration which, in the ensuing years, was to be featured by units of the British Army of the Rhine. On 30 August 1945, 1st R.T.R., mounted in their Comet tanks, drove up the Autobahn with other units of 7th Armoured Division, to enter Berlin prior to taking part there in an Allied victory parade. Four abreast, the Comets, led by Major J. J. Dingwall, swept down the Charlottenburger Chaussee and through the Tiergarten to dip their guns in salute to Marshal of the Soviet Union

George Zhukov. This rôle was an honour in itself, but it is more than likely that the R.T.R. took even greater pride in its own, subsequent, regimental parade held in Berlin on 20 September. On this occasion, 1st R.T.R. was inspected by its newly-appointed Colonel Commandant, Field Marshal Sir Bernard Montgomery, who had replaced General Sir Hugh Elles when he died in June. Thus the man who had won the first great tank victory gave way to another whose victories were largely won with armour.

This event marked a turning-point in the R.T.R.'s history, symbolizing as it did the changeover from war to peace-time soldiering. 'Monty's' associations with the R.T.R. could be traced back to the day he had married Betty Carver (née Hobart) in 1927 and thus found himself exposed frequently to the influence of her brother 'Hobo', one of the R.T.R.'s most forceful and far-sighted leaders – who, before the war, had raised 1st Tank Brigade and 7th Armoured Division and, during its course, 11th and 79th Armoured Divisions. Since then, as C.-in-C. of Eighth Army, of 21st Army Group and now of the British Army of the Rhine, there was scarcely a unit of the Regiment that the Field Marshal had not, at some time or another, taken under his command in winning victories in which tanks predominated. With Sir Percy Hobart in close attendance, and the 1st under the command of Lieutenant-Colonel P. R. C. Hobart, he now presented medal ribbons to officers and men from several other R.T.R. battalions in recognition of their services in the war, and spoke to a gathering which included many senior members of the R.T.R., besides those who one day would become its leaders. He remembered past glories and the rôles that the R.T.R. had played between the wars in fostering 'the tank idea', '. . . in spite of the many obstacles put in its way and of obsolete equipment'. He recalled that it was the trained men of the Regiment who had made it possible for the cavalry regiments to change over rapidly to armour. Turning to the future and, with the authority vested in him as Chief of the Imperial General Staff, designate, he declared:

'We now need in England a strong establishment devoted to research and experiment in all types of A.F.V. This has already been started, and the R.T.R. must play a leading part in its organization and development. The Regiment has made a great name for itself both in peace and in war. We must see that that name prospers in the years that lie ahead. I myself am sure we will not experience again the great difficulties with which the Regiment was faced before the war. I personally shall do everything in my power to promote the interests of the Regiment

23

in every possible sphere. I am confident that in exactly the same way as the R.T.R. has played a leading part in the Armoured Corps during the war, it will continue to do so during peace.'

The roll of those who were in Berlin for the parade contained the names of men who had been bound together by the travails of the past and would guide R.T.R.'s destiny in the years to come. Besides Sir Percy Hobart, there was Major-General G. P. B. Roberts, Brigadier N. W. Duncan, Brigadier R. M. P. Carver, Colonel A. Jolly, Lieutenant-Colonel R. E. Ward and Lieutenant-Colonel P. R. C. Hobart, all of whom, within the next thirty years, became colonels commandant, and much more besides, in the Army's hierarchy. Neither of the other two colonels commandant, Broad and Major-General G. M. Lindsay, was able to attend, but the number might have been larger had not an aeroplane run into difficulties over the Alps, compelling its crew and passengers to take to their parachutes. Fortunately for the R.T.R., Major-General H. L. Birks, and Brigadiers J. L. C. Napier, C. W. M. Timmis and H. R. B. Foote, V.C., landed safely on a mountain side and shared nothing more serious than a broken leg and a broken ankle between them. At this time, however, the Regiment's impetus came as much from Sir Percy Hobart as from Broad. He was behind the notion that the Regiment should be more closely knit. The informal discussions he promoted (though not in Berlin) would, in due course, create a Regimental Council.

The Field Marshal's remarks about research and development into new A.F.V.s were already in process of translation into fact. At the end of the war, the units of the R.T.R. were equipped with Comets, Cromwells, Shermans, Churchills, Grants, Stuarts or a mixture of a strange specialized menagerie of armoured vehicles such as Crocodiles, Crabs, Kangaroos, Buffaloes and Arks. But of these, only the Comet could be reckoned as a match for the best tanks that the Germans had fielded, or which the Russians possessed in immense quantities. A few Centurions (Operation 'Sentry') had been sent post-haste to Germany in the closing days of the war, but had not arrived in time for action. This tank, with its well-sloped armour, was quite clearly far in advance of anything Britain had built hitherto. Armed, in the first instance, with the obsolescent 17-pounder gun, whose accuracy in elevation fell off beyond 800 metres, it was in need of development, and its introduction into service would also be curtailed by stringent cuts, as money was quickly diverted from armaments to the needs of peace.

In June, the Army Council set up a Land Movement Committee under Professor C. D. Ellis, with the D.R.A.C., Major-

General R. Briggs, and the veteran tank engineer, H. R. Ricardo, among its members. Its task was to produce a paper on 'The Present State of Land Movement – A.F.V.s' – the intention being to see what measures might be taken to make these vehicles independent of civil resources in their mobility. This problem was acute because at the end of the war some fighting tanks in service were so large as to be demonstrably immobile. The Germans had employed Royal Tigers, weighing 68 tons, and Jagd Tigers of 70 tons, and were experimenting with Maus which was in the region of 190 tons; already they had appreciated that these machines were too clumsy. The biggest of the Russian Josef Stalin tanks then in service – the JS3 – weighed only 47 tons but it had a 122mm. gun. The British were experimenting with the Tortoise S.P. gun of 78 tons, a bit below the 85 tons which the Director of Royal Artillery, as it happened, specified as the expected weight of the future, heavy S.P. anti-tank gun which the Royal Artillery required to fulfil its anti-tank rôle. Eventually, reason would prevail and weights would be reduced, but at that time the British and the Americans, who felt they had suffered from lack of a tank like the Tiger, were anxious to copy their late enemy. Simultaneously, specialized armour, Hobo's interest, was enjoying a vogue. It was the intention to establish in the Far East, under Brigadier N. W. Duncan, a Headquarters similar to that of the old 79th Armoured Division, with a task that was not only operational, but also to carry out Trials and Development.

Tank design policy went into the melting-pot once the war was over. The development of current vehicles was either stopped or delayed, while deep consideration was given to an entirely new range. Nevertheless, Sir Percy Hobart's scheme for a Specialized Armoured Development Establishment (S.A.D.E.), in England, was allowed to begin at a time when his immense experience and enthusiasm, allied to the strong support he was then receiving from the C.I.G.S., Field Marshal Sir Alan Brooke, and from Montgomery, made him difficult to resist. At the first R.A.C. Conference, held at Bovington in November 1945, S.A.D.E. (later named S.A.E. because F.V.R.D.E. claimed exclusive rights for development) was publicized by its commander. Indeed Hobo's was the only voice to sound a *fortissimo* note in a conference chiefly spent, apart from domestic issues, in confirming the validity of existing armoured establishments and practices. The Corps would have to wait until the R.A.C. Conference of 1947 before it heard open discussion of the policy which Montgomery had evolved, when he came in person, as C.I.G.S., to propound his views.

In the Chair at the '45 and '46 conferences was Briggs who had been well grounded by Hobo in experience of directorate matters before the war and who, since then, had commanded 1st Armoured Division at El Alamein before becoming D.R.A.C. in 1943. In the audience, apart from the senior members of the Corps, sat representatives from all the overseas theatres as well as the War Office and the Experimental Establishments. Taking as his creed the philosophy that armoured warfare had a distinct and vital future, Field Marshal Montgomery outlined his views on the sort of tank which would be needed to make that possible. The Centurion, he said, was a very good tank, and its successor, the A 45, would be even better; an A.F.V. to be known as FV 201 and designed to satisfy Montgomery's demand for what he called a 'universal tank' – one belonging to the FV 200 series which were intended to perform every desirable armoured rôle. It was intended that FV 201 be a well-armoured gun tank, capable of engaging enemy armour on at least equal terms, of being readily convertible to flame, for swimming and as a bulldozer. Some would be built specially as flails. In addition, there would be a wide range of supporting armoured vehicles to replace the hotchpotch of British and American machines then in service. But for financial reasons, it was explained, they would all be a long time in arriving.

For the officers and men of the units, therefore, it was a question of making the best of what equipment they had, of endeavouring to improve their living conditions and waiting in an atmosphere of national economic gloom while the shape of the post-war army became more clearly defined. Again, it was Montgomery who, in June 1946, pronounced to the Army Council, in his inimitably clear manner, what he believed to be the correct Army policy, a policy, it must be emphasized, which was the product of consultations with his contemporaries and subordinates in addition to his own experience in peace and war.

This boiled down to the need for a force which was:

1. Balanced between its regular and citizen elements.
2. Deployed, in so far as the regulars were concerned, as garrison and internal security troops throughout the Empire with strategic reserves in the U.K. and Middle East.
3. Trained and educated to deal with modern warfare.
4. Used to working in close co-operation with the Royal Air Force.

Because the C.I.G.S. placed man management first in his list of requirements, he attached a high priority to his call for much improved standards of accommodation, and far more constructive training and employment than had often been the case before war. Employing his well-developed technique of public relations promotion, Montgomery drew the attention of the Press to the weaknesses and needs of the Army, at a time when it was still populated by the residue of wartime servicemen. When he spoke of each man having a room to himself and being treated in a milder way than was often the case, it seemed as if a revolution were in the offing – as indeed it was to some extent. How this would work out once the Army had become entirely regular remained to be seen. Recruitment of sufficient men of the right quality would be crucial – as the Army Council realized long before Montgomery became C.I.G.S. One mark of their concern was the totally revised Pay Code announced in the spring of 1946, a subject as dear to soldiers as it was to the vast majority of the world's workers.

Nobody would have denied that, in the war's aftermath, pay scales had evolved to a state of such complexity that nobody really understood them, waste as much time as they might in attempting to do so. In addition to his basic rates of pay and marriage allowance, an officer might be entitled to many other kinds of allowance. Soldiers could receive all kinds of supplements of a nature related to their location or their trade, as well as for long service and good conduct. It required a walking computor to understand it all in the days before electronic computors, and before the Royal Army Pay Corps began to attach its specialists to regiments to save regimental soldiers from the worries and errors induced by so complex a subject. As every army unit knew to its cost, injustice and avoidable fraud were only too frequently generated in unit pay offices staffed by officers and clerks who did not fully comprehend a specialist's task the performance of which, they hoped, was only of temporary duration.

The War Office with its financial advisers tried to simplify matters with a revised Pay Code brought into force on 1 July 1946. At one swoop, most officers' allowances were abolished in an attempt to dispense with anomalies. Only ration and marriage allowance would continue, and additional pay would be granted only for such activities as parachuting and piloting aircraft, as well as for special technical and staff qualifications. Prospects were improved when advancement in rank was put on a more generous footing than before the war. Promotion up to the rank of major would take place at clearly specified intervals so that, after 13 years, an officer was assured of the rank of major (providing he passed an exam) with gross emoluments of £867 per annum.

This was fairly easy to grasp, but the same cannot be said for the arrangement wished upon the other ranks, whose pay would depend upon a complicated Star System geared to trade qualifications, rank and service. For fifteen years it would baffle the Army, the R.A.C. units, with their high proportion of tradesmen, suffering more than most. In an effort to create incentives, fairness may also have been sought by those who devised the system, but it was small wonder that it was misunderstood, and the War Diaries repeatedly refer to the damaging effect the Star System had on morale. Anomalies there continued to be. Margins, for example, were narrow; a three star corporal with an increment of 6d per day after four years service received 10/– per day, while a newly-promoted sergeant, with the highest trade qualification, received but 12/–, and one without a normal crew trade, as little as 10/6d. Another problem concerned the decision to lower the age for marriage to 25 in the case of officers, 21 for other ranks. Again it was decreed, in equity, that a man married prior to 1 July 1946, the date of implementation, would be paid the new and higher rate even if he were still below the statutory age. As a result, a number of members of the R.T.R. (and other regiments), for quite original reasons, had to hasten forward their nuptials.

While reorganization from the centre was moving in what, in retrospect, can be seen as a purposeful and well-intentioned manner, events on the periphery of the Army's zone of responsibility were producing strains to which the Government and the War Office had to react by varying their plans. In India and in Palestine, pressures were already mounting before the end of the war, and these will be described in the next chapter.

In Greece, the 40th, 46th and 50th in 23rd Armoured Brigade spent their time in contented comfort among a populace who were enduring severe deprivations in the aftermath of the civil war which the British Army had helped to end early in 1945. Had it not been for massive Allied aid, conditions might have been a lot worse. Were it not for the extremely friendly relations enjoyed by the Army with the people among whom they often lived in close association, the turmoil of a classic Balkans imbroglio might have been even worse than it was. Equipped initially with Sherman tanks, and latterly with a mixture of Shermans plus Staghound and Daimler armoured cars, the brigade was spread about the country, sometimes in squadron detachments, between Athens and Salonika. The rôle was one that would become increasingly familiar to the Army as the years passed. Peace would be maintained while the local indigenous army was reconstructed and trained to deal with a Communist threat. At the same time, every effort would be made in a foreign country to enhance morale among the soldiers, many of whom dearly wished to be back in Britain and out of uniform. But in Greece, throughout 1945, the atmosphere was relaxed and there were compensations. The days often passed in a holiday and carnival fashion. At one period of September 1945, the 50th had 422 men absent on leave simultaneously; on another occasion, it ran an Olde Englishe Carnival at Loutraki, a popular watering-place on the Gulf of Corinth, and raised £200 for the R.T.R. Benevolent Fund.

By the end of the year, the process of rehabilitating the Greek Army had advanced so promisingly that all three R.T.R. units were scheduled for suspended animation early in 1946. But the danger of disturbances at the forthcoming elections delayed this stroke until April when the entire 23rd Armoured Brigade, with its three T.A. units, was expunged from the Order of Battle. They left but a few days before the second civil war erupted along the frontiers with Albania, Yugoslavia and Bulgaria and led to a conflict in which the British Army was to play mainly a watching rôle.

No sooner was one confrontation over than another took its place, and often there would be several going on at once. At the same time as guerilla activities simmered along the southern frontier of Yugoslavia with Greece, a new threat attracted the public eye in the north, centred upon the long disputed territory of Venezia Giulia, claims to which had been lodged by both Yugoslavia and Italy.

2nd R.T.R. had gained experience of Yugoslav partisans during the immediate aftermath of the war, when A Squadron had been sent to an area near Jalarea on Austria's southern border. Here, rival bands of those owning allegiance to Marshal Tito's Communists and those loyal to the Royalist General Draja Mikhailovich, confronted each other in open hostility. The task of the tank squadron was to keep the protagonists apart, and this they did by diplomatic consultations coupled with the deployment of the tanks in positions separating the two sides. When a partisan attack was threatened, the tanks would fire their guns in a harmless direction to cause confusion and disrupt the respective predatory schemes. But at one desperate moment they felt the need to rearm German prisoners-of-war to stiffen up the peace-keeping force. At the end of 1945, however, the emphasis of policing shifted from Austria to Italy when it looked as if the Yugoslavs and Italians might clash over Venezia Giulia. The 2nd found itself hastily transferred with its tanks, in winter, to draughty, ancient 'summer' barracks at Palmanova, which had been designed in the past for horsed units. Standing among medieval fortifications, the narrow entrances were not designed for tanks, which consequently had to be parked outside the fortifications.

A clear impression of the task awaiting the 2nd, and a description of the means at its disposal, is provided by its Operation Instruction No. 1, laying down the procedures to be adopted if it became necessary to move to a forward concentration area in order to maintain law and order. It was a problem beset by the usual manpower difficulties, aggravated by the change of station having coincided with a conversion programme from Sherman to Churchill tanks. Whoever wrote the instruction may have indulged himself, but at the same time he outlined the state of so many armoured units at that time:

'The regt is at present organized mainly on a peacetime basis in that crews have not been organized, squadrons have not been practised and a great many administrative arrangements are static and could not be made mobile without considerable preparation. There is no intention at present of departing from the routine of individual trng or normal peace-time adm, but it is necessary to make various preparations to ensure that both sqns and the regt adm machine could function efficiently on a mobile basis if called upon to do so. It is not possible to give any period of notice but it may be assumed that more than one day would be available.'

Seemingly trying not to appear alarmist at what might be in store, but determined that his regiment could go into action 'efficiently and rapidly', Lieutenant-Colonel H. A. Lascelles (who was acting Brigade Commander at that moment) divided 2nd R.T.R. into an operational and a non-operational element:

'Operational
RHQ.
A Sqn, equipped mainly with Churchill Tanks.
C Sqn, equipped with Sherman Tanks.
Recce Tp, equipped with Stuart Recce Tks and Scout Cars.
HQ Sqn, containing the adm vehs.
In addition all available crews of B Sqn will accompany the operational portion of the regt [as spare crews and for a variety of other tasks].
Non Operational
B Sqn less operational crews.
All vehs, baggage and eqpt which does not accompany the

operational element.

All personnel of the regt due for early release or early PYTHON. For the present this will be:

Release up to Gp 27 incl.

PYTHON due for release before end of Mar.

Personnel under trng in C Sqn who are not yet sufficiently trained.'

The call to intervene in the squabble between two jealous nations soon came. Everyone had to be on his guard against becoming involved in arguments between excited citizens. Those who ventured into Trieste and the towns which were hotbeds of dissent had to take care. Training went on in an atmosphere of tension and, as fighting seemed imminent between the rival factions in the summer of 1946, the troops and squadrons moved into the hills or became engaged on the ranges in Northern Italy, living in their tanks and practising drills which had partly been forgotten in a year of peace. Some contemporary accounts portray this period as one of benign contentment for the 2nd, and for the 4th as well when they were sent to Italy in January 1946, there to join forces with the 6th (Lieutenant-Colonel G. Gaisford) which had returned there in October 1945. But it was not always so, and a lot of hard work was demanded. Among other things, a victory parade was held in Trieste on the orders of the corps commander, not as an expression of triumph but, as Lascelles recalls, 'as a device, since there was reason to believe that on a certain day, a massive infiltration would take place from Yugoslavia to seize the city. The victory parade, by a display of strength, was intended to frustrate this.' As Lascelles writes, 'Yugoslav orators who hoped to inflame the population found their voices drowned by the noise of the assembling tanks. Later it rained and this helped too. There were several other crises, but none so bad.'

The 4th (Lieutenant-Colonel F. I. C. Wetherell) would occupy Palmanova in August 1946 after the 2nd moved out. In the meantime, families began to arrive from the United Kingdom now that, at last, sufficient houses were available and the transport services had acquired adequate facilities. For hitherto, it had been normal practice for soldiers on the so-called Medloc Route to travel in cattle-trucks reclining on straw, while, even if they were lucky enough to be put in carriages, there was every likelihood that the windows would be missing, even in winter. The presence of four units of the Regiment (2nd, 4th and 6th in Italy, and the 8th (Lieutenant-Colonel N. E. B. C. Mahoney) in Austria) within motoring distance of each other was stimulating to regimental spirit. Sporting fixtures could be played and visits could be exchanged amid the rich variety of lakes and mountain slopes to be found in this historic corner of Europe. Despite the rather primitive accommodation that was sometimes provided in an area permeated by bandits – a ruined factory in Zaule and a cave at Costova, for example – this was a popular posting, even when the Bora blew and its icy blast penetrated every corner of rickety rooms. It was a time which each of the four regiments would recall nostalgically, after they had left for their next destinations – and found themselves in circumstances of deprivation, as the nation to which they belonged entered a state of economic siege.

CHAPTER II

The Initial Withdrawals
1945-1947

Of all the R.T.R. battalions, none can have spent a more frustrating time during the Second World War than the 43rd. Converted to armour in 1938, from the 6th Battalion Royal Northumberland Fusiliers, it remained in Britain for most of the time, engaged initially on anti-invasion duties until the winter of 1941, when it became part of 33rd Armoured Brigade, preparing itself for the day when it would take part in an invasion of the Continent. It nearly went to Sicily during the summer of 1943, but at the last minute the Canadians were sent instead. As a reward for the experimental work it had done for the specialized armour of Hobo's 79th Armoured Division, it might have led the invasion of Normandy, but it was diverted and was not given another opportunity for action until February 1945. This time, equipped with Grant C.D.L. tanks and Shermans, it trained for a rôle in the closing campaign against the Japanese in the Far East, and sailed from Britain in July. But just a few days prior to arrival at Bombay, the Americans dropped the atom bomb on Hiroshima and so, by the time 43rd unloaded its last tanks on 6 September, the war was over. Then, as a final insult, it was denied a part in Operation 'Button' (the reoccupation of Malaya) and the troops had to console themselves with the delights of soldiering in India, accommodated in good barracks, working when the temperature allowed and engaging in sport and expeditions to those parts of the sub-continent which had fascinated their forefathers.

The 43rd (Lieutenant-Colonel E. H. Gibbon), joined a few months later by the 7th, were the last units of the R.T.R. to be granted these unrivalled facilities. Before the war, the political struggles of the educated minority of Indians had gained them the promise of independence. Throughout the war years the threat and occasional outbreak of dissidence had prevented the Government from being able to rely entirely upon Indian collaboration, although the loyal part played by the Indian Army in nearly every theatre of war had been of incalculable value to the British war effort. The Indian Army's cavalry regiments, whose mechanization owed much to the training provided by the Royal Tank Corps and the school it had established before the war at Ahmednagar, were soon able to stand on their own feet, and the Indian Armoured Corps, formed on 1 May 1940, was the natural growth from that mechanization. In the Middle East, on their own soil and in Burma, the Indian armoured regiments had fought hard along-side their mentors and by the end of the war were a force to be reckoned with. But, as peace returned, the seeds of partition and dissent were sown. In September, amidst intense political activity and an undercurrent of communal disorder, the British Government of Mr. C. R. Attlee admitted that, when the British eventually withdrew, the sub-continent might have to be divided between Hindus and Muslims – a split which would separate the regiments of the Indian Army quite as funda-mentally as it would undermine British power in India.

The British Army in India, of which the 43rd became part, was in a bad way. Their infantry element had been disrupted by **PYTHON** and a mood of discontent permeated some units, bordering on (and sometimes crossing) the line of mutiny. On the one hand, the Army had to be ready to support the Civil Power, whose police forces were as susceptible to infection by the current trend of rebellion as was every other element of the community. On the other hand, it had to be ready to deal with trouble within its own ranks (such as men refusing to get up in the morning or of declining to embark in troopships), and it was from this source that a serious outbreak of unrest stemmed early in 1946 and involved the 43rd.

A mutiny by members of the R.A.F. in Calcutta, conducted under the guise of a strike, and settled by negotiation, coincided with unrest among the Indians over the court-martialling in Delhi of three officers who had belonged to the renegade (in British eyes) Indian National Army, which had fought along-side the Japanese as a means to win Indian freedom. Taking their cue, the Royal Indian Air Force also mutinied, rather ineffectually, for a short period in January. At that moment, A and C Squadrons of the 43rd happened to be collecting tanks in Bombay and they were placed on stand-by, but, fortunately, did not become seriously involved. They were in the middle of a major redeployment throughout India, with tank squadrons on the eve of departure to Calcutta, Nowshera and Agra, besides the one that would remain in the vicinity of Bombay and were, therefore, ill-prepared for serious .trouble. But a month later, when serious rioting broke out as the Royal Indian Navy mutinied at Bombay and its members came ashore to lead the mobs and criminal element into extremes of violence, they were ready as the trouble spread to the other great cities. A naval mutiny at Karachi was brusquely and efficiently quelled by British troops; in Calcutta, communal disturbances (which were, in any case, a fairly frequent occurrence) got right out of hand. Here, C squadron of the 43rd saw its first, and virtually only, action.

At the height of the trouble, as the city throbbed with rioting, a detachment of two C.D.L.s, under the command of Captain F. N. Lees, was put in support of, respectively, the 2nd York and Lancaster Regiment and the 2nd Green Howards. Debouching from Fort William, the York and Lancasters aimed to clear the main streets of rioters and looters by night and gain control of the key-points, while the Green Howards and 4th/3rd Gurkhas moved in from another direction. A C.D.L. was put in the lead, playing its powerful searchlight ahead, while the infantry stayed to the rear in 15cwt. trucks and sheltered in the shadows created by the light. Then, at moments of tactical advantage, as the screaming crowds gave way, the infantry debussed to seize the key-points, usually against only minimal resistance. In this way, the Chowringhee Road and Sham Bazaar were quickly dominated, but when the crowds dispersed it was usually into the myriad unpoliced side streets where robbery and murder proceeded unabated. Indeed, not until the energy of the rioters was spent on 15 February would there be quiet. And yet, by the standards of the day, this had been a successful and well-conducted operation.

The same cannot be said, however, for the venture in which six Shermans under Lieutenant H. E. N. Wilshaw became involved at Bombay on 24 February, when rioting again broke out in conjunction with a sympathetic insurrection on the part of the local Indian Electrical and Mechanical Engineers. D Squadron stood by in case it was necessary to arrest the mutineers, while A Squadron engaged in an operation of dubious conception. Ordered to clear a route and facilitate a tour of the disaffected area by the Governor of Bombay, they had no machine-guns and no small arms ammunition, and had first to borrow these before setting out on the morning of 24 February. Three tanks and two armoured cars advanced under the command of Lieutenant J. W. Potts, but found themselves totally unimpeded since, not only were no barriers found, but none had ever existed. An angry Potts, in a pithy report, made the sensible suggestion that not only had the operation been quite unnecessary, but that, in the context of the principle of using only minimum force in support of the Civil Power, it was positively harmful. This does, in fact, appear to have been the last strong-arm action by the 43rd, although tanks of the Indian Armoured Corps continued to be employed with dubious results. The unit now awaited disbandment in 1947, becoming, in the meantime, 2nd/43rd R.T.R. when a new Territorial Army 43rd R.T.R. was formed in England.

In those days it seems not to have been fully comprehended that tanks were far from being an appropriate weapon for crowd control. They lacked the speed, mobility and reliability of armoured cars which, with their lighter armament, were more fitting to the employment of minimum force. That this lesson was beginning to be understood was reflected in the composition of 7th R.T.R. (Lieutenant-Colonel R. B. P. Wood) when it was withdrawn from Germany at the end of 1946 for service in India. After a spell for reorganization (and little or no training) at Barnard Castle, it was sent to the Punjab, where it arrived in January (bringing 60 wives and children) at a moment which almost coincided with outbreaks of a typically racial and religious nature. Based on Sialkot, and equipped in each squadron with two troops of light Stuart Mk VI tanks and two troops of G.M.C. Fox armoured cars, it was the 7th's task to help keep the peace between the Muslims and the Hindus and Sikhs who largely comprised the population of that part of the country, and who dwelt uneasily in communities that were inextricably intermingled. Indian politicians and agitators, aware that the British were stretched to breaking-point as fresh troubles broke out in Bombay and Calcutta, did all in their power to accelerate a breakdown. But when the British Government announced on 20 February that Admiral Lord Louis Mountbatten would take over as Viceroy from Field Marshal Lord Wavell, with the task of completing the handover of power 'by a date not later than June 1948', they switched to a more distant objective, making ready for the struggle as to who would control those parts of the land which were marginal to the rival communities.

During its seven months' operational spell in the Punjab, the 7th had little respite and virtually no time for such acclimatization and training as the 43rd had enjoyed. Its crews found themselves equipped with a tank which was quite different from the Churchill Crocodile flame-throwers they had known before, and armoured cars of which they were totally ignorant. Fortunately, many of the men who would man the Foxes were already in India, having been transferred *en bloc* from 146th Regiment R.A.C. (Duke of Wellington's Regiment) after that unit had been disbanded. But whereas the tanks were already at Sialkot, the armoured cars had still to be drawn from a depot near Rawalpindi, and the first batch was not available until February. Training had hardly commenced, moreover, when an urgent request was received from one of the four separate headquarters – each of which had varying powers of command over the regiment – to send as many armoured cars as possible within 24 hours, to deal with Muslim attacks on a Hindu minority at Murree near Rawalpindi. Agitators who were proficient in creating disorders which led rapidly to killing, looting and burning, were working up the countryside into a ferment. The scattered infantry detachments of 23rd British Brigade Group and the Indian Army were barely able to cope with a situation which demanded that they should concentrate on controlling the closely congested cities. Twelve Foxes could be assembled, and these were formed into a squadron of troops drawn from the entire regiment and placed under Major K. V. Fidler. On 13 March, within the time prescribed, it had moved 140 miles to come under the command of 7th Indian Division, and was attached to the 2nd Royal Norfolk Regiment with the task of employing its mobility to calm the rural districts.

At once, the squadron entered a countryside in which villages and temples were burning and the dead lay unburied. Troops were spread over a wide area in support of detached infantry companies. Radio contact by means of the 19 Set was often tenuous in an area where static interference was high. As a result, a troop leader frequently found himself confronted with difficult decisions in situations involving the use of a mixture of English and Urdu (no one had yet learned the latter) to communicate with a populace consumed by fear, mistrust and hatred. By moving troops rapidly from one threatened village to another, it was hoped to deter itinerant gangs from their sporadic raids and, to some extent, this was achieved along with several arrests. On 16 March, 1 Troop (Captain J. Russell) found itself confronted by a crowd of 200 at the village of Daultala, whose mainly Hindu population was being threatened by marauding Muslims. It was a sign of the deteriorating respect the local Muslims had for their erstwhile rulers that, when told that fire would be opened if they did not disperse, a ringleader blandly answered Russell that 'The Sahib no longer fires.' There was some justification for his belief; the inhibiting effects of legal processes, which made a junior commander extremely vulnerable in the courts, had taken its toll. Tragically, this particular hothead had not been informed of the wider discretionary powers recently granted to the troops by the Governor of the Punjab who, almost alone among the ruling hierarchy, fully envisaged the holocaust which might come if law and order were not at once enforced rigorously. In this instance, the banner instructing the largely illiterate crowd, in three kinds of script, to 'Disperse or we Fire', went unheeded. Two rounds of .300 Browning were fired and two Muslims were seriously wounded. Word quickly spread that the 7th seemed to play the game to a different set of rules, but, sadly, that was not enough since, later that night, the infantry had to open fire, and killed five more Muslims.

Throughout the rest of March and into May, the armoured cars took their turn in patrolling a vast area, covering high mileages along dusty tracks, often intersected by irrigation channels that were difficult to cross. A dire shortage of spares hampered operations, and the drivers and fitters performed miracles in keeping a high proportion of vehicles on the road; their metal became so hot by day that they could only be worked on at night. As temperatures climbed, the dangers of heat exhaustion and disease multiplied, but all ranks quickly learned the value of taking salt and water, and of dressing lightly to reduce skin complaints. There were no major losses from ill-health (though many of the drivers were badly fatigued) and only one case of malaria (the present writer as it happens) – and in his case it was proved beyond doubt that the infection had been caught during a night patrol, after all proper precautions had been taken.

On 3 June, the Viceroy announced that British India was to be separated into two nations – Pakistan and Hindustan (present-day India), the actual boundary to be notified in mid-July. Since an immediate flare-up was expected, a firm hand was placed upon the obvious trouble spots. R.H.Q. stayed in Sialkot (mostly Muslim) where Indian troops were also deployed; A Squadron was sent to Lahore with 23rd British Brigade; B and C Squadrons were, respectively, in Amritsar (mostly Sikh) and Jullundur (mostly Hindu), these two squadrons coming under command of 4th Indian Division, which the Regiment had last fought alongside in North Africa in 1941. In the towns, the light tanks, carrying infantry, proved particularly useful, because their propensity to overheat was less of an impediment to short-range operations. The armoured cars were the maids of all work, both in the towns and in the outlying rural districts; one troop, for example, covering 350 road miles in two days, dashing from village to village. But wherever they went they discovered the same pattern of mounting terror and disorder as the rival factions prepared, in a sinister atmosphere, for the day when the British withdrew. And in the inaccessible back streets and bazaars the toll of murder by gun, bomb and sword mounted, barely checked by troops and police who did what they could at one outbreak or another.

Typical of many incidents was the occasion on which a Sikh threw a small bomb among some workers outside the Lahore Railway Works, killing one Muslim. Immediately his companions retaliated by killing twelve Sikhs – mostly using the Sikhs' own Kirpans, the religious swords they insisted upon carrying, and which the law allowed. A stand-by troop of armoured cars from A Squadron (Major I. G. Thwaites) turned out with the police and found corpses strewn about and the crowd contemplating further mischief. But all they could do was disperse the crowd and subdue the area by intensive patrolling – and wait for the next outbreak. Arrests they could make, weapons they might confiscate by the hundred, but the tide of opposition was too strong to be held back.

Amritsar, the scene of the celebrated killing in 1919 when British troops under Brigadier Dyer had opened a devastating fire, was a hotbed of trouble and probably contained more hidden illegal arms than anywhere. Here, B Squadron (Major D. N. Moir) confronted unyielding intransigence among the populace of all three races, who were consumed with fear and hatred. Magistrates would not co-operate, doors were kept locked to prevent arms searches, and there were instances of the police divulging the intentions of the security forces to interested communities. Intrigue was rife. At Fatehahab, a Muslim leader suggested to one troop leader that if a mock attack were staged upon the Muslims it would cause the Hindus to rally with arms and they could then be arrested – the converse, that the same reaction might provide an excuse for similar action against the Muslims having, it seemed, been overlooked. Moir writes: 'We captured an impressive array of home-made spears and clubs which included some usable hockey sticks . . . Once or twice we fired a few shots, but I think only to get people out of some houses so that the Infantry could round them up . . . as soon as the tanks or armoured cars appeared in a cloud of dust the crowds hastily dispersed. We were well received by most of the locals who, I think, felt that a tank or two in their village added to their prestige and their security.'

When the end came, in the middle of July, it arrived too quickly for comfort and conscience. Once the alignment of the frontier had been announced, a two-way traffic started along the roads as the richer, better-informed members of minority groups shifted house quickly to territory which would be friendly to their particular race and religion. Those who could not afford to move, or who would not believe that the British they had befriended over the centuries would desert them, stayed on. Tanks, armoured cars and equipment were handed in on 22 July, the families were brought down under escort from the hill-station at Dalhousie to Sialkot on the 23rd, and on 1 August the 7th entrained for the four-day journey to Kalyan and Deolali, where they had to wait until 9 September before embarking for the U.K. with the remnant of 2nd/43rd R.T.R. (Lieutenant-Colonel G. M. Hawtrey) in the same ship.

They left behind a chaotic situation wherever Muslims, Sikhs and Hindus rubbed shoulders, as they did in such large numbers in the Punjab. Members of the 7th whose departure had been delayed, brought harrowing tales from the north of the holocaust which, inevitably, followed the removal of the British Army's presence. The Indian troops who remained, were quite unable to prevent the disaster because their units turned against each other. The police were spent. A terrible slaughter left corpses piled high, with which even the vultures were unable to cope, and disease became prevalent.

Of the part the 7th had played in helping to keep control up to the last, General Sir Frank Messervy, C.-in-C. Pakistan, wrote that they were '. . . the best troops I had in this Command. They were keen, efficient and ready to take on any job. Their discipline was excellent and they were always happy and smiling. . . .' The hearts of those who realized what had happened were heavy. Yet this was but the first step in the long retreat from Empire that was to follow.

* * * * *

It was fortuitous that the intention of the War Office to station a Strategic Reserve in the Middle East coincided with the need to have troops in that region to deal with a succession of internal security problems during the post-war years, very few of which had been thoroughly envisaged in 1945. Before the war there had been only tribal disputes to settle and local riots in an area where nationalism assumed a somewhat random form. Only in the mandated territory of Palestine had the confrontations between Arabs and the small, but vigorous Jewish community been so prolonged and deadly as to tie down large numbers of British troops on internal security duties. The Arabs, who had rebelled against Jewish immigration, suffered heavy casualties, but during the political bargaining received a promise from the British Government in 1939 that only 75,000 Jews would be admitted each year for the next five years, and that, thereafter, no more would be allowed in without Arab consent. Thus a struggle between Arabs and Jews was assured. The Jews formed secret forces such as the Palmach, the Irgun

Zvai Leumi and the Stern Gang to fight the battle they intended after the war. The Arabs depended on the British for protection. When the World Zionist Congress demanded in August 1945, in the aftermath of the European holocaust, that a Jewish state be established in Palestine, an emotional confrontation was inevitable at a time when the main British force was 1st Division, soon to be joined by 6th Airborne Division as part of the Strategic Reserve. Armoured support was provided in October by the Staghound armoured cars of the 3rd King's Own Hussars, and it was not until June that the first unit of the R.T.R. put in an appearance.

The 8th R.T.R. (Lieutenant-Colonel N. E. B. C. Mahoney) had existed nomadically since it had left Italy for England in 1945 and England for Austria in January 1946. By the time it reached Palestine it had travelled 8,000 miles in one year. In Austria its equipment was a hotchpotch, each squadron comprising four Churchills, two Snowmobiles and an assortment of Daimler Scout Cars (Dingos), jeeps and half-track carriers. They spent their time guarding a German prisoner-of-war camp at Graz and searching for suspected Nazis in the surrounding hills. But it was a languorous life, particularly for R.H.Q. and H.Q. Squadron in the Schloss Eggeburg where an attempt was made, it seems, to revive an old Viennese spirit; and for the detached squadrons, too, there was the replete satisfaction of not coming too closely under the eye of the upper echelon of command. In August, this idyll came to an end abruptly when the 8th was sent to join the 2nd in Venezia Giulia. Here they lived under canvas in conditions which compared most unfavourably with those they had vacated. But far worse was to come, when the unit was shipped via Egypt to Palestine, where the situation was tense and nobody could afford to be off his guard.

Rapidly re-trained to operate a medley of petrol- and diesel-engined Sherman tanks, the bulk of the 8th was placed under command of 2nd Infantry Brigade at Lajjun, where it undertook the relatively unexacting task of patrolling a large area, which remained peaceful because it was mostly populated by Arabs, who laid low at a time of intense Jewish activity. A Squadron, with a section of the Reconnaissance Troop, was sent to Gedera to support units of 6th Airborne Division who were heavily engaged in the aftermath of the kidnapping of five officers from the Officers Club at Tel Aviv on 18 June, operations that were extended after the dynamiting of the King David Hotel in Jerusalem by Irgun on 22 July. Yet A Squadron took no part in 6th Airborne Division's activities, though available to do so at any time. Indeed, it was the other squadrons which were more gainfully employed, 'rumbling the odd troop of Shermans up and down off-stage', as Lieutenant K. C. Dudley put it, during arms searches by the infantry, although mainly these tasks excluded tanks. Throughout July and August, the regiment escorted 200 Jewish detainees from Athlit to the Rafah detention camp; sent out recce troop patrols; set up road-blocks and guarded the Haifa oil dock. Also, illegal immigrants had to be controlled, as on 17 August, for example, when 30 men in 3 half-tracks found themselves responsible for embarking these unfortunate people for shipment to Cyprus.

There existed an abiding bitterness among the embattled factions. Mutual hostility between the British troops and the Jewish guerillas was counter-balanced, to some extent, by the revulsion of the 'official' Jewish Haganah and Palmach units for the extremist Irgun. Mistrust by the Arabs of British intentions produced a callous ostracism of soldiers who, even if lying alone and wounded, would be fortunate to receive aid from bystanders. In these circumstances, as one, R.T.R. officer put it, the soldiers had no chance of obtaining a 'poppet' and his lot was hard. The men of 8th R.T.R. were fortunate to avoid the worst excesses of this fierce internecine struggle; the nature of their tank establishment frequently precluded them from becoming engaged when the armoured car units were often in the thick of it. In a document defining its rôle and the manner of carrying it out, Major J. Prichard, the second in command, pointed out that 'Unless open warfare breaks out, the use of tanks is almost ruled out by the principle of minimum force.' Various rôles were envisaged, however, such as forcing an entrance through wire and gates into settlements and removing inhabitants when they lay on the roads to resist arrest. 'This may be done', it was written, 'by driving slowly towards them or, with Sherman type of exhaust, reversing towards them and revving up. The exhaust smoke is blown downwards and proves very effective in moving anyone on the ground.' But the most useful vehicles, it was adjudged, were the armoured half-tracks manned by a crew of ten men, 'drawn from the tank crews, and armed with Bren guns, rifles and T.S.M.G.s – not pistols'.

8th R.T.R.'s days in the operational rôle were numbered. By stages they were withdrawn to Rafah in the now famous Gaza Strip, leaving B Squadron temporarily at Acre to give demonstrations to the Middle East School of Infantry, a task which placed high demands upon manpower to the detriment of the rest of the regiment. For, as the Quarterly Report said, as it recorded the disbandment of C Squadron, 'the personnel question has become acute'. It certainly had. The commanding officer, Lieutenant-Colonel N. E. B. C. Mahony, was in the United Kingdom on long leave. The camp at Lajjun, being poorly wired and having a large perimeter, required very heavy guarding at night, and duties were coming round far too frequently – this at a time when the Jews were doing everything in their power to steal arms and ammunition from the British Army. No cook sergeants were available in the theatre and no one was fit for promotion, it was reported, and there was also a shortage of clerks since, no sooner had a learner gained experience, than he became due for release. And yet, of all the R.T.R. units in Central Mediterranean Forces at that time, the 8th, according to the War Diaries, was the only one which appears to have had few worries about morale.

Towards the end of 1946, as the violence worsened in Palestine, the 8th continued on its travels, sending A Squadron on exercises to Trans-Jordan in December, prior to the entire regiment returning overland, on transporters, to Egypt where they were put under canvas at Shandur. This camp was to know an R.T.R. presence for many years to come, situated as it was on the airfield which also accommodated the Royal Armoured Corps Schools Middle East. And here they remained until embarking for the United Kingdom in August 1947, after what may have been one of the most varied tours in the shortest time ever completed by a unit of the R.T.R.

For a brief period, however, there were three units of the R.T.R. in Egypt at the same time, the 4th having arrived from Italy in June and the 6th in July. The latter would stay only until the end of the year when it would also return to Britain, but the 4th was destined for a long sojourn and it was they who would be next to carry the R.T.R. badge into Palestine and this time, into serious action.

Strangely enough, in 1947, the only R.T.R. unit to have had intimate experience of the fomenting Jewish problem was the 3rd (Lieutenant-Colonel E. C. Mitford), stationed many hundreds of miles away in Germany. That summer a detachment of 40 men, initially under the command of Captain W. S. Rice and subsequently, Captain D. S. Squirrel, had the unpleasant task of organizing a camp and guarding several hundred unfortunate Jewish immigrants who had been intercepted at sea by the Royal Navy while on their way to the so-called homeland. The event received much adverse publicity, especially in the U.S.A., and the troops had to endure a measure of abuse from the Jewish fraternity. But Press comment on the post-war Army, with its high citizen content, was something that had to be understood, dealt with patiently and, if possible turned to advantage.

In February 1947, Ernest Bevin, the Foreign Secretary, gave up hope of reconciling Arab and Jewish interests and referred the dispute over who should rule Palestine to the United Nations. In September, the Colonial Secretary advocated partition of the country. Immediately, the deterioration in law and order accelerated as Jews and Arabs adopted attitudes related to their territorial claims. Simultaneously, the authority and morale of the police declined and a heavier load was thrust upon the Army. Bomb attacks and ambushes by the Jews became regular features of the day, and were borne almost entirely by the Infantry, the Royal Artillery, the Royal Engineers and the armoured car regiments. At the end of November the Arabs joined in the fighting.

Both the 4th (Lieutenant-Colonel F. I. C. Wetherall) and the 6th (Lieutenant-Colonel G. Gaisford) together with the Queen's Bays and 9th Royal Lancers, might also have been involved if a War Office plan to re-form 2nd Armoured Brigade and 1st Armoured Division as part of the Strategie Reserve had been implemented in the summer of 1947. It was for this reason that all four units had been concentrated in Egypt and located at Qassasin, in a camp which had been designed for a single regiment. 'Set in a bleak and arid desert north of the squalid Sweet Water Canal', as the 4th R.T.R.'s contemporary report puts it, 'it consisted of tents, a few ill-constructed buildings, a crumbling cookhouse and innumerable deep trench latrines and, of course, Egyptian flies and mosquitoes galore'. The brigade was meant to be there for only three weeks, but it stayed for five. For no sooner had they arrived than an obviously unsound scheme was abandoned. Not only was it clearly an error to commit units which were totally unsuitably equipped to deal with the Palestine imbroglio, but also lack of manpower was taxing the ability of the regiments to survive. Indeed, at the end of the year, both cavalry regiments and the 6th were to be sent back to the United Kingdom and reduced to cadre strength while the 4th was to move to Shandur – a Nissen hutted camp that was easier to guard, and where there was more room.

In November 1947, the United Nations General Assembly voted in favour of partitioning Palestine. The Mandate would terminate on 14 May 1948, giving Arabs and Jews six months' grace to prepare for the war that all knew must ensue. The British were to complete their evacuation by 1 August and in the meantime would revert to the task they had endured in India, that of keeping two hostile sides apart while protecting themselves as best they could. Typical of the sort of volatile situation which could arise was that which confronted Captain D. A. Windeler on 20 December 1947. At that time, he was seconded to the Mechanized Regiment of the Trans-Jordan Frontier Force, and, in company with a troop of the 17th/21st Lancers, was called to a village where fighting had broken out between a large Arab force and a few Jews. The Arabs, being stronger, were in a very excited mood and it was mainly Windeler's arrival and his presence among them which persuaded them to give up their aggressive intentions and allow him to evacuate the Jews to safety.

Both sides were ready for a major test of strength. The conditions for intervention by tanks were now present at last – but at a time when training in the 4th was at a low ebb. For no sooner had the unit settled at Shandur than it was loaded with Lightning Patrols (trying, unavailingly, to prevent the Egyptians from stealing telephone cable) and the 40-man Guard for the C.-in-C. who happened to be General Sir John Crocker, the R.T.R.'s most distinguished serving officer. As a result, training was mainly of an individual nature and never took place out of camp. Moreover, it was nothing unusual for a trooper to carry out four guards in eight days.

The call to send a troop of Comets (with which the 4th was now equipped) to Rafah, for the defence of the British garrison on the Egyptian border with Palestine, came as a relief. And, under Lieutenant L. G. Burgess, they had their moment of glory when, on 1 April 1948, at the very moment when all four Comets were in workshops, they were called into action. Two Jewish, improvised armoured cars (3-ton Chevrolets with an armoured cab) had sallied forth from a nearby settlement and burnt an Arab truck. Two of the 4th's Comets, fully fit, but sticky with wet paint, set out in pursuit and tracked down one of the offending vehicles. Next day, an attempt by the accompanying infantry to enter the settlement of Mitvahen was resisted, and the Comets fired about 30 rounds of 77mm. high explosive at the water-tower and neighbouring villages, killing one Jew and wounding two others. This effectively put a stop to further episodes of a similar nature.

From then on, this troop (later commanded by Lieutenant R. G. Morris) acted as a transit camp for the rest of the 4th when it was called forward into Palestine at the end of April. For, as the time for partition approached, it could be seen that minimum force would no longer prevail, and that there might even be considerable difficulty in extricating the 70,000 British troops, 5,000 police, innumerable members of the civil administration, and some 210,000 tons of military stores, on which both Arabs and Jews were anxious to lay their hands. At this juncture, Crocker, who was invariably anxious to make decisions based on his own observations, took the bold decision, as C.-in-C., to go incognito to Palestine in order to see for himself, unhindered by the usual entourage, what help was needed.

The 4th was jerked out of its routine existence on 27 April by an unexpected signal ordering it to move, 48 hours later, to Palestine to relieve pressure on the troops in Jerusalem and Tel Aviv and assist in the withdrawal which had begun on 1 April. After handing over the C.-in-C.'s Guard to the luckless 16th/5th Queen's Royal Lancers, it was barely possible to man two squadrons of 14 Comets, supplied by an improvised echelon. Most of the crews were National Servicemen, the command half-track was driven by the regimental cobbler and another was driven by H.Q. Squadron's pay clerk – tasks that were accepted with what the Regiment's report calls 'gleeful enthusiasm' – and yet they achieved a high standard of maintenance. By dint of feverish hard work, A Squadron (Major T. H. Gibbon) was made ready to cross the Suez Canal on the 30th, for embarkation on tank transporters which then took 48 hours to travel the 200 miles to Rafah. The transporters had just been taken out of 'mothballs', the drivers were unfamiliar with them and they were not up to the weight for Comets. Tyre blowouts were frequent because of overheating and, every time, the tanks had to be off-loaded to effect repairs. While the remainder of the Regiment waited at Sarafand, a troop went to Jaffa and Gibbon took A Squadron to Jerusalem where, on 3 May, he was greeted by Lieutenant-General G. H. A. Macmillan with the remark that 'he had been waiting for us for a week and nobody had taken longer to cross the Sinai since Moses'.

Fighting between Jews and Arabs was already widespread and yet B Squadron found that, even when interposed in No Man's Land between the two sides, they encountered little trouble and were actually able to partake in some infantry tank training with the infantry they were supporting. As a deterrent they were a success and on 15 May they pulled back safely into Egypt via Rafah, acting as escort to 3rd Infantry Brigade. From there they watched the Egyptian Army advancing in the opposite direction, making for Bethlehem in their invasion of Palestine. The Rafah troop also saw them go, commenting, with the amused indifference of the British soldier towards his Egyptian counterpart, on the manner in which they by-passed the Israeli settlements, and how 'a stream of Coca-Cola vans crossed the border to the thunder of artillery into a completely unoccupied waste.'

For Gibbon, parked with A Squadron adjacent to a cesspit amid rubble between the Jewish Agency and the Jewish Library in Jerusalem, and 'in constant terror of losing a tank or a weapon', it was much more difficult. At first, the tanks were employed on 'Flag Marches', to impress the populace, and for the purpose of knocking down road-blocks as soon as they were built. The prices offered by the Jews for British equipment were high, and a few sales took place – but not by the 4th! The tension was electric. With every move by Jews or Arabs posing the likelihood of action, the escorting of every convoy became a full-scale military operation. The Arab Legion was deployed in the vicinity of Jerusalem and was in action in a battle between its armoured cars and those of the Jews near Latrun on the 12th (where A Squadron less one troop had been dispatched on 10 May) which ended to the distinct advantage of the Arabs, who knocked out a Jewish car. As a result, the Jews, who presumably placed responsibility for their setback on the British, mortared A Squadron in Latrun police station, but drew retribution upon themselves when the Comets returned fire and knocked out another armoured car. For a few hours, as the Jews became more threatening and produced two 75mm. self-propelled guns, it looked as if a major battle were in prospect. But it died down as the Jews came to realize their mistake and reverted to overcoming the Arabs.

The final withdrawal from Jerusalem to the port of Haifa, as Gibbon writes, was brilliantly carried out by 1st Guards Brigade, with 40th and 42nd Royal Marine Commandos, 4th/7th Dragoon Guards, 17th/21st Lancers, 6th Field Regiment R.A. and the Chestnut Troop R.H.A., Freddie Plaistowe [Captain F. G. Plaistowe] and a half-squadron led the advance guard and soon after midnight on the 14th, arrived at the entrance to the Latrun Pass where he was fired upon [by mortars] and put down a smoke screen. I brought up the rear with the other half-squadron . . . As I passed the hotel where the newspaper correspondents lodged I was hailed in American and we evacuated 'Time and Life' on the engine deck. Jim Pulzer [Captain W. Pulzer] had the Command Cashier and the strong boxes on the floor of his tank. Every time we halted he thought his last hour had come.' Next day, however, they all arrived safe and sound in Haifa where they remained for ten days until evacuated by sea.

It was a memorable operation, if only because of the success it had achieved after such improvisation with men whose training was, to say the least, uneven. 'Morale was raised out of all recognition', reports the 4th's account, which goes on to comment on the capability of the modern army to adapt itself to conditions and be capable of endurance. These qualities, indeed, would be required in abundance during the months to come. With little prospect, for the moment, of action, and drastic economies already biting hard, the struggle to retain some semblance of purpose in peace-time, at a time of national financial crisis, was entering a most testing phase.

CHAPTER III

Montgomery's Army
1946–1950

The parlous state into which the Army had fallen by the autumn of 1946, heavily underlined, as it was, by the impoverished condition into which units on operational duties had been reduced (let alone those units whose rôles were mainly concerned with occupation or training duties), was fully shared by regiments of the R.T.R. The experiences of the 4th, 7th, 8th and 43rd R.T.R., described in the previous chapter, were endemic to the Army. Field Marshal Montgomery had become C.I.G.S. on 26 June 1946, and in the interim had acquired considerable publicity for himself as well as the Army by the pronouncement of his schemes for the Army's future well-being. At the Camberley Conference on 6 August 1946, he said that the soldier must have 'a good life' as part of 'the social fabric of the nation, with living standards in step with the nation. Better married quarters must be provided, bedrooms and sitting-rooms should take the place of barrack-rooms, messing must be equal to good civilian standards and there should be a minimum of such infringements on the privacy of the soldier as 'Lights Out', short leave passes and minor parades. 'Why', he asked, 'should not a soldier have a bedroom light to enable him to read in bed?'. These were sentiments which, on the whole, received a favourable response from the Army, but, for reasons partly outside the C.I.G.S.'s control, were a far cry from implementation at the time.

Lack of money and shortage of manpower confounded almost every project. The state of the British economy, damaged by the war and heavily dependent, as it was, upon outside aid – principally from the U.S.A. – gave the Labour Government under Clement Attlee very little room for manoeuvre. Traditional Labour Party views, and the unhappy relationships which developed between Montgomery and successive Ministers of War and of Defence, exacerbated a difficult situation which could only be successfully resolved by cool negotiation. And for this, Montgomery was neither qualified nor temperamentally suited. Once the withdrawals from India and Palestine had considerably reduced the armed forces' commitment, the arguments in favour of spending more than the Government's announced ceiling of

£600 million per annum, on all three Services, were harder to support. Until the dangers of Soviet intransigence and provocation were made manifest by the Communist *coup* in Czechoslovakia in February 1948 and the suspension, in June, by the Soviets of land transport between West Berlin and the outside world, making it necessary to supply the city by air, there was little inclination in political circles to put the West's defences in order.

Central to the military debate in Whitehall was the proposal to establish National Service permanently in peace-time, once the system of wartime call-up had ended. From the outset it was the opinion of the War Office that a period of two years' service was necessary, followed by time on the reserve, but for political reasons this was whittled down to 18 months when the Bill was introduced to Parliament. In April 1947, however, the Minister of Defence (Mr A. V. Alexander), beset by stiff opposition from within the Labour Party, asked if the Chiefs of Staff would accept a reduction to 12 months, and when the Bill became law this was the period agreed. Each man would serve one full-time year with the Colours, followed by six years on the Reserve or with the auxiliary forces – with the provision, according to Montgomery, that Britain's overseas obligations be liquidated and that there would be no operational commitment.

To the technical Arms and Services such as the Royal Armoured Corps and the Royal Electrical and Mechanical Engineers, for example, it could not be expected that the product of a mere year's training would be of much value to a first-line unit. Moreover, the regular element would be so heavily involved in training the never-ending flow of recruits that there would be a further diminution of their combat potential. Some idea of what this would mean to a tank unit can be gleaned from reports made, respectively, by 8th and 4th R.T.R. in the summers of 1947 and 1948. After the 8th was relegated to a minor Internal Security rôle in Egypt early in 1947, it had rapidly to convert one squadron to armoured cars when the Life Guards were transferred at short notice to Palestine. But from March until August, the 8th was mainly engaged upon converting to crewmen 467 infantrymen who had been made redundant when their battalions reverted to Suspended Animation. This they did so well that only 20 men were rejected, but the 447 successful candidates only temporarily filled gaps in the Middle East R.A.C. units to which they were sent. A year later, in July 1948, Lieutenant-Colonel H. J. B. Cracroft, who had taken command of the 4th from F. I. C. Wetherall in June, was reporting to G.H.Q. and 8th Infantry Brigade the virtual inability of his regiment, recently back from Palestine, to fulfil its rôle.

'The unit is smart, keen and well turned out,' he wrote, but '. . . due to many changes in personnel and general commitments of the unit, the technical knowledge and training . . . is at present far from satisfactory'. He went on to point out, for example, that of an Establishment of 73 driver-mechanics, only 19 were on strength and there was only one electrician where there should have been five. Aggravating the situation was the fact that 'So-called potential tradesmen arrive only having done half their training, e.g., Gunner-Operators are trained in gunnery only or vice-versa . . . There is no trace of when the unit last fired an annual range practice . . . It is no use moving an Armd Regiment to a scene of trouble if it cannot shoot if required to do so.' Cracroft complained bitterly of the manner in which the 4th was plundered by higher formations for guards, patrols, courses and station duties. 'I have a squadron commander at H.Q. B.T.E. [British Troops Egypt] for two months [setting and running an exercise] on higher training and have now been asked by G.H.Q. to provide another squadron commander to set a combined operation exercise . . . my task would be easier if I served one master instead of two.'

Cracroft's complaint could be, and frequently was, echoed by almost every other commanding officer finding himself beset by conflicting orders from senior commanders and staff, who sometimes seemed incapable of understanding that the days of plenty were over and that units were at breaking-point at a moment of institutional change. Half of the R.T.R. was now in the process of reduction to what amounted to cadre strength, although for some, the experience was less harrowing than for others. Five out of the eight regular units would serve in the United Kingdom where, in December 1948, there were no new barracks and only 1,559 officers' quarters along with 14,551 other ranks' quarters. With only 600 under construction and 488 huts being converted, the waiting-list numbered 1,233 officers and 3,507 other ranks.

The 7th, after returning from India, and having been sent to stage for two months in a dilapidated hutted camp at Wrottesley Park near Wolverhampton (where there were no organized training or leisure facilities), was moved to Tidworth to undertake the duties previously carried out by the Land Wing of the Specialized Armoured Establishment (S.A.E.) originally set-up by Sir Percy Hobart as the means to pursue the development of his 'Funnies'. Here a most extraordinary collection of vehicles were to be found, most of them obsolescent, some of them, such as a tank that was intended to jump across minefields with rocket assistance, bizarre and rather dangerous to approach. The epigram was declaimed by Lieutenant-Colonel R. A. H. Walker as he inspected the dummy armament of a Churchill A.R.V. when he took command early in 1948: 'Even the bloody gun's bent.'

8th R.T.R. was destined, along with three cavalry regiments, to assume the rôle of a training regiment at Catterick Camp – in their case to replace the 57th which was in the process of being disbanded by Lieutenant-Colonel L. P. Crouch, an R.T.R. officer of redoubtable reputation. At least they had the satisfaction of assuming a rôle in which manpower was abundant, for they would be dealing with the stream of National Service recruits in the initial stages of their year of full-time service. But, inevitably, the unit forfeited its expertise as a combat unit; within a few months, trained tank commanders and crewmen would become out-of-date as they were converted to become teachers and administrators of an educational sausage-machine. And, whereas its strength before leaving Egypt in August had been 39 officers and 714 other ranks, at Wrottesley Park, where it staged throughout the rest of the year, it had fallen to 38 officers and 152 other ranks (60 per cent of these were Regulars) on reversion to what was called R.A.C. Regimental Reduced Cadre.

When they returned from Germany and the Middle East, 2nd and 6th R.T.R. fared, if anything, worse than the others. For them, awaited the task of Territorial Army assistance, the provision of support in administering T.A. camps, drawing-up, maintaining and then returning to depots the vehicles which the part-time soldiers used, and assisting with training. In other words, the part-timers, not necessarily from any desire of their own, depended upon regular soldiers to perform the donkey-work while the training of the regulars fell into decline. The 2nd (Lieutenant-Colonel R. H. O. Simpson) were stationed at Crookham, in rickety wooden huts. Some of these had to be converted to married quarters because there was nothing else available for families in a land that was critically short of houses. On 14 August 1948, the unit's strength had been reduced to 213 all ranks, a draft of 44 qualified regular crewmen having been sent to join 4th Hussars in Malaya, where the Communist-inspired uprising had led to a state of emergency and outright guerilla warfare. To assist its rôle as part of 56th (London) Armoured Division T.A., two of the three tank squadrons were disbanded. This left H.Q. Squadron to carry out the task of administration; create a training wing to perform that function; and keep A Squadron in being to hold the eleven Comet, two Cromwell and three Stuart tanks together with six Scout Cars and eight 15cwt. wireless trucks, which were all that could be maintained by the manpower available. Even so, the maximum number of men that could be allotted to each troop averaged only nine or ten and these, after deductions for fatigues (such chores as coal deliveries to barracks and married quarters in the days before civilian labour was provided), compassionate leave and sickness, fell to five or six. A serious lowering of morale was envisaged by Simpson if, to quote a letter he wrote to H.Q. 22nd Armoured Brigade, driver-mechanics were employed 'purely as garage hands on the maint of A.F.V.'s for week-end use by the T.A.'.

Manpower shortages similar to those which afflicted the 2nd also affected the 6th (Lieutenant-Colonel A. Dow) which was sent to occupy Scofton Airfield near Worksop, to provide assistance to 49th (West Riding) Armoured Division T.A. Most of the accommodation was in draughty and leaking Nissen huts, but the officers were lucky to dwell in a wooden spider complex which had once been the Station Hospital. The tanks were kept in Romney hangars. Married quarters simply were not available and, as one expedient, a large country house was purchased for a number of officers' families (legend says 14 at one time) in which the wives, each with her own cooker, shared a central kitchen and cooked 14 separate meals for 14 cheek-by-jowl families. The airfield, vast in circumference, was also partly occupied by squatters. Lieutenant A. R. Bissett who, like a great many other officers, was compelled in 1947 to relinquish his commission in the Indian Army and transfer to the British Army, arrived at Worksop as the 6th was settling in. He describes the atmosphere of gloom which prevailed. 'The place was dilapidated and a great deal of effort in the early days was put into surviving, maintaining – just that – no exercises, no training worth the name . . . We couldn't guard it . . . patrols had to be mounted to prevent the squatters from establishing themselves and I reckon this went on for a year . . .' At one time, it was decided to train men to handle guard dogs, just another diversion from the intended rôle of the regiment. When one studies the conditions under which 6th R.T.R. existed, and reads the accounts of those who endured quite appalling conditions for a home station, one wonders that this unit was ever able to recover in the way that it quickly did when the time came. The fact that it did so will be shown later as one of the accomplishments which demonstrated the inner strength of the R.T.R. as a whole.

Of the R.A.C. units which came to England, the 3rd fared best of all. Sent from Flensburg to Gosport in January 1948, it lived partly in semi-subterranean forts of the 'Palmerston-folly' type, and partly in barracks, engaged (less A Squadron) upon the rôle of the amphibious 'C' Wing of S.A.E., equipped for the most part with Sherman DD tanks. In March, A Squadron was sent to Warminster to act as demonstration squadron to the

School of Infantry, and in September, the remainder of the regiment handed over at Gosport to D Squadron, 7th R.T.R. and departed for Bovington Camp. Here it became the armoured element of the War Office Reserve in the United Kingdom, and at once began to receive the reinforcements in manpower and Comet tanks which were to bring it up to something approaching full strength by the end of the year. Under Lieutenant-Colonel D. J. O'Flynn, it began intensive individual, troop, squadron and regimental training, such as was denied every other armoured regiment in Britain, and which was the envy of those stationed overseas. Within a matter of months, following a spell on Salisbury Plain in March 1949, the 3rd had recaptured many of the skills which had last been possessed in 1945. Motoring on their tracks from Warminster to Bovington, its tanks covered the distance at speed, with only one breakdown. The revival was not a moment too soon. To the steadily worsening political climate in Europe was now added a new threat in the Far East, where the Communist Armies of Mao Tse Tung had routed Chiang Kai Shek's Nationalist forces and were rapidly taking control of the entire country. With very little warning, it became apparent that the Crown Colony of Hong Kong was in danger and badly in need of reinforcements. At short notice, the regiment was told to move, a story that must wait until the next chapter.

With units in such a state of flux, officers and men underpaid by comparison with civilian standards, and a state of stress induced by shortages in practically every department, it may seem surprising that these lean years imbued those who lived through them with a unique spirit, and that there were triumphs to be recorded among the tragedies. Quite naturally, a great deal of attention was paid to diverting the minds of men deprived of the martial aspects of soldiering to those activities that might absorb surplus energy. Foot drill parades were more frequent than would be the case in the future, but church parades, after 1948, were no longer compulsory. Sport assumed a high place in unit activities at a time when National Service was injecting into the Services men whose prowess at games was of a quality not normally to be found in the peace-time Army. Although nobody in any section of the Services would admit it, there was ruthless competition, and conspiracy with their Records Office, by some corps and units to acquire players of above average performance in order to win the highest honours in sport. The 7th, whose R.S.M. from 1949 to 1951 was W. R. Armit, who had been one of the members of the 4th Battalion team which won the Army Soccer Cup in 1934, had ambitions of emulating this feat under his tutelage – until operational commitments in 1950 thwarted the scheme. The 2nd achieved honours, such as few units have done before or since, by winning the Army Hockey Cup three years in succession from 1948 to 1950, taking on and beating 8th R.T.R. in the finals of 1949 and 1950, both games going to extra time. Simpson was to be seen, file under arm, with papers to prove each man was legitimately on strength, shouting them on from the sideline. Meanwhile the 3rd, swept away by their close proximity to the Royal Navy, took to rowing and became so proficient that they had the temerity to win the Naval Cutters race in 1948, thus becoming the first soldier crew in history to beat crews of the Senior Service – a feat which has nothing to do with the 3rd's adoption of 'On the Quarter Deck' as its Regimental March. Over the years, members of the regiment were to be found to the fore in most sports, and for each of those to achieve distinction in the higher reaches of endeavour, there were scores who simply played for a troop, a squadron or the regiment.

By comparison with the difficulties experienced by the Regular R.T.R., those of its Territorial Army counterparts in the post-1946 period were perhaps less trying, even though they underwent a complete metamorphosis. By the time the T.A. was due to be reborn in April 1947, all the old T.A. R.T.R. units that had survived the war had, with the exception of the 43rd, been disbanded. But the units that were reinstated took their shape, as well as many of their officers and men, from the old units which had fought so well as part of the regular forces since 1939. Each drew heavily upon old comrades, and many were commanded and led by officers, warrant officers and N.C.O.s who were civilians again. Of the six R.T.R. regiments and three yeomanry regiments affiliated to the regular R.T.R., seven were commanded by part-timers, all of whom had had distinguished careers during the war. Upon these commanders, with their close contacts among the civilian community and assisted by the Territorial Army Associations, fell much of the responsibility (in addition to their daily work) for raising, enthusing and training the cadres which would absorb the intakes of National Servicemen, whose year of service with the colours had ended. Yet none of these units could have long survived had it not been for the provision of a regular nucleus of higher quality than had been the norm before the war. To each T.A. unit was affiliated a regular unit, and within each T.A. unit would be found one or two regular R.T.R. officers and some dozen other ranks who might fill any of a number of key-posts ranging from R.S.M. to storeman. The nomenclature, location and regular affiliation of the reformed T.A. units are shown in the following table.

Title	Location	Regular Affiliation
Lothians and Border Horse Yeomanry (Lieutenant-Colonel C. J. Y. Dallmeyer)	Edinburgh	4th R.T.R.
2nd County of London Yeomanry (Westminster Dragoons) (Lieutenant-Colonel D. J. O'Flynn)	Westminster	2nd R.T.R.
3rd/4th County of London Yeomanry (Sharpshooters) (Lieutenant-Colonel The Earl of Onslow)	St John's Wood	2nd R.T.R.
40th (The King's) R.T.R. (Lieutenant-Colonel J. L. Finigan)	Bootle	1st R.T.R.
41st (Oldham) R.T.R. (Lieutenant-Colonel J. B. Whitehead)	Oldham	3rd R.T.R.
42nd R.T.R. (Lieutenant-Colonel W. J. Wykes)	Clapham Junction	8th R.T.R.
43rd (Northumberland) R.T.R. (Lieutenant-Colonel P. Gardner)	Newcastle-on-Tyne	7th R.T.R.
44th R.T.R. (Lieutenant-Colonel E. D. Rash)	Bristol	5th R.T.R.
45th (Leeds Rifles) R.T.R. (Lieutenant-Colonel R. H. Holden)	Leeds	6th R.T.R.

Service for a part-time soldier, whether volunteer or National Serviceman completing his Reserve Service, obliged a man to attend for training on a specified number of evenings or weekends, in addition to a fortnight's annual camp each year. Unfortunately, there were a great many unavoidable hazards in the way of a constructive training programme and these were succinctly summarized in 1947 by Captain J. Saxby (a regular, serving with the T.A.), long before the first National Service reservists were due to report.

'. . . the problems', he wrote, '. . . may be tabulated as follows:

    a. Shortage of good instructors.

    b. Unpredictability of attendance.

    c. Shortage of good training equipment.

    d. Need of maintenance of vehicles. '

    e. Shortage of classroom space, it being almost impossible to hold 10 classes nightly in any drill hall used by an armoured regiment.'

Attendance was statutorily compulsory, but it was intended that time be spent as enjoyably as possible. Montgomery declared that it was for each local T.A. unit to turn itself into the 'best club in the district', and there is no doubt that the comradeship founded upon wartime associations gave the majority of units a good start. For the regular element, apart from helping with instruction, it was extremely hard work, and it would be idle to claim that they preferred this task (i.e., preparing training sessions for part-timers, taking a back seat during the major training sessions and clearing-up afterwards) to that of work in a regular unit. That there were advantages is also undeniable. Most units had extra-mural affiliations which could help provide future employment and give aid if the need were dire. 43rd R.T.R., for example, was well officered by lawyers, and 45th R.T.R. had strong connections with a firm of brewers.

From the established affiliations with T.A. units grew the territorial roots which not only the R.T.R., but almost all the R.A.C. units lacked. Regular R.T.R. soldiers living among the populace made friends, married local girls and, by their example, began to accustom civilians to a military presence which they came to respect. From these contacts would stem a recruiting structure which, when the time was ripe, would provide the Regiment with its regular manpower. And from the cadet units attached to T.A. regiments in, or adjacent, to their drill halls, would come many future crewmen and commanders.

As Montgomery's 'Citizen Army' began to take shape, fundamental decisions were being made within the R.A.C. which would affect the R.T.R. The first post-war R.A.C. Conference in November 1945 had done little more than confirm the *status quo* so far as establishments and equipment were concerned. But it had been agreed to ask His Majesty King George VI to become Colonel Commandant of the R.A.C. and that there should be five colonels from the Cavalry and two from the R.T.R. in the Corps – a scheme which did not give complete satisfaction. Content as the King was to accept the titular leadership of the Royal Armoured Corps, in addition to that of some of its Regiments, including the R.T.R., it was clearly desirable, in the interests of clarity, to avoid repetition of the title 'Colonel Commandant'. In due course, a most appropriate amendment was adopted – at whose suggestion it is impossible to discover – that, instead, His Majesty should become 'Captain-General of the R.A.C.'. This most happy solution, reminiscent, as it was, of the joint association of the Cavalry and R.T.R. with 'Ironsides', was adopted in August 1949. Yet it was never announced at the R.A.C. Conference, nor was the listing of this important appointment given much publicity within the Corps, and after August 1954 (two and a half years after the King's death) it disappeared. No reason can be found for the lapse, but the preference for Regimental loyalties within the R.A.C. is of fundamental significance to this history in the pages to come.

Affecting the officers far more closely was the suggestion, in 1945, that they all be included on a Common R.A.C. List. At the same time, it was agreed that for the time being, Cavalry units should operate Armoured, Armoured Car and Reconnaissance Regiments, while the R.T.R. provided Armoured and Specialized Armoured Regiments. Both these proposals were divisive and neither would withstand the test of time. In its thinking, the R.A.C. remained the marriage of convenience between Cavalry and R.T.R. it had been at its formation in 1939, and the failure, in 1946, to become a true Corps would have dire consequences when reductions in strength became unavoidable at a later date. As it was, little progress was made at this time with a Common List, and it was found expedient the following year to suggest that R.T.R. units, being separate, should be allowed to change their function as required. For notwithstanding that both Cavalry and R.T.R. units had, since 1944, been compelled by operational circumstances to man armoured cars, there still existed the rule that armoured cars were reserved for the Cavalry. And although it was the decision of the 1947 R.A.C. Conference to permit a freer interchange of Regiments between rôles, the armoured cars remained the exception on the spurious contention that it was extremely difficult to convert to that rôle. Naturally, the benefits in peace-time of being mobile on wheels instead of tracks were abundant, if only because far greater variations of location were assured, in those interesting parts of the world where the Cold War was being fought. Certain Cavalry units could not be blamed for attempting to retain a choice, adventurous rôle everybody relished, until, as time went by, it became obvious that this worked to the detriment of the R.A.C. as a whole. Only a select body of regiments became eligible for purposeful use during the Cold War and they, quite often, were to be overburdened by repeated operational tours in countries such as Malaya, while the others felt deprived of opportunities for active service. To some extent, worry lay at the heart of the matter, the fear of what would happen when, as the result of the dwindling commitment in India, the Army would have to be reduced in size. A decrease in the R.T.R.'s size was already inevitable, Montgomery told both the Hobarts in a private meeting at the War Office on 22 August 1947.

A study of successive R.A.C. Conference reports fails to reveal any pronounced attempt during this period to achieve unity within the R.A.C., although behind the scenes there were some who tried indirectly to achieve it. A rationalized policy was thrust upon the R.T.R. by Montgomery, in a letter he wrote to commanding officers on 7 March 1947. Reminding them that it was he who had been responsible for the decision that there should be only one R.A.C. Depot at Bovington instead of separate ones for R.T.R. and Cavalry, he told them, too, that the officers mess at Bovington should not be the sole preserve of the R.T.R., as many old R.T.C. officers regarded it, but should be for the R.A.C. also. He was adamant that '. . . all units of the R.A.C. should be prepared to take on any rôle . . .; in this way we shall gradually obtain that high degree of flexibility which is so essential in war, and will also widen the experience of officers and men'. Turning then to the unity of the R.T.R. itself, he dealt uncompromisingly with those who short-sightedly envisaged devolution: 'Breaking up the R.T.R. and making it into eight individual Regiments; similar to the Cavalry Regiments. This will NOT be done', he wrote: 'The Royal Armoured Corps consists of twenty Cavalry Regiments and the Royal Tank Regiment. The R.T.R. has eight Units. Officers will be posted within the R.A.C. in accordance with the needs of the Army, due regard being paid to the claims and wishes of an Officer to serve with his own Regiment whenever that can be done.' But desirable though it was to have cross-posting within the Corps, little progress was made towards this, probably, it must be faced, because the will did not yet exist, and each unit thought it could survive without the others.

Finally, the Field Marshal laid down that although all correspondence should be sent to the Representative Colonel Commandant at Bovington, 'there is no objection to C.O.s of Units writing direct to me if they wish . . . From my point of view, I find it necessary to have an officer in the War Office who will be my Staff Officer for R.T.R. Affairs. I have appointed Lt-Col P. R. C. Hobart, R.A.C. 3, to do this work. . . ' Hobart, in fact, cannot remember a single occasion when he was called upon to do any regimental work for Montgomery, and this is hardly surprising in the light of the impending changes in the Regimental hierarchy and the methods of consultation and control. On 1 May 1947, Major-General G. M. Lindsay, who had been a Colonel Commandant since 1938, retired from the appointment and was replaced by Sir Percy Hobart who simultaneously became Representative Colonel Commandant in place of Sir Charles Broad. Lindsay, who had delivered a rousing speech at the Cambrai Dinner in 1946, stressing the need for unity within the Regiment while recalling the days when the struggle for survival against hostile influences was omnipresent, had for long been remote from the mainstream of R.T.R. affairs, even though he had contributed strongly to the ideas which had driven the Regiment into the forefront of military thought and practice. Broad's postwar part in placing the Regiment on a firm organizational footing has been described above, but he too was detached from the centre of affairs because he was living in Ireland. The appointment of Hobart would bring management into the hands of a dynamic man, whose contacts with the younger officers, as well as with the latest thought and the ruling members of the Army Council, was much more recent. He was still to be counted among those who had struggled hardest for the Regiment's survival in the 1930s, and compromise did not come easily to him; he had made many enemies, but also, many friends.

Throughout the closing months of the war, the brothers-in-law, Montgomery and Hobart, had been in close and frequent consultation when planning the assault into North-West Europe, which had owed so much to the Specialized Armour Hobart had helped develop and train. In the campaign which had culminated in the German surrender on Luneburg Heath in May 1945, their collaboration burgeoned. Although there are no records of the close contacts that existed, there is no doubt that they were very much in each other's minds. Now the co-operation of the battlefield was extended to the post-war period. In 1945, Hobart instigated a recommendation that Montgomery be made a Colonel Commandant. Montgomery promoted the appointment of Hobart as the Representative Colonel Commandant in 1947. These moves coincided with informal conversations, led by Hobart, in the immediate post-war period, with the trusted R.T.R. officers who had worked under him at various stages in his career, notably N. W. Duncan, A. Jolly, and A. W. Brown. To them he propounded his determination to see that regimental unity be paramount. From them came the proposals which shaped his policy when he became Colonel Commandant. Central to the ideas that arose was the concept of far closer control, with decisions made by commanding officers (and the wives, too) through the creation of a Regimental Council which would meet once or twice a year. Its members were to be the Colonels Commandant and the commanding officers of regiments, its advisers, co-opted senior officers of great experience. The first meeting of this Council was held during the first post-war Corps Week, which was run by 1st R.T.R. at Hobart Barracks, Detmold, from 29 June to 3 July 1947.

Paradoxically, as the threat of a reduction in R.T.R.'s size grew imminent, a determined and successful effort was made to increase its number of Bands from the one existing Staff Band to a mooted figure of eight – each unit having expressed the desire to have its own music. As a first stage, in 1947, two Regimental Bands were formed out of the Staff Band, a loss of official status which also allowed members to transfer to any other band, and produced a drop in fees from performances. In fact, most members stayed on, proud as they were of being 'Tankies', and the 'A' and 'B' Bands under, respectively, Band-masters (later Lieutenants) T. Davies and W. J. Lemon, prospered until, in 1949, both Bands were re-granted Minor Staff Band status, and were joined by a 'C' Minor Staff Band under Lieutenant R. Jarvis. At this stage, too, they took the names Cambrai, Alamein and Rhine.

The day by day running of the Regiment devolved upon Duncan as Commander of the R.A.C. Centre at Bovington (McLeod had handed over his regimental responsibilities in 1947), although there came an important shift in emphasis when Hobart moved to the Royal Hospital, Chelsea as Lieutenant-Governor in October 1948. Here, well-placed to have personal dealings with the War Office branches, and with members of the Regiment passing through the capital city, Hobart initiated the arrangement which, eventually, was to lead to the transfer of the Representative Colonel Commandant's office to London. At the back of his mind was the installation of an independent staff, although this was not yet feasible in 1948 because of financial objections and because, if the R.T.R. were given an official establishment of that sort, other R.A.C. Regiments would demand the same. Eventually, changes in the appointments of the D.R.A.C. made possible the official transfer. At the end of 1946, Major-General R. Briggs had handed over as D.R.A.C. to Major-General R. H. B. Arkwright (late 12th Lancers) as the first Cavalry D.R.A.C. Arkwright, in his turn, had handed over in October 1948 to Major-General G. P. B. Roberts, of whom the R.T.R. was proud; at forty-two, he was one of the youngest General officers in the Army and one of the most able and experienced armoured commanders. Unfortunately, he was to remain for only a few months before retiring to take up a post in industry. He was replaced by Duncan. At about the same time, too, on 1 January 1949, Sir Charles Broad retired and General Sir John Crocker succeeded him as one of the three Colonels Commandant. The team which had carried the R.T.R. through the war had thus passed from the lists. In their stead were to be found the men of the war years who, between them had done so much to make the invasion of Europe successful – Montgomery as C.-in-C., Crocker as Commander of 1st Corps on the beaches, Hobart as leader of the Specialized Armour. And in 1951, when Hobart retired, it would be Duncan (for a few months with Colonel T. C. A. Clarke as Secretary) who would take his place as Representative Colonel Commandant in addition to his duties as D.R.A.C.

It was, therefore, a logical step to appoint an official Secretary to the Colonel Commandant in the War Office, an innovation that became feasible in 1951 at a time when rearmament was in full swing and the lean years were, for the time being, over. In March 1952, Lieutenant-Colonel R. N. Wilson became the official Secretary to the Representative Colonel Commandant in the Grade of R.O. II and was located by Duncan in a room in R.A.C. 1 at the War Office where, apart from doing his assigned job, he could keep an ear to the ground as R.A.C. policy evolved. He was made responsible for a wide range of duties, such as liaison with A.G. 17 in connection with the careers of R.T.R. officers and (also with R.A.C. Records) senior W.O.s and N.C.O.s, and editor of *The Tank*. Also, he was in charge of liaison with Regular and T.A. Regiments, as well as with 'Old Comrades' branches, the arrangement of council meetings, ceremonial and social events plus a host of other tasks. He was assisted by one civil servant clerk, Mr. A. L. Jenkins, and one R.T.R. corporal clerk.

It is a strange paradox that when, at the latter end of the 1940s, it became necessary to prevent units of the R.T.R. from splitting apart, the R.A.C. was being drawn closer together. Unification of the Corps, laggardly and, sometimes, tedious though it was, advanced irresistibly. Although they had to join their individual units eventually, recruits and officers were, invariably, first inducted into organizations of an Army or Corps nature. Until 1948, when the 8th R.T.R. (Lieutenant-Colonel H. M. Liardet) and three cavalry regiments assumed the task, a Regular or National Service trooper would join an R.A.C. training regiment at Catterick Camp or Carlisle, and be taught for fifteen weeks by officers drawn from every unit in the Corps, a system to which the R.A.C. was to return early in 1950 when R.A.C. training regiments were reformed. A man with aspirations to a Regular commission would spend a minimum of four months in the ranks (mostly at an R.A.C. training regiment) before being sent to the Royal Military Academy, Sandhurst, where the first post-war course opened in February 1947, during one of the coldest and most miserable winters in memory. Here, from the entire Army entry, the selection of candidates for Regiments went on in parallel with the course of fifteen months, and it was a source of comfort to the R.T.R. and its first Regimental Representative at the Academy, Major A. R. Leakey, that from the outset, the number of available vacancies was over-subscribed so that young officers of a very high standard could be chosen. A National Service officer cadet, on the other hand, would be sent to the Mons Officer Cadet School, Aldershot, where he would receive a much more intensive course of twelve weeks under R.A.C. instructors that was intended only to fit him as a troop leader.

And in due course, regular officers and N.C.O.s would find themselves attending courses at the R.A.C. Centre where they would meet old friends from many regiments and make many new ones, thus widening their knowledge of the Corps and absorbing its spirit. In January 1952, the process was extended when a Boys Squadron R.A.C. (the brain-child of Duncan as D.R.A.C.) was formed at Bovington Camp under Major B. O'Sullivan and the foundations were laid of an establishment which was intended to produce R.A.C. N.C.O.s in the same way as the officer training units produced R.A.C. officers whose thinking was on Corps as well as on Regimental lines.

An outward sign of the way in which units as well as individuals of the Regiment had begun to go their own way could be seen in the clothes they wore. All manner of different kinds of lanyard were being sported in addition to varieties of service dress, shirts and shoes. 1st R.T.R. wore its red lanyard – and this was not in dispute – but the 7th, for example, went in for a red and green lanyard and its officers took to carrying canes instead of ash-plants with a knob. Sartorial splendours and irregularities were frowned upon. In May 1950, the Regimental Council felt the need to reinforce the Regulations of Dress by insisting upon officers at extra-Regimental Duty conforming to the standards that were being enforced in units, the units having already been brought to heel. Except in the 1st, black lanyards would be worn. Shoes would be black, with a stitched toe-cap. Brogues would not be worn. Khaki socks would be worn with battle and service dress, black socks with No. 1 Dress or blue patrols. Gloves would be of brown leather, later changed to black. For a while some sort of regularity did appear, but, as everyone who has served for long in the British Army must know, the mere appearance of a Dress Regulation acts as a spur to change. The story of dress in the R.T.R. is one of frequent alteration as one fashion superseded another. But one item of clothing remained constant, the envied black beret which so many other armies enviously copied as did some units and corps of the British Army, quite illegally, until officially prevented. Yet not even this jealously guarded headgear was proof against development, as became evident in 1959 when the Regimental Council, after many years of investigation and experiment, managed to obtain authorization for a design by Mrs Susan Hobart of the officer's dress beret in Furleen (imitation astrakhan). To say the least, its reception was mixed. Some professed to like it and a few tried hard to avoid wearing it, while others resorted to derision by comparing their new hat to a small poodle, and asking if it would walk to heel. Over the years, its popularity waned until it was discarded in 1977.

Before passing to consideration of the major events which were to govern the Regiment in the 1950s, and which were to lift it out of the depths of deprivation into which it had been driven by extremes of Government defence policy, it is essential to record two measures, one transitory, the other permanent, which had a marked effect on morale. The transitory measure concerned a surplus of senior and substantive W.O.s which was produced as the Army contracted in size and who could not be absorbed within existing establishments. Not only did they block the promotion of the many excellent junior N.C.O.s throughout the regiment, and who began to leave the Army because of lack of encouragement, but they were virtually a wasted asset since there were insufficient places for them at extra-Regimental employment. In consequence, a scheme, graced by the abbreviation SURWONCO, was introduced to employ senior ranks at Regimental Duty, in tasks at a level below those to which their rank suited them. As an expedient it served the purpose of utilizing men of considerable ability and experience. But as a deterrent to promotion and recruiting it was far from welcome, at a time when many people were concluding that a sound recruiting programme and good promotion prospects were essential to counter-balance the detrimental effects of National Service. Fortunately, the improvement in circumstances through expansion in the 1950s removed the need of this scheme.

The measure which hit hardest at Regimental loyalty, even though it was intended to and, in fact, actually did improve the lot of the most highly-skilled men in the Regiment, was that announced in 1949 as R.E.M.E. Phase II. In essence, those artificers and fitters who, up to 1950, had been centrally trained and posted to regiments, were to be transferred, if they agreed, to the R.E.M.E. A larger organization, it was reasoned, would make fuller use of the highly trained and specialized men charged with the task of maintaining the entire Army's technical equipment. The benefits to the Army of such a centralized organization were quite apparent, and were eagerly presented by the R.E.M.E. As a further attraction it was also pointed out that promotion prospects would be improved. The rub came when loyal members of regiments reached the moment when they had to change their badge and join a Corps of which they knew nothing, and which knew little or nothing of them. For the most part, in fact, the transformation went smoothly, eased by assur- ances that there would not be an immediate and wholesale transfer of fitters from the units in which they had served for many years. The sheer necessity to retain fitters at work in which they were expert demanded nothing less, if the maintenance of armoured units were not to collapse overnight. The vast majority of men agreed to the call to change, albeit with an outward display of disgruntlement. Some, however, refused point-blank to make the change, preferring to wear the black beret with a tank badge, instead of a blue one and a badge that had no emotive impact – and sacrificed their career prospects by so doing. Such can be the effect of the tugs of regimental spirit in its most fervent form.

*   *   *   *   *

Field Marshal Montgomery handed over as C.I.G.S. to Field Marshal Sir William Slim in November 1948, just as the international situation had reached the point where the Western Powers could no longer remain indifferent to their security. Western Europe stood in danger. As Soviet Russia maintained the siege of Berlin, only a few understrength British, French and American formations were available to prevent a possible invasion, and, for the most part, they were ill-equipped and undertrained.

Stage by stage, as public opinion was gradually brought to accept the perils of the situation, the Western Powers began to put their joint defences in order. In March 1947, the Treaty of Dunkirk had created a fifty-year defensive alliance between France and Britain; in March 1948, on the eve of the commencement of Marshall Aid to Europe and of the Berlin blockade, the Brussels Treaty brought into existence Western Union, comprising Britain, France, the Netherlands, Belgium and Luxembourg. And in November of that year, Montgomery left Whitehall to become Chairman of its permanent defence organization. Six months later, in April 1949, the Western Union powers joined with the U.S.A., Canada, Denmark, Iceland, Italy, Norway and Portugal in establishing the North Atlantic Treaty Organization. In the meantime, Slim had succeeded where Montgomery had failed, in that he had managed to change the mind of the Government so that, when National Service came into effect on 1 January 1949, the eighteen months period which the War Office had always deemed essential was agreed. It was further extended to two years in the summer of 1950, at the time of the political crisis associated with the Korean War, when it was decided to make a very large expansion in the size of the armed services.

In 1950, Soviet military strength was heavily concentrated upon the Red Army, with a preponderance of resources allocated to its armoured forces. Estimates as to its real strength varied, but a conservative figure suggested that, in addition to a very large number of infantry divisions, each with its own medium tank battalion and self-propelled gun units, some 50 tank divisions were available, each with about 300 T 34/85 and JS 3s, plus 30 mechanized divisions each having about 150 tanks. The current Intelligence forecasts contemplated a high proportion of this enormous force being launched against the British Sector guarding the North German Plain between Hamburg, in the north, and the Harz Mountains in the south, and the blow, if it came, was expected to be *en masse* and so rapid that little or no time would be available to reinforce the Allied troops stationed in the theatre. Already it was becoming apparent, as information about Soviet strength was acquired, that the chances of the British Reserve Citizen Army formations arriving in time were extremely poor. Such defence as could be mounted would depend upon the attenuated 2nd Infantry Division, the 7th Armoured Division, a weak Dutch corps, a Belgian armoured division and a Canadian infantry brigade. The main hope lay in the threat of an atomic deterrent from the U.S.A.

The plan which H.Q. B.A.O.R. devised based the main defences on the Rhine, with the 200 tanks of 7th Armoured Brigade, under Brigadier H. R. B. Foote, V.C., deployed ahead to delay the Soviet mass. This amounted to the height of military optimism. The state of the two R.T.R. units in 7th Armoured Brigade (the other units were The Scots Greys and the 5th Royal Inniskilling Dragoons) was fairly representative of early 1949. The 1st was regarded as a National Service training regiment, while the 5th, also entirely engaged in lower level training, had a squadron detached to the Infantry School at Sennelager for demonstration purposes. Neither was battleworthy, but both had converted slowly to Centurions, though only the Mark 1 and 2 versions, with 17pdr. guns. So Foote, who had earned his V.C. in a forlorn charge in 1942, could have had few illusions as to this brigade's prospects should it be called upon. As it was, the emergency did at least rescue his units from menial tasks and project them on the first of the intensive round of tactical training programmes and exercises which were to be a feature of life in B.A.O.R. from that moment onward.

It is very difficult to visualise what sort of army the British Army would have become, if the system Montgomery was driven to permit had come fully into being – or if the international situation had not deteriorated to the extent that it did, in order to enforce a virtual abandonment of the scheme for a Citizen Army. How long the Regular element would have survived intact amid the punishing round of classroom work is conjectural. The opportunities for adventure and to practise the art of putting theory into practice in tactical exercises, if nothing else, were essential as a means of retaining the loyalty of men of character. As it was, the various organizations upon which Western Europe's defence would be based had yet to come into existence and it would be 1950 before a pronounced change could be felt within combat units of the Army. And it would be 1951 before convincing N.A.T.O. forces could take the field.

Lack of trained manpower would be one cause for the delay, since it would take time to re-organize the training establishments and convert run-down Regular units to an operational state. Shortage of equipment, especially equipment powerful enough to compensate for numerical inferiority, was another. In this realm, too, the post-war effect of Montgomery's tank policy on the R.A.C. and the R.T.R. could be felt. Not that Montgomery can be accused of producing that policy entirely off his own bat. Certainly he knew from his own experience that tanks such as the Sherman and Comet, with their universal capability of engaging in a variety of combat tasks, were more useful than such specialized heavy tanks as the Churchill, but the concept of the 'Universal Tank' had been formulated in 1943 before these ideas had time to take root in his mind. As an infantryman and high commander, he was bound to seek and accept advice from armoured experts and in this respect he was likely to be influenced to a larger extent by R.T.R. than by Cavalry officers. For example, apart from Sir Percy Hobart's voice, he had listened since 1943 to his B.R.A.C. in Eighth Army, Brigadier G. W. Richards, who stayed with him as Armoured Advisor when he took command of 21st Army Group in 1944; and the tank policy he inherited in 1946 when he became C.I.G.S. had been produced by the previous D.R.A.C., Briggs. In their turn, these officers had been swayed by the impact of their own recent experience in battle, and by digesting the reports of their subordinates as well as operational research scientists. The former were prey to the worst that the enemy could do, the latter were few in number and not, as yet, wholly convincing in their findings.

At the end of the war, an informed consensus would have shown that tank soldiers, while adamant that armoured vehicles were essential to the pursuit of war on land, were in some doubt as to the best means needed to implement their use in the future. Two weapons threatened a tank's existence on the battlefield, and a third frustrated it. The threat came from the large, high-velocity gun, such as the German 88mm. (mounted either on a very heavy and clumsy wheeled mounting or carried in a tracked vehicle such as a tank), and the light-weight, man-portable, bazooka-type, rocket-propelled missile, fitted with a hollow-charge, chemical energy warhead. The frustration was caused by mines, which were difficult to detect and sweep. All were feared by tank crews, though possibly it was the bazooka which was disliked the most because it was in greatest supply on the German side during the closing stages of the war. In general, it was realized that the counters to these weapons were to be found in refined tactics (whereby armoured vehicles, infantry, artillery and engineers worked in closer co-operation, in order to make the best use of their characteristics to deal with each kind of threat) and improvements in the tank's protection and hitting power along with mine-sweeping devices. It is by no means insignificant that the one new, major technical proposal to be found in the last wartime R.A.C. half-yearly report, issued in June 1945, called for new radio sets using the very high-frequency range to replace the existing 18 and 38 high-frequency range sets which had failed to satisfy the requirements of infantry/tank cooperation. To prevent penetration by solid shot or hollow-charge weapons, the only solution seriously considered at that time was the classic one of increasing armour thickness as well as sloping it, and of introducing space between surfaces wherever possible. Both methods could be seen in the A 41 (Centurion) the design of which had begun in 1943, and would be found to an even greater extent on its intended successor, FV 201, which was selected at the end of 1945.

It was with this machine that Montgomery concerned himself when he addressed the R.A.C. Conference in November 1946, shortly after taking over as C.I.G.S. He spoke of the need for extensive research and development and of the financial stringency that would allow only low production of new tanks. Announcing that the Centurion would be the new main battle tank, he also said that FV 201 would be running in 1947. But only the wooden mock-up was ready by that date, and it was not until October 1948, when Montgomery was about to lay down his job as C.I.G.S., that the first prototype was on the road. But because of the requirement that it should perform numerous rôles, it had become too complicated and expensive. Several important design changes had been introduced as development proceeded, to such an extent that when the prototype made its first appearance it was obvious that the project could no longer be supported. At the R.A.C. Conference, on 27 October 1948, it was announced that FV 201 would be abandoned, though not solely because of technical difficulties. Under the new D.R.A.C., G. P. B. Roberts, a close study had been made of tank philosophy, from which emerged a clarified statement of policy to the effect, as declared at this conference, that the R.A.C. must be in possession of a tank 'which is armed with a gun capable of penetrating frontally the best enemy tank'. This was fundamental. Equality with a potential enemy, which had been the case virtually since 1918, was no longer acceptable. Simultaneously, a reassessment had been made of the armament and armour protection likely to be found on the best Soviet Russian tank, considered at that time to be the JS 3 with its 122mm. gun. From this it was concluded that the 20pdr. gun, which was being mounted in the Centurion and would also have been given to FV 201, was inadequate. It was merely the last nail in FV 201's coffin when, in 1949, it was discovered that the latest tank landing craft (LCT 8) produced by the Navy was not wide enough or high enough to let the D.D. (swimming) version go through its doors.

Tank design and development are the products of teamwork. To no one man can the credit be assigned for any one concept, and this applies with particular force to the change in policy with took place under Robert's direction at the end of 1948, shortly before he handed over to Duncan in March 1949 and left the Army. Roberts himself embodied the distilled essence of armoured warfare knowledge, having experienced practically every aspect of tank combat, from adjutant to divisional commander, from the initial phases of the desert campaigns in 1940, to the culminating battles of 1944 and 1945 in Europe. He knew what it meant to be outmatched in a qualitative as well as a quantitative manner. His G.S.O. 1 in R.A.C. 3, who was responsible for formulating D.R.A.C.'s technical specifications in conjunction with the staff of the Director General of Fighting Vehicles (D.G.F.V.) at the Ministry of Supply, was Major D. B. Wormald (13th/18th Hussars). And the D.G.F.V., whose responsibility it was to coordinate the design, development and production of A.F.V.s with establishments such as the Fighting Vehicles Research and Development Establishment (F.V.R.D.E.), Armament Research and Development Establishment (A.R.D.E.) and Signals Research and Development Establishment (S.R.D.E.) (quite apart from the other Services) was Major-General E. M. Clayton, a Gunner, with Lieutenant-Colonel R. M. P. Carver as G.S.O. 1 in F.V.A. 1.

These departments and organizations were permeated by officers of the R.A.C. and R.A. whose knowledge and attitudes were heavily influenced by personal involvement in battles in which, all too often, they had been at a technical disadvantage. It was inevitable, therefore, that the specifications they wrote for any future A.F.V.s would reflect their experience and that, seeking to remedy all the deficiencies in equipment that had become apparent during the war, they tended to ask for rather more refinements than were technically or economically feasible at that time. Additional complications were introduced by attempts to standardize tank procurement policy with Allies. That this was rarely possible emerged during and after an A.B.C. (America-Britain-Canada) standardization conference in 1948, when one of the few agreements reached was that all three should have three types of tank – a heavy with a 120mm. gun, a medium with a 90mm. and a light with a 76mm. gun.

World events and technological improvements then took a hand in 1949. By studying the picture of a JS 3, which appeared on a foreign postage stamp, Major A. Cooper, in R.A.C. 3, had managed to calculate the armour thickness of that tank's frontal armour belt, as well as deducing a great deal of further information. In due course, the JS 3 would be revealed as a less dangerous foe than had been feared, but at the time it was reckoned that the 20pdr. gun was inadequate to kill it; something much more powerful was required. Only an American 120mm. gun was immediately available and suitable, and this was too big to go into the Centurion, which had now assumed the mantle of Universal Tank. It was decided, therefore, to produce a heavily armoured tank, mounting the 120mm. gun in an entirely new turret, and utilizing the hull and running gear of the discarded FV 201. Duncan says he was bullied into it by Mr. E. Masters of F.V.R.D.E. – but the need was seen as urgent and it did satisfy the A.B.C. agreement. The vehicle was known as FV 214 and would be running in 1952, by which time it would be graced by the name Conqueror. Simultaneously, the most careful scrutiny was being focussed on tank gunnery; on the accuracy of guns and their associated optical instruments and firing gear. It was now appreciated that, against an enemy fielding vastly superior numbers of A.F.V.s, only the delivery of rapid and accurate gunfire would prevail. Therefore, a better system was required than the existing one whereby, to quote H. B. Starr, who was to become one of the R.A.C.'s most experienced gunnery instructors, '. . . tank crews were taught to estimate range, to fire and observe the fall of shot, apply a correction and eventually hit the target'. For one thing, such was the muzzle velocity of the 20pdr. (1,432 metres per second), and such the obscuration caused by its discharge, that it was virtually impossible for the commander to observe the fall of shot from his turret. And in any case, the estimation of visual range had never been accurate. The 120mm. gun, with a muzzle velocity of 1,300 metres per second, would be no easier to range than the 20pdr. and so it was decided to solve the problems by technology.

In Conqueror, the commander was located in a sub-turret which was fitted with a range-finder. Sophisticated facilities enabled him to override the gunner by laying the main armament accurately on the target himself, leaving the gunner to complete the engagement while the commander selected another target. Brilliant in concept though this was, the state of modern technology at the time proved inadequate to field conditions, with the result that, from the outset, Conqueror had many teething troubles. Moreover, by the time it had begun trials in 1952, certain devices and methods were in the offing which could, with relative ease, improve the Centurion's capability to such an extent that Conqueror became less of a necessity. To begin with, the invention of the R.C.P. (Reflector-Cum-Periscope) Sight in 1948 (work on which had begun in 1943) enabled a Centurion's commander to lay the gun on the target, and went some way to matching Conqueror's far more complicated machinery for achieving the same object. But the main improvements in shooting techniques, accuracy and the sheer penetrating power of Centurion's main armament – which would extend its life potential for a generation at least – were reserved for the mid-1950s and are described in Chapters VI and IX.

Typical, however, of the pitfalls which were omnipresent in all technical advances, were those associated with the creation of the proposed new range of radio sets described by members of S.R.D.E. at the 1949 R.A.C. Conference. The projected V.H.F. (38–60 m/cycles range) 42 Set to replace the H.F. 19 Set, which was becoming progressively inadequate in a crowded wave-band, offered advantages in communication which could not be gainsaid. The main debate focussed on the need of a 'B' Set (B 45) and was carried in favour by an unscientific (if democratic) show of hands (!) with only one dissentient. Unfortunately, no mention was made of what might be possible in a few years' time, if the development of prototypes were delayed until the newly-invented transistors could be utilized in place of valves. True, the transistor had yet to be evaluated, but by 1955, when the new sets were first displayed at the R.A.C. Conference, and the transistors' advantages in efficiency and reliability were revealed, things had gone too far. In 1960, the Army would get a set which it desperately needed. Had it waited a little longer it would have fared a great deal better – but this is the classical progression in technical improvement.

In 1949, however, a world-wide threat to British interests had to be countered by whatever means existed. First, a rapid expansion of the Services, able to confront a variety of threats in a wide range of climates, had to be started. These demands would tax the Army quite as heavily as had the negative restrictions of poverty, but at least they would stimulate units by giving them a military goal, as they began to emerge from the limitations imposed under Montgomery's régime to a relatively blissful state under Slim.

CHAPTER IV

Defence in the East
1949-1953

When 3rd R.T.R. (less B Squadron) found itself at anchor off Liverpool in a broken-down H.M.T. *Orduna* on the morning of 5 July 1949, it must have seemed an ill-fitting reward for the efforts they had made to sail for Hong Kong at what, by the standards of the day, was very short notice. At that time not even the units of the War Office Reserve were geared to quick moves. The receipt of an instruction in mid-April to include an all-Regular squadron among the reinforcements for Hong Kong, against the threat posed by the approaching victorious Chinese Communist Forces (C.C.F.), made it necessary to reshuffle the the officers and men of B Squadron to meet the Regular requirement. And that squadron, under Major D. C. F. Chute, was chosen mainly because it was the only one in the 3rd which had recently fired its annual armament classification course. Five weeks were allowed to prepare vehicles and equipment for shipment, to undergo innoculations, take fourteen days' embarkation leave and load the tanks into merchant ships. It would take the squadron commander five days (with night stops in that pre-jet airliner era) to fly to the Colony, and the squadron with their vehicles two months to complete their journey. Moreover, when they did arrive, they were placed under canvas in a paddy-field, their intended accommodation being as yet uncompleted, because it had never been foreseen by the authorities that an armoured regiment might one day be needed in Hong Kong.

When the remainder of the regiment arrived, a month later, it was to share the discomforts of a station in which heat and high humidity sapped the men's stamina, and where typhoons could wreck a tidy camp within a few minutes, in a location where the difficulty of deploying tanks among the hills, paddy and built-up areas was unique in the R.T.R.'s experience. First of all, however, they had to restore the tanks to fighting fitness after a voyage in which many items of kit had been pilfered, and the spillage from the cargo of flour, with which some of the tanks had been over-stowed, had to be removed. But as to a confrontation with the potential enemy, there was anti-climax. A comprehensive plan had been made by the newly-formed 40th

Division and 27th Brigade, to which the 3rd R.T.R. belonged, to hold the high ground overlooking China from the New Territories. But it was not until October and, fortunately, on a Sunday when, at last, the imminent arrival of the C.C.F. was reported. The officers had congregated in the mess for drinks and, as a result, orders were speedily given. A Squadron (Major W. D. Bazley), which was standing by at one hour's notice to move, deployed to hull-down positions on the frontier within ninety minutes. There they waited, tensely watching the arrival of an advanced guard of refugees, but without a Chinese soldier in sight. Next day they returned to camp, thus concluding the only occasion, in Hong Kong, when the 3rd was required to stow ammunition in A.F.V.s in readiness for offensive action. The Communists, as it turned out, preferred to leave the Colony in British hands.

It was in another part of the Far East that the 3rd was to find action – in Malaya – and it was to do so there only because there was nowhere in Hong Kong where it was possible to fire armour-piercing shot from the Comets' 77mm. guns. On the direct intervention of the C.-in-C. Far East, General Sir John Harding, himself no mean exponent of tank operations, land for a full-sized field firing range some fifteen miles deep was taken over at Gurun in North Malaya – an area which happened also to be infested by some exceedingly active Communist terrorists. In March 1951, in compliance with Harding's instructions that, 'if the Japs could do it so can we', Major D. C. F. Chute selected and set up a range in undulating country that was sufficiently open to allow shooting up to 3,000 yards, and bounded by rubber estates and secondary jungle. Within a remarkably short time, a camp was built and the first crews to arrive had pioneered routes into the training area and had built bridges for their tanks over the many streams which intersected the approaches.

During the coming months, several troops from the regiment would be sent to spend six weeks firing their annual open range course. To some, however, training was an incidental. Always they had to be alert against ambush. Occasionally an opportunity came to join in the fight against the Communists. Once their camp came under fire and in July 1951, they were instrumental in carrying the fight to the enemy after an armed terrorist had voluntarily surrendered to Trooper Duke of 6 Troop who was driving along the range road.

The information given by this deserter led to the mounting of what grew into the first all-arms operation against terrorists in Malaya, involving tanks, infantry and artillery controlled by a spotting aircraft. The discovery of the terrorist camp on a hilltop enabled the Gunners to engage it with a 15-minute concentration while the Comets of 6 Troop, carrying a platoon of infantry on their engine decks, advanced to within 200 yards of the area thought to contain the objective. Here, the infantry debussed and the tanks moved round to a flank, firing Besa machine-guns and 77mm. H.E., while the artillery shifted its fire to the jungle edge beyond. Tactical theory and standard practice went hand-in-hand until, quite unintentionally, one tank actually blundered straight into the camp, ahead of the infantry, to capture a large quantity of supplies. In the meantime, the infantry, to their astonishment too, came across another camp, whose existence had not been suspected. But the birds had flown, and so the operation is left to history as just another in which a ponderous blow directed at guerillas hit thin air. To the satisfaction of the R.T.R. however, it had been shown that modern tanks could operate in jungle and that they did have a rôle to play in South-East Asia, despite the disparagement of those who thought otherwise. 'British armour', as an officer in 3rd R.T.R. wrote, 'is at present ahead of that of other nations [in the movement of A.F.V.s in jungle country]; world conditions to-day demand that the early development and perfection of this technique shall not be overlooked.'

But the days of the Gurun detachment, unpopular as it was from the start with Lieutenant-General G. Evans, the Commander, British Troops Hong Kong, were numbered. As an infantryman with desert experience, he placed great reliance on armour and resisted any reduction to his tank strength when the Chinese were so bellicose. In November 1951, the detachment suffered its only death from enemy action when a subaltern was ambushed in the training area. In February 1952, it was closed down just prior to the 3rd setting sail for the U.K.

* * * * *

In the early 1950s the depredations of the Chinese attracted considerable world attention and succeeded in diverting a significant proportion of Britain's relatively slender military means from other threatened areas. They gave encouragement to the North Koreans when, in June 1950, the latter invaded South Korea, thereby initiating the war which was to involve the U.S.A., the British Commonwealth and many other nations in a rescue operation under the banner of the United Nations. In August, 27th Brigade was sent at short notice from Hong Kong to reinforce the hard-pressed U.N. defenders of the Pusan bridgehead, but 3rd R.T.R. did not accompany them. Not only was it believed that the security of Hong Kong should not be put in jeopardy, but it was also felt that the contingent should be equipped, for prestige purposes, with Britain's latest and best tank – the Centurion, and at that time the 3rd had only Comets. Indeed, there were only enough of the latest Centurion Mark 3, armed with the Metrovik stabilized 20pdr. gun, to equip one other R.A.C. Regiment – 4th R.T.R.

Before it was decided to send 27th Brigade, the Government had announced its intention to send the 29th Brigade to Korea from Britain – a formation under the command of Brigadier T. Brodie and consisting, when it sailed in October, of the 8th King's Royal Irish Hussars, 1st Battalion Royal Northumberland Fusiliers (R.N.F.), 1st Battalion The Gloucestershire Regiment and 1st Battalion Royal Ulster Rifles (R.U.R.), plus units of the Royal Artillery, Royal Engineers and the supporting Services. This, as the Press described it, was to be a 'Rolls-Royce' force. But as was usual in those days when a so-called 'Fire Brigade' formation was committed to its task, it was impossible to assemble the force without extensive surgery, alterations and additions to its existing structure. One of the designated infantry battalions could not go because it did not have enough N.C.O.s and Regulars; they had to be relieved by 1st R.N.F. who, at three days' notice, gave up their job as demonstration battalion to the School of Infantry, Warminster. Because it was ruled that no National Servicemen, except volunteers, were to go, they had to be posted away, with the result that the Government was compelled to call up reservists to make good the shortfall in manpower. The brigade which eventually left for Korea consisted of an average number of 75 per cent reservists, some of whom had recently purchased their discharge and many of whom were Second World War veterans who were unfit and out of date, and who had been torn, none too willingly, from their homes and jobs. Rich in experience though they were, and excellent though their performance in trying conditions would be, they were not necessarily the right men to call upon.

Originally, it had not been intended that an R.T.R. unit be included in the 29th Brigade, although many ex-members of the regiment were to be found within the 8th Hussars. But, as an after-thought, it occurred to the Army Council that a squadron of Crocodile flame-throwing tanks might be useful and, with this in mind, 7th R.T.R. (Lieutenant-Colonel J. G. S. Compton) was ordered to produce such a sub-unit and make it up to strength with what would amount to 35 per cent reservists. The order arrived at a bad moment. An under-strength 7th was scattered in no less than four places. C Squadron was guarding the U.S.

Strategic Bomber base at Marham in Norfolk, D was performing as the Amphibious Wing at Gosport, a detachment from A was running a T.A. summer camp at Lulworth, and the remainder were living in penury at Bovington. By plundering the Regiment, with the exception of R.H.Q., the bulk of D Squadron, the men who were administratively indispensable or medically downgraded and, with undue emphasis as it seemed at the time, A Squadron's Clerk (because he was a very good racing tipster), the cadre of a new C Squadron, under Major A. J. D. Pettingell, was formed. Within eight weeks it had drawn its equipment, given rudimentary training to the influx of new men, sorted out the multitudinous welfare problems of the reservists, taken embarkation leave, loaded its tanks into merchant ships and set sail in H.M.T. *Empire Fowey* in company with the 8th Hussars. At that time, there can have been few squadrons that contained so high a percentage of experienced tank soldiers. When 4th R.T.R. lined the banks of the Suez Canal to see them pass, the cry 'Get your knees brown' came from ship to shore – and there was no audible retort.

By the time the complete 29th Brigade arrived in Korea on 17 November, the war looked as if it were over. The North Koreans had been routed and flung back into the northern end of the country, where they clung tenaciously to a bridgehead, sustained by increasing help from the Chinese. Eight days later the Chinese Army struck massively at the U.S. Eighth Army (which included 27th Brigade) near the Yalu River, and hurled it back. Meanwhile, C Squadron had disembarked its tanks at Pusan and with the 8th Hussars was brought northward on rail flats in conditions of bitter cold. One troop arrived at the North Korean capital of Pyongyang just in time to off-load and retreat southward on its tracks, swept up in the precipitate U.N. withdrawal. By stages the Brigade was moved to a defensive position at Changdan, standing in rear of the Imjin River defences, held by the 6th Republic of Korea (R.O.K.) Division. On New Year's Eve these were broken by a Chinese attack.

At this moment, C Squadron, 7th R.T.R. contributed half of 29th Brigade's armour, but had sent its flame-throwers' trailers to the rear (less those of one troop) so that the Churchills could move more freely in the difficult hill and paddy terrain. The remaining armour came from an *ad hoc* unit called Cooperforce under Captain Astley Cooper of the 8th Hussars, with 12 Cromwells assembled from 8th Hussars' Reconnaissance Troop and from 45th Field Regiment R.A. For a sudden fear that the loss of a Centurion might prematurely prejudice the tank's secrecy had led to their removal to the south, thence to Japan, leaving Brodie without his most powerful weapon. 1st R.U.R., with Cooperforce, held the left of the Brigade position in Happy Valley. 1st R.N.F. was on the right with C Squadron, in Compo Valley. Early on 3 January, both battalions were attacked simultaneously and, by mid-morning, enemy infantry had penetrated the valleys between the R.N.F. company positions in the surrounding hills. The battalion telephone-exchange in the village at the centre of the defended area, had been captured. W Company was ordered to turn the enemy out of the village, and 5 Troop, under Lieutenant B. H. S. Clarke, supported by two tanks of Squadron H.Q., was sent from the squadron concentration area in rear to support them.

The ground over which the action was to be fought was intersected by narrow, frozen water courses, and was overlooked by R.N.F. companies pinned on the surrounding hills, from which the Chinese could not eject them in face of accurate rifle, mortar and machine-gun fire. The tanks could only move in single file along the narrow track leading to the village, firing as they went, while W Company moved slightly in rear and to the flank like a line of beaters. 'As I was the leading tank I think I fired more than the others', writes Clarke, 'and I was getting very short of ammunition by the time both my guns fell to pieces in the middle of the battle! Sgt Dowling then took up the lead and did a lot of shooting as well. . . . I was never conscious of anything coming back, but I recall trying to shoot at a machine-gun with my Bren [from the top of the turret] and having difficulty making up my mind whether to show myself or whether safety was the better part of valour. We wreaked terrible execution . . . The only anti-tank weapons they had were long bamboo poles with a very crude explosive charge tied to the end, and which on rare and brave occasions, they would ram against the side of the tank.'

The village was retaken without much difficulty, and by nightfall the position had been restored. But already the Americans had pulled back on the flanks, and orders came to retreat under cover of darkness, a manoeuvre which passed off without serious incident. The tanks came out last, with each commander walking in front to guide his driver down the crumbling track. To this day, Clarke cannot understand why the Chinese did not press their initial penetration on the flanks and cut the escape route. As it was, Cooperforce and the R.U.R. on the right, having also withstood the assault throughout the day, were caught in the dark and suffered heavily. Cooperforce was wiped out by hordes of Chinese who ran to the tanks' sides to knock them out with their primitive charges.

Along with the rest, C Squadron retired until they came to a standstill at Osan-ni, south of Seoul. These were miserable days, often spent in the open in temperatures of 48 degrees of frost, dressed in clothing which gave insufficient protection and boots which fell to pieces in three weeks, and trying to prepare hot meals from frozen food in inadequate cookers. Sleeping-bags arrived later; meanwhile the British blankets were supplemented by others looted from the U.S. Army. During some of this period they were placed under command of 25th U.S. Infantry Division, but on 12 February, they rejoined 29th Brigade to take part in its first offensive operation – a move which coincided with the return to battle of the 8th Hussars' Centurions. The Chinese were exhausted and the initial U.N. advance in the direction of the River Han met with little opposition. Not until Hill 327 was tackled on 16 February was there a serious fight and here, 7 Troop (Lieutenant R. J. Shackleton) became involved, along with 5 Troop, in the final assault on the hill, which cost the infantry 43 casualties and the enemy a great many more. By now the Chinese were in full retreat and once again Seoul was to fall, 6 Troop (Lieutenant G. R. Merrell) being the first to enter, on 1 April (in a blaze of publicity) the industrial suburb of Yong-dongpo where 2,000 gallons of beer were discovered. For C Squadron, as for the bulk of the 29th Brigade, this operation virtually brought an end to mobile operations. It would remain on call, and in support of units guarding vital points, such as the Han bridges and Seoul airfield. During the Battle of the Imjin River, when the Chinese attacked again on 20 April, it stayed in reserve while 29th Brigade fought the memorable engagement which, as much as anything else, brought the enemy to a halt and covered the 1st Glosters with glory.

The front now settled along a line that was to remain stable, if embattled, near the 38th Parallel, until the end of the war. Mobile warfare, in which C Squadron had been mostly engaged, gave way to trench stalemate, with the Centurions of the 8th Hussars dug in along the hills. In mid-July, at about the time the British and Commonwealth units were being organized into 1st Commonwealth Division, preparations for a return to Britain began and, finally, the squadron embarked on 8 October. Not once had it used its flame-throwers in anger, and for most of the time it kept only one troop in readiness for that rôle. It had lost only one N.C.O. in action, but, in the three months of its full commitment to war, had undergone rather more fighting than any of the other British armoured squadrons engaged hitherto. In many respects, the Churchills had proved ideal for the conditions, their excellent cross-country performance being superior on the steep slopes where Centurion tracks slipped, and better still in the soft going of the paddy-fields which covered the valleys. It was fortunate that they were never called upon to fight an enemy equipped with modern weapons.

* * * * *

When 1st R.T.R. (Lieutenant-Colonel G. C. Hopkinson) arrived in Korea early in December 1952, its C.O. and squadron commanders were an all-star cast of battle-hardened veterans, whose presence denied younger officers the chance to gain vital experience. Selection of crewmen, on the other hand, had been affected by the need to weed out those of the unit who were not yet 18, and whose remaining service would not allow seven continuous months in Korea. There was a shortage of junior tank commanders and double tradesmen, which had to be filled from other R.T.R. units and the cavalry. The 1st was to occupy a line which had altered very little since C Squadron, 7th R.T.R. had left. Positions which had been successively held by the 8th Hussars and, later, by 5th Royal Inniskilling Dragoon Guards were, from long occupation, much stronger. Infantry company positions were a warren of bunkers and tunnels dug into the hillsides and surrounded by wire and minefields. Peace negotiations, with little progress made, had been going on since the summer of 1951 and neither side wished to indulge in further attempts at conquest. Such fighting as was initiated by the Chinese and South Koreans was keyed to making an impression on the negotiators, while the other U.N. forces sought merely to retain the existing alignment. Tanks were employed as semi-mobile pill-boxes, in an artillery rôle against enemy guns and infantry. No Chinese tanks were seen.

Arriving at the front after a journey in an unheated and windowless railway train, some members of the 1st R.T.R. may have reflected that this, their first experience of active service in 7½ years, was a considerable change from the interminable round of exercises to which they had become so accustomed before leaving Germany the previous September. Within 24 hours they had to complete the relief of the two 5th Innis.D.G. Squadrons which were holding a line reminiscent of Dartmoor, the Welsh hills and the Scottish highlands. They had half their tanks dug-in forward and the rest lying back. By day, the tanks would be used to harass the enemy, by night, to fire defensively, close in to the front, deal with enemy raids and to support friendly patrols. When an enemy gun, deeply dug into some opposite hillside, became troublesome, the extremely accurate 20pdr. gun would fire H.E. with the fuse caps left on, to achieve maximum penetration of enemy tunnels before exploding. For the rest of the time it was a question of survival.

By now, the type of winter clothing issued was excellent and space heaters made tents more habitable than they had been in 1950. Yet the extremes of cold were hard to bear and there were cases of frost-bite among sentries in the turrets of tanks on exposed hill-tops. Cooking breakfast, when the eggs were frozen solid and had to be peeled instead of broken, and milk had to be served on a knife, was irksome. Each tank position usually consisted of a solidly constructed shelter called a Hutchie. These, Lieutenant G. Forty recalls, were dark, dank and infested by rats. 'I remember waking up in the middle of the night and seeing one sitting at the end of my bed eating my underwear. The tank', he continues, 'was normally parked close by during the day so that maintenance and gun cleaning could be carried out more easily. Towards evening, or if the position was being attacked, we would motor forward up the hill into our firing pit. . . It was necessary to be in exactly the same place each night. We therefore used a system of marker posts to denote where the tracks should be and then traversed the gun on to another pair of 'in line' posts. We then zeroed the traverse indicator and measured all our night DF tasks as switches so that it was merely a question of reading them off in my notebook when we were called upon to fire.'

Within 24 hours of taking over, A Squadron (Major S. I. Howard-Jones) was in action in support of a raid by 1st Battalion Royal Australian Regiment, the troop involved being commanded by an Australian (Lieutenant D. J. Duff) who was on attachment for experience. He received it in the shape of five hits from enemy shells and returned the compliment by destroying a tunnel sheltering a Chinese gun. Throughout January, and until relieved early in February, the unit was frequently active within the limits of its entrenched confines. B Squadron (Major R. E. Ward) supported raids by the 1st Battalion Duke of Wellington's Regiment. From reserve, C Squadron (Major R. E. Maunsell) occasionally sent up a tank to engage special targets which could not be reached from the established positions. One of these fired 26 rounds of H.E. into tunnels on 26 January without attracting much response.

At the beginning of February, 1st Commonwealth Division was relieved by 2nd U.S. Division and sent into reserve for rest and retraining. It was a good time to go. After the frosts and before the monsoons, the Centurions could go anywhere, so that, on the journey back to a base camp at Gloucester Valley and during the subsequent exercises, the tanks covered a greater mileage than at any other time in the regiment's stay in Korea. In rotation, officers and men spent five days R. and R. – Rest and Recuperation Leave (or Rack and Ruin as some called it) – in Japan, sampling the delights of Tokyo or Kure. It was 6 April before they were called back into the line to hold the same positions as before.

The war was now entering its final phase as the issues which had prevented political agreement were gradually overcome. Paradoxically, activity at the front intensified. Shelling and mortaring grew heavier, with, occasionally, up to 200 projectiles arriving in a troop's position in a single day. In May, sporadic raiding gave way to deliberate Chinese attacks culminating in very heavy fighting on the left sector – the celebrated and exposed Hook position – where C Squadron (now commanded by Major W. D. P. Sullivan) was in support of the 1st D.W.R. Throughout the month, preparations for a major assault by the Chinese were apparent, prefaced by a mounting volume of shellfire. Forty recalls that he rarely managed more than three hours' sleep a night, and that most of the day was taken up with climbing up and down hills, clad in a heavy flak jacket, visiting each of his five tanks in turn.

The Hook jutted out to within only a few hundred yards of the Chinese positions – a wide separation by First World War standards – and the tanks often had to deploy their standing D.F. tasks to help standing patrols escape enemy attentions. Forty says, 'We would on occasions stir up the Chinese using our searchlights [a few Centurions had Canadian lights mounted on their turrets] one tank illuminating while the others fired like hell at anything they saw. We caught a number of digging parties but unfortunately the lights were without any form of protective shutter and they did not last long when battle commenced . . . One day we were engaged by a Chinese rocket launcher detachment – they must have dug a crawl trench to within a few metres of the Hook – and the first I knew was when something like an express train went overhead. Thereafter we always went up in pairs in daylight, one watching for short range parties while the other engaged the selected target.'

But on 28 May, the time for engaging pin-point targets ended, when the Chinese launched a massive artillery concentration of 10,000 shells followed by infantry waves advancing with fanatical courage. At the same time, a diversionary attack was made on the extreme right-hand sector of the Divisional front in which a Centurion of B Squadron experienced a rare event with a hit from an 85mm solid shot which failed to penetrate the tank's glacis plate. The really heavy fighting fell to C Squadron and the

1st D.W.R., and particularly, in the early stages, on Forty's troop in the exposed Company position in the Hook, which was overrun by the enemy. Intensive, indirect fire by the guns of the Royal Artillery backed up by rapid direct fire from C Squadron's 20pdrs. and co-axial Besas, held the assault at arm's length. Each tank could be subjected to a personal bombardment, that of Corporal (Acting Sergeant) A. J. G. Wallace being no exception when it received three hits and had its searchlight destroyed. But remaining in action, Wallace, Sergeant N. Mcfarlane and others were able to dominate the enemy to their front and force them back with direct fire. In all, the tanks fired 504 rounds of H.E., 22,500 rounds of Besa and 4,500 rounds from the cupola-mounted Brownings. In return, each of those engaged suffered an average of five hits from shells and mortars and every searchlight was destroyed. But apart from superficial damage and a few wounded, their positions remained intact.

This was by no means the end of the fighting, but it was the last major assault on the 1st Commonwealth Division. Until 27 July, when an armistice came into effect, the shelling and patrolling continued much as before. To celebrate the Queen's Coronation on 2 June, the artillery put down concentrations of red, white and blue smoke, while tanks of the 1st R.T.R. fired a salute of live ammunition at an unappreciative enemy. The big battles took place on the flanks where, at one place, the South Koreans sought to gain political advantage from local victories, and at another, the Chinese endeavoured to show the world that, by striking hard at the Americans, they were making peace from a position of advantage – as well as saving face. As late as 24 July, B Squadron, taking a turn in the Hook, found itself heavily engaged helping 2nd Battalion Royal Australian Regiment when an enemy attack directed against the U.S. Marine Division, on the left, over-spilled into their sector. Sergeant F. J. Brundish, indeed, positively resented being deprived of an appearance at the last curtain. Wounded in the initial action, he refused medical treatment until the attack had been halted and, after having been evacuated to the Forward Dressing Station, made his way back under his own steam, so as to be at his post, though to some extent incapacitated, at the last. The 1st was in action right up to the moment when the cease-fire sounded on 27 July. To young Lance-Corporal Roy Fawkes, Ward's radio-operator in B Squadron, fell the historic task of transmitting the cease-fire order to the squadron. As he wrote home to his parents at the time '. . . at 10 o'clock I gave the cease-fire over the wireless to all the tanks on the air. I am glad it is all over!'.

When the guns fell silent, and the U.N. troops turned to clearing the battlefield, retiring from the forward demilitarized zone, constructing the defensive Kansas Line and making plans for recommencing the battle should the Chinese break faith, 1st R.T.R. could look back on five months in the line which were almost as hectic (if not nearly so mobile) as any they had known in the past. They had fired 23,800 rounds of 20pdr. and had received 68 direct hits, but had not lost a single tank. They had suffered 20 wounded and only one man killed by shellfire as he drove back from the line in a scout car.

For 5th R.T.R. (Lieutenant-Colonel S. D. W. Seaver) their transfer from Germany to Korea via U.K. was an anti-climax. After 8½ years in B.A.O.R., which put them among the most exercised of all the units of the R.A.C., they would have preferred an active service rôle instead of being sent to a theatre where the action was finished before they had relinquished their rôle in Europe. Not for them an exciting relief in the line such as the 1st had experienced the previous year. Instead, they were committed to helping construct the Kansas Line, with occasional time off to exercise in mobile warfare. One exercise, called 'Impetus', involved the tanks in higher track mileage than had been achieved by 1st R.T.R. during the entire year they had spent on operations. For the rest of the time it was a matter of waiting for the rundown in strength to come, while practising, once a month, to occupy the Kansas Line at four hours' notice.

At the end of September 1954, the 1st Commonwealth Division was reduced in size to that of a brigade group, and the 5th R.T.R., as its account of the year's sojourn among the hills and paddy-field tells, '. . . became virtually a labour Battalion at the beck and call of the Divisional Staff'. The tanks had to be placed in heavy preservation for shipment. Quonset huts had to be dismantled and guards mounted to deal with armed gangs of Koreans who broke into camps to steal petrol, food and vehicles as units began to load kit or move out. On 28 December, the 5th sailed from Pusan, bound for Cyrenaica where further frustrations were in store for them. An outpost of the Western Powers' defences was gradually handed over to the care of the indigenous South Korean Army, and the forces of the United Nations were redeployed for confrontations elsewhere. The departure of 5th R.T.R. also eliminated, for the time being, the R.T.R. presence in the Far East.

*   *   *   *   *

In 1952, 7th R.T.R. (Lieutenant-Colonel M. J. Woollcombe) had begun what amounted to an enjoyable, if rather uneventful

– from the operational point of view – tour of Hong Kong. In May 1953, Lieutenant-Colonel J. K. Greenwood had taken over, and for him the year ahead was one of consolidation, in a station with notoriously restricted boundaries, and sharp contrasts in the semi-isolation of Sek Kong camp deep in the New Territories, and the prosperous and vibrant life of the nearby city. By early in 1953, the Colony was full of British and Gurkha troops, and the 7th found themselves acting as Divisional Regiment R.A.C. to 40th Infantry Division (Major-General R. Cruddas) mainly serving as operational and training support to 35 Infantry Brigade (Brigadier R. W. Urquhart) and 27th Infantry Brigade (Brigadier W. Stirling) and other supporting arms, all crammed into the New Territories. None of the five infantry battalions of these brigades had any experience of working with armour, and so the demand for the tanks (usually in groups of two or three troops) was consistently high throughout the year. Much mileage in low gears on paddy put a considerable strain on the ageing Comets, and this in turn caused a great deal of work for the crews and L.A.D., and much ingenuity over the provision of spares, all of which had to be carried out in the 'weather of the time' in a virtually open tank park. The large number of personnel, including the Royal Navy and the Royal Air Force, enlarged the scope of sports and social functions, and many soldiers went 'to sea' or 'flying' as part of their training in co-operation with other Arms, and to see the Colony through the eyes of an invader.

By the early summer of 1954, troops had started to leave the Colony, and it was the 7th's turn to face the monotonous routine of preparing for handover to the 7th Hussars, a routine familiar to armoured units the world over, and depicted in the July 1954 issue of *The Tank*: 'Little has happened during the past month. Within Squadrons nothing but sten and rifle classification firing, Adjutant's parades and preparation for, and holding of education exams in addition to the normal fatigues, padres hours, current affairs, lectures, tool checks, too hot weather, too wet weather, sports and eating and sleeping have interfered with preparation for, and 'necessary action' after, the C.I.V. [Central Inspectorate of Vehicles] inspection.'

The Brigade Commander's remarks attached to the final Annual Administrative Inspection report in August 1954, a month before handing over to the 7th Hussars, give a clear impression of the difficulties to be surmounted besides the results achieved: 'The administration of the unit is very good . . . there has been a slight improvement in the B Vehicle accident, and a decided improvement in write-off, V.D. and preventable disease rates. The discipline record is marred by the behaviour of a particular draft from Korea base-employed men. Apart from this, the discipline is good and the administration of discipline firm. The unit has an enviable team of experienced and effective senior N.C.O.s. . . It has the atmosphere and feel of a thoroughly good fighting unit.' It was their fate to be forced to dissipate this expertise in the limbo of duties as a training regiment in Catterick Camp.

CHAPTER V

The Canal Zone Pivot 1949-1956

In advance of the Korean episode, and even before the first reinforcements which would accrue as the result of National Service being extended from twelve to eighteen months, 4th R.T.R. had found itself again under heavy stress in the Middle East. From its nadir in the aftermath of the Palestine withdrawal, the unit had steadily recuperated in strength at Shandur, saved as it had been from further immediate operational commitments. Of course, no unit in the Canal Zone was ever entirely absolved from some sort of security duty. Even when the Egyptian Government of the day was not exerting political pressure allied to military undertones, members of the local criminal populace were preying on all and sundry, including that most obvious of targets – the British. There was, too, the threat posed by the Israelis who, having defeated the Arabs in the war of 1948, were industriously building their new nation while seeking ways to expand their defences. For example, on 3 January 1949, they sent an armoured column 35 miles into the Egyptian territory of Sinai, where it remained for two days, and always they were sparring with the Jordanians, to whom the British Government was bound by treaty obligations, agreed in 1946.

When, early in March, reports of overt Israeli movements in the vicinity of Aqaba became known, 4th R.T.R. was engaged in an orgy of painting prior to taking part in a parade for the C.I.G.S., Field Marshal Sir William Slim. At first, only one battalion of infantry (1st Royal Lincolns) held the port, and now the only issue which seemed open to argument, when it was decided on 10 March to reinforce them, was the size of the tank component to accompany 'O' Force which consisted of a troop of 43rd Royal Marine Commando, a battery of Light A.A. guns and a troop of S.P. anti-tank guns. Initially, a troop of Comets from A Squadron (Major T. H. Gibbon) of the 4th was considered sufficient, but when the latest Intelligence reports spoke of eleven Israeli tanks in the area, Gibbon was prompted to recommend strongly that a complete squadron be sent, and this was agreed. To the ordinary trooper, warned to be ready to take his tank aboard an L.S.T. within 24 hours, the problems posed are often different from those envisaged by the officer giving the orders. To Gibbon, who issued his instructions at 17.00 hrs., it was a matter of seeing that the correct kit was taken, that ammunition was stowed and crews brought up to strength. To Trooper J. Cannon it meant reassembling a 77mm. gun in a Comet dripping with fresh paint, and working throughout the night by the light of B Vehicle headlights – 'bombing up', packing personal gear and then driving to the hard to embark in the L.S.T. *Humphrey Gale*. 'In the rush', recalls Cannon, 'we had packed everything except rations'. But these reached the L.S.T. on time, and the squadrons arrived at Aqaba on 13 March – a performance which represented a marked improvement over that connected with a similar emergency move less than a year before, but which was spoiled on this occasion when the L.S.T. hit the beach at 7 knots and damaged some of the tanks.

'Aqaba was like a ghost town', continues Cannon. 'Nothing moved, we had no idea what to expect. The first tank off was fully prepared for action and ran the whole length of the docks with caution . . . The squadron moved to a site where it could guard the desert air landing strip, the docks and the pass. The enemy were in the range of hills opposite. Early days were spent fully prepared at all times, stand-to first and last light, sleep in trenches with troops out guarding the pass at what we knew as the 'Oyster Beds'. The only enemy activity was the firing of Very lights . . . We on our side retaliated with the same trick.'

Another trick, noticed by one of the troop leaders, Lieutenant R. G. Lawson, concerned a female voice which was heard on the squadron's radio frequency. 'She said her name was Mitzi. She sounded a nice little thing and she made us all kinds of sweet promises if we would drive across the border and sell our tanks to the Israeli Army. For some reason, which I cannot remember, the squadron did not take her up on her offer . . .'

For a couple of days the two sides glowered at each other, but a month later the tension had relaxed and the squadron went under canvas. In June, B Squadron, with its new Centurion 3s, relieved A and three weeks later it was deemed safe to reduce the squadron to troop size, and as such it remained until finally withdrawn in 1952. Undoubtedly this small garrison was closely watched by the Israelis who were soon strenuously engaged in constructing their new port of Eilat as a substitute for Aqaba. A live-firing range had been built by the British, with its firing point on the frontier and its danger area in Jordanian territory. Here the Comets had fired their 77mm. guns. But when at last, in 1951, some 20pdr. ammunition was released for the Centurions to fire, the troop officer, Lieutenant W. F. Woodhouse, was astonished to see '. . . the entire Israeli garrison deployed and digging in furiously a mile or so away. Eventually their commander must have noticed that the British were firing the other way and the furore subsided'. Perhaps the Israelis were anxious to observe in action a tank which one day would be the best armoured vehicle their army possessed.

For the next two years, 4th R.T.R. led a relatively domestic life, ruffled only by the coming and going of National Servicemen, by courses, by the departure of those whose overseas tour of duty was complete, and by the occasional major exercise. As the only Centurion unit in the Canal Zone they were of great interest. In the summer of 1949, C Squadron (Major A. H. Austin) sailed in an L.S.T. to Tripoli to take part in the first exercises, outside Europe, to involve this tank, and to demonstrate the immense fire-power of its gun. The opportunity was also taken to visit some of the Second World War battlefields along the coast and in Tunisia. To these young men, the majority of whom, just four years after the war, had not seen a shot fired in anger, the scene at Wadi Zig Zau was an eye-opener in terms of both professional and historic interest. In this desolate place, where they had been knocked out in March 1943, lay the charred and rusted carcasses of the Valentine tanks which had been fought to the death by 50th R.T.R. In some the guns were still loaded. Memories of this chilling experience might have been lost to posterity when, a few days later, in stormy seas on the voyage back to Port Said, a line of Centurions on the tank deck of the L.S.T. *Humphrey Gale*, broke lose and slid sideways against the tanks on the other side, damaging their side plates severely. The danger of their shifting back and straight through the ship's side as she rolled to and fro was obvious. No mean feat of courage was demanded of those who went below to shore up the runaway tanks with baulks of timber to avert a disaster. But an indication of the poor supply of spare assemblies and parts at that time (in this theatre as in all the others) was that, for some months, the tanks of this squadron wore a lopsided look, because it was found impossible to replace the damaged side-plates immediately.

For nearly two years, exercises and parades were to be the principal occupations for the Middle East garrisons. While the Far East stole the news headlines and N.A.T.O. forces were gradually brought up to strength in Europe, life in Egypt for the 4th (now commanded by Lieutenant-Colonel J. B. Robertson) was relatively tranquil, although not without sporadic change. In 1950, a half-squadron visited Cyprus for exercises, and this was matched in interest by manoeuvres to the east of the Canal, where the Centurions showed their ability to operate effectively in the soft sands near the Mitla Pass, on ground where, in years to come, some of the fiercest tank battles of the century would take place, with Centurions in the van. It would be the last opportunity the British Army in the Canal Zone would have to indulge in routine activities. Already the political temperature in Egypt was rising as the Nationalist Government demanded freedom. But overt nationalism first came to the surface in April 1951 in Persia, where the Premier, Dr Mossadeq, to the cheers of the crowd and against a background of assassination and anti-British demonstrations, announced that his government intended to nationalize the Anglo-Iranian oilfields and take over the running of the great refinery at Abadan.

World reaction was one of concern at the prospect of an oil famine, for it was expected that the Company might be compelled to shut down the refinery. Recourse to diplomacy and to the International Court of Justice at the Hague were abortive, since Mossadeq was intransigent and the Court did not feel competent to give a ruling. A British Labour Government, which could call on only a small majority in Parliament, and whose armed forces were weak, felt unable to take a strong line. As the crisis deepened and the lives of the Company's employees at Abadan seemed to be at risk, steps were taken to evacuate them. A combined force of Royal Marines, Royal Artillery and 4th R.T.R. was to be sent to the Gulf under the guise of Exercise 'Shakedown'. On 30 June, B Squadron (Major T. R. Newton-Dunn) was ordered to load 12 Centurions, 3 Cromwells, 4 scout cars and supporting vehicles in the L.S.T. *Snowden Smith*, with a view to sailing on 4 July. 'It was a change', remarks the 4th's chronicler, 'to be given such notice'. Moreover, the frequent practice the crews had experienced in this sort of movement now stood them in good stead and, as usual, it was the L.S.T.s which created delays and difficulties. To begin with, they were late arriving at the hard, and then it was found difficult to fit the B vehicles onto the top deck. There was insufficient accommodation for all the crews, so that some, the lucky ones as it turned out, had to be left behind in Egypt, ready to fly out at a moment's notice. For C Squadron, which was also earmarked to go, there was no L.S.T. Their tanks were loaded into a Liberty ship with derricks of 50-ton lifting capacity, and sent to the Gulf in the care of one R.E.M.E. Staff Sergeant whose task it was to keep the batteries charged. The crews stayed at Shandur and passed the time in infantry training.

When at last the *Snowden Smith* arrived at the small Kuwaiti port of Merg Al Ahmadi in the Gulf, those on board were suffering from the oppressive heat. Fortunately, several ships of the

Royal Navy had already arrived and they saved the day by doing all they could to alleviate the men's suffering. So hot had been conditions below deck in the L.S.T. that maintenance had proved impossible to carry out, and on arrival in Kuwait, a primary task was to build a ramp and off-land the tanks in order for work to be done on them on land. Meanwhile the Kuwaiti Oil Company came to the rescue by providing the crews with air-conditioned accommodation, of which every man had a share on a roster system. They stayed in Kuwait throughout August and September, ready for action which never came, and listening to news of diplomatic rebuffs in the Gulf, and of serious trouble brewing in Egypt where their families and most of the 4th were in residence. They began to feel forgotten and morale started to suffer. It was noted, without rancour, that while the ships of the Royal Navy were relieved constantly, the Army remained in a temperature of 120 degrees, with humidity, at times, reaching 100 per cent. Prickly heat was rife, aggravated by septic sores and boils. Patience and tempers began to fray. It was a profound relief when, on 7 October, the decision to retire to the Canal Zone was taken, and the L.S.T.s and the freighter containing C Squadron's tanks were ordered to sail. Members of the freighter's crew – all Europeans – had busied themselves, meanwhile, in systematically pilfering the tanks' equipment.

Whatever history may conclude about British rule during the years of their occupation of the countries of the Middle East, it will be unable to ignore the attitudes of the soldiers who, for much of the time, were the principal instrument by which power was asserted. The British soldiers took a prejudiced and contemptuous view of Egypt and the Egyptians, their experience of of the latter being limited almost exclusively to those they encountered in and around the military cantonments, or in the places they frequented when off duty.

The Anglo-Egyptian Treaty of 1936, which had provided for close cooperation between the two nations in the event of war, and had made provision for a gradual modification of the British occupation of the previous 53 years, was due to terminate in 1956 and had long been the subject of Egyptian discontent. No nation with a proud history enjoys being dictated to by outsiders and, as time went by, the reasons given by the British for extending their occupation grew less and less acceptable in Egyptian eyes. The desire of the Western nations to retain close control of the vital trade route and strategic link to the Far East, the Suez Canal, and access to the oil supplies which lay beyond (now cut off by the Arab embargo on supplies by pipeline to Haifa in Israel), weighed but little with Egypt's leaders who wished to control their own destiny. The time to free their nation of foreign occupation was ripe. The British, having withdrawn to the Canal Zone under pressure of rioting in 1946, had revealed their vulnerability. The exodus from India and Palestine and now, the failure to stand up to the Iranians, underlined an unwillingness on the British Government's part to engage in an outright confrontation to the bitter end. In any case, the British were clearly stretched to the limit by their commitments elsewhere.

The proposal in a joint British, American, French and Turkish plan in 1951, for a combined Middle East Command to defend this vital area against the threat of a Communist takeover, served only to precipitate the crisis. At that moment, the Egyptian Government under Nahas Pasha (elected the previous year) was in local difficulty and in need of a distraction. On 15 October 1951, Nahas formally abrogated the 1936 Treaty, and was instrumental in instigating riots, arson and looting directed primarily against the British community. This came at a bad moment for the British Army in the Middle East. An attenuated 'O' Force was still detached at Aqaba, and the 'Shakedown' elements were still in transit from the Persian Gulf. A dangerous situation was made even more delicate by the exposure of the Army's families who lived, in many cases, among the local community or in places which were difficult to protect. From the outset, on 16 October, they were almost as liable to be the target for insults and stone-throwing as the troops themselves. Those in Ismailia and Suez town had to be brought at once to safety within the Army camps. There they could be housed only temporarily and in discomfort as, in the weeks to come, an ugly series of riots burgeoned into an undeclared war.

4th R.T.R. (commanded by Lieutenant-Colonel J. R. D. Carlton since September) with less than a squadron (A) of tanks available (and some of those in workshops), could contribute little more than manpower and administrative capability in the early stages of the emergency. While the tank squadron stood to arms in case the main body of the Egyptian Army intervened, it was left to the armoured cars of the 1st Royal Dragoons, later reinforced by a squadron of Comets of 4th/7th Royal Dragoon Guards shipped in from Tripoli, to provide the principal armoured force, as part of a rapid and massive strengthening of the garrison. Troops were returned as quickly as possible from Aqaba and from the Gulf, in addition to those brought in from Tripoli and Cyprus. Men of the 4th, whose tanks were on the high seas, erected tents for 70 women and children, in the vicinity of the Sergeants Mess at Shandur, and mounted guard on the camp and certain vital points. Those who were fortunate enough to have fighting vehicles went forth in improvised groups to do battle on 16 October.

At that moment, the Egyptian Army was deployed partially in the Sinai, to the east of the Canal, preparing for the day when they would resume hostilities against the Israelis. The remainder were in Egypt, centred upon the Cairo area, and the British in the Canal Zone lay across their lines of communication. Hence, it was easy to place a stranglehold on the forces in Sinai by controlling the ferries across the canal. Each ferry was surrounded by British troops on 16 October, a detachment from the 4th was sent to the site at Kubri, while a combat team of a troop of Centurions, a company of the 1st Royals and a Field Battery R.A. (known as 'Willforce') established a road-block under Major G. N. Williams at Kilo 99 on the Suez to Cairo road, where it was to remain for several weeks. Meanwhile, the detachment at Kubri (called 'Wetbob' and consisting of men of the Reconnaissance Troop not in the Gulf) mounted on a jeep, two 3-ton trucks and a Gunner O.P. Cromwell tank, awaited orders.

As rioting and acts of violence against the British increased throughout 17 October, reports began to arrive of a Battle Group of Egyptian tanks (two squadrons of Shermans and two of armoured cars, plus infantry and artillery) advancing along the Cairo to Suez road in the direction of 'Willforce'. Therefore, Lieutenant-General Sir George Erskine, the G.O.C. British Troops in Egypt (B.T.E.), felt compelled to stiffen further the resistance he had so far exerted in maintaining the safety of his formation. Until this moment, he had had no authority to intervene in the interests of keeping the peace, which was strictly an Egyptian responsibility. But now that he was threatened by what looked like an act of war, the measures he took were relative to that. Orders went out to seize the Canal ferries and deny their use to the Egyptians, whose forces on the east bank consisted of infantry and anti-tank guns and, on the west bank, officials and members of the Egyptian police. When the ferry was at the end of its westward journey, the detachment commander (Lieutenant J. A. Withers) closed in and informed the ferry's engineer that it would not be permitted to sail again – a declaration implemented with such firmness that the engineer concluded, with some justification, that the British intended to destroy the ferry. For, unbeknown to the detachment commander, an over-zealous R.E.M.E. fitter had removed the cylinder head from the ferry's engine and dropped it in the Canal. In the diplomatic uproar which ensued, the matter, as 4th R.T.R.'s chronicle recounts, 'was straightened out and the police officer and his squad did not reappear'. The ferry would not move for the time being, and the Egyptian Army on the opposite bank (which had failed to intervene) was immobilized, its future supplies being rationed by the British.

On 18 October, to meet the threat posed by the Egyptian Army coming from Cairo, Erskine formed, near Fayid, the largest mobile striking force at his disposal – two troops of Centurions led by the Regimental Signals Officer, Lieutenant W. F. Woodhouse, who was the only officer available. These tanks, prised out of the L.A.D. by the superhuman efforts of the fitters, were joined by some of the Royal's armoured cars, an infantry battalion and a battery of 25pdr. field guns. Legend surrounds the outcome of an incident which, for a few hours, looked as if it might develop into a full-scale tank battle in which, without much doubt, the vastly superior Centurions would have defeated the Shermans. Suffice to relate that Erskine, who, it is said, threatened to blast the Egyptians off the face of the earth and had a message dropped by the R.A.F. saying 'Go away – or else', succeeded in his object of avoiding an exchange of fire. The Egyptians thought again, halted, dug-in and finally began to withdraw. A most perilous situation had been resolved by a display of determination. From 17 October onwards, the flow of reinforcements was overwhelming and the arrival of C Squadron's Centurions at Adabiya in their Liberty ship on 24 October, at last restored to the 4th a strong measure of its striking power. The initial crisis was over and the war – which is what it was – moved into its next, more harmful phase.

Intimidation of the civilian labour force which served the British garrison was now applied by the Egyptians concurrently with guerilla warfare. Within two days, only the bravest civilians remained in the Canal Zone and the rest left for Cairo or went home. For a while it looked as if the administration of the Base would collapse, but Erskine refused to be intimidated and for a few weeks, until fresh labour could be recruited from Mauritius, Cyprus, Malta and the United Kingdom, the troops who could be spared from essential operational duties took their turn running the docks, the power-stations and the lines-of-communication installations. Meanwhile, the Egyptians began the formation of a uniformed partisan army, a so-called auxiliary police force called the Bulak Nazim, which began to establish itself at key-points, such as police stations, and to harass British troops. In addition, natives in plain clothes were given arms and began to terrorize outlying districts and hinder movements by road.

An early decision was taken by Erskine to evacuate the families, since it might soon be impossible to ensure their safety. Those belonging to the 4th, together with several hundred women and children from other units, had to be escorted by scout cars in a convoy of buses to Port Said. Chaos reigned throughout the operation and reached its climax when it was discovered that the ship provided was not a regular Trooper, but a small passenger vessel of ancient vintage and with appallingly bad accommodation. The sight of her drove a militant R.T.R. officer's wife to complain personally to Erskine and insist that he come to see for himself – which he did! He was sympathetic, but nothing could be done. The ship sailed – to be greeted at Liverpool by press reporters who managed to create a certain amount of unfavourable publicity at a time when the Citizen Army was the frequent target for criticism in Press and Parliament.

4th R.T.R., with their tanks restored, began serious infantry/tank exercises with 16th Parachute Brigade who had arrived by air from Cyprus. They stood by to deal with any renewed threat from the Egyptian Army, while the remainder of Erskine's force tightened its grip in dealing with the sniping which provided a foretaste of the battles to come in the Canal Zone. The next major threat was directed against the crucial water filtration plant, just to the north of Suez, from which the garrison drew its supplies. The route to the plant passed through the village of Kafr Abdu which sheltered snipers' nests whose occupants fired on the supply convoys. To guard these vital supplies, Erskine took the difficult decision to demolish part of the village, after a bomb attack on the plant on 4 December had caused damage and a serious loss of water. At first it was believed that the village consisted of mud huts, but they turned out to be much more substantial. In the end, Operation 'Flatten' involved a Sherman dozer tank and 10 Troop from 4th R.T.R., escorted locally by 1st Battalion The Parachute Regiment, and screened to the west by 'Willforce'. And although, apart from sporadic sniping, there was no opposition, not unexpectedly there was a fearful outcry in Cairo when the news was announced. Moreover, the threat to the water was not eliminated because, on 3 January, further sniping started from the houses which had been left standing. As a result, the 4th were called in again to fire (under the personal direction of Erskine) three carefully aimed rounds of 20pdr. high-explosive, laced with Besa, to drive out the enemy.

One thing led to another. The Egyptians now retaliated with heavier weapons, including machine-guns. The British replied with mortars and further use of the 4th's Centurions when 5 Troop was ordered into action near Suez. But they got stuck in soft sand and were fortunate to complete their recovery undisturbed by the local snipers who, fortunately, had called it a day. As this sort of action became commonplace, while the situation grew progressively more unpleasant, it is interesting to find the Regimental recorder writing of a high level of morale. Notwithstanding a chronic manpower shortage, alleviated by holding men back from repatriation (four months delay as a rule), separation from families, over-crowding at Shandur, little time for recreation, none for leave, and the experience of being spread throughout the Canal Zone on a frontage estimated at 2,000 miles, from Suez to El Ballah to the north of Ismailia, with a solitary troop still far away to the south at Aqaba, the soldiers were steadfast and cheerful. Hitherto the tanks had been used sparingly, despite the situation having long ago passed beyond the point at which 'Minimum Force' was deemed appropriate. But events were rising to a climax at Ismailia, which had always been the most volatile of the hot-spots, and here it was that A Squadron played a leading rôle in what may have been the turning-point of the war.

The trouble began on 19 January, when a mine killed two men of the 1st Royal Lincolns, and gunmen took possession of a convent as a fire-base. In the fighting which broke out (resulting in the death of one nun), a major clearance operation, supported by 3 Troop, which fired Besas and Sten guns, culminated in the search of a Muslim cemetery which yielded a considerable arsenal of arms and explosives. At the same time, it was decided that, since nearly all the trouble-makers – the police and the auxiliary Bulak Nizam – were based on the police barracks, these should now be compelled to surrender their arms. On 25 January, a request to this effect was delivered to the Egyptian authorities who replied that they had orders from Cairo to resist. It was then left to Brigadier R. K. Exham, the Commander of 3rd Infantry Brigade, to carry out the operation, which was named 'Eagle' and entrusted to 1st Battalion, The Lancashire Fusiliers, supported by a squadron of the Royals' armoured cars and by A Squadron of the 4th, with two Centurion troops under the command of Williams.

Of the two police headquarters buildings, one, the Caracol, was tardy to surrender, but eventually did so after a prolonged parley of three hours' duration, attended by a desultory exchange of fire. Casualties were minimal and the Centurions were not called upon to use their main armament.

It was a very different matter at the Bureau Sanitaire. Here, a loud-hailer request for the occupants to surrender their weapons was rewarded by the sight of the Egyptians being deployed in fire positions at the windows and on the roof. A blank 20pdr. round, fired by the troop leader of 3 Troop, 2nd Lieutenant J. A. Goodwin, provoked machine-gun fire which was silenced by the Besas of his Centurions. Six rounds of 20pdr. were then fired into one wing of the building, but the Egyptians stood bravely to their posts and returned the fire. More appeals to the defenders to come out were ignored. An assault by C Company of the Lancashire Fusiliers, covered by smoke from the Royals and six more rounds from 3 Troop, enabled the infantry to enter the inner compound and come to closer quarters, but such was the resistance that eventually they had to withdraw. The Bureau Sanitaire, engulfed in dust and smoke, was the target for fire from every tank, armoured car and infantry weapon. Casualties within were mounting as each tank, met by petrol bombs, was sent in to fire a final fusilade of 20pdr. which brought down a lot of masonry, killed many more men and, at last, persuaded the survivors to surrender. Forty dead and 63 wounded were counted among the ruins, a price which was justified on the spot by the feeling that, if 3rd Brigade had made less effort, the British casualties of 3 killed and 13 wounded might have been far higher. But the ultimate effects, despite the immediate cessation of major terrorist activities in Ismailia, were far-reaching politically, and resulted in immense destruction elsewhere.

When news of the battle reached Cairo, the Egyptian propagandists instantly whipped up a storm of protest and vilification not only against the British, but against almost all foreigners. Led by well-briefed activists, the mob roared and howled through the city, burning alien property, including such famous buildings as Shepheard's Hotel and the Turf Club; the police took no counter-measures except to protect the British Embassy when it was threatened. In the Canal Zone, 1st Division stood by on 26 January to launch 2nd Infantry Brigade, 16th Parachute Brigade, the Royals and 4th R.T.R., in a bid to occupy Cairo and enforce order – a prospective move which caused Erskine and the British Ambassador, Sir Ralph Stevenson, acute concern since there was no knowing, in the light of the Egyptian determination at Ismailia, what might be the outcome. Cooler reconsideration, reinforced, on the instructions of King Farouk, by the intervention in Cairo of the Egyptian Army to restore order, brought an almost immediate end to hostilities. The dismissal of Nahas Pasha by the King next day brought a return to sanity, and his successor began the search for a diplomatic solution.

For the next fortnight 1st Division stood to arms, waiting for the call to advance. But as time went by and the tension eased, the aims of the operation were modified from that of the wholesale rescue of the foreign population, to one designed, specifically, to save the members of the British and American Embassies. Prime objectives would have been the Farouk and Almaza airfields.

It obviously intrigued 4th R.T.R.'s chronicler that the defences adopted by the Egyptian Army to bar the way were the same as those which had been discussed at a Staff College Exercise during the war, when Egyptian officers were present. Fortunately good sense prevailed again, and a battle, the result of which might well, some thought, have been uncertain against so large a force as the Egyptian Army, did not take place. Nevertheless, a political decision had been assured. The British would soon leave of their own volition. And there are historians who are convinced that it was the violent action at Ismailia, with its inevitable aftermath, that was decisive in bringing this about. For the next four years, friction within the Canal Zone was minimal. Egypt would achieve notoriety because of her internal difficulties and political man-oeuvring, but of these the 4th would see little. In May 1952, the troop from Aqaba returned and at the end of the year the regiment sailed for the U.K.

*   *   *   *   *

In the meantime, the latest source of trouble for the Army had arisen in Kenya, where the Mau Mau terrorists were making life extremely unpleasant for the population at large. No sooner, in fact, was one outbreak doused than another took its place. The R.T.R.'s participation in the Kenya Emergency, which began in 1952 and continued in being until 1960 (although active opera-tions virtually ceased in 1956) was one of contributions by individuals. At one time, the Deputy Chief of Staff (later Chief) to the G.O.C.-in-C. East Africa, General Sir Gerald Lathbury, was Brigadier R. M. P. Carver, and for the greater part of the period the principal mobile force, which was of an infantry com-plexion and, only in the slightest part armoured, consisted of the East African Armoured Car Squadron commanded initially by Major H. Huth (8th Hussars). This unit, originally formed in 1939 from the Kenya Regiment, recruited its troops mainly from the King's African Rifles. It had taken part in operations against the Italians in 1940, and had been expanded into two squadrons in 1941, to play an important rôle in the conquest of Ethiopia. As the Kenya Armoured Car Regiment, it had gone to India in 1943, but it had not seen action and was reduced to squadron strength in 1949.

When the Mau Mau oath-taking ceremonies of the Kikuyu tribe were translated into murderous and bestial attacks on the civil population (regardless of race or colour) in the summer of 1952, the squadron, which was recruited from all the principal

Kenyan tribes, was organized into five operational troops plus the usual Command administrative troops. Each troop consisted of two Landrovers, five 15cwt. trucks, and a few Dingo scout cars armed with bren guns, and was self-contained for movement up to a range of 1,000 miles for the period of a week. Weapons were of the conventional infantry type, communications were provided by infantry 88 Sets and one 52 Set per section – a section being the 15cwt. truck with its crew of Askaris who sat back-to-back and hung on to a safety rope during cross-country travel. It regarded itself as an élite and it had an important part to play in the campaign.

The troops operated independently at long range and often for weeks on end. All the troop officers and senior N.C.O.s were drawn from the Royal Armoured Corps, several of whom were from the R.T.R. While on patrol they would sometimes march 30 miles in a day through jungle, across desert or scaling glacial slopes in temperatures which varied between 90 degrees and zero. For most of the time they were engaged on long-stop missions, setting up ambush patterns to deal with Mau Mau parties on the run. The squadron had its successes in the widely scattered series of operations in which it was almost constantly engaged. It had its losses, too, although contacts were few in number. Lieutenant C. H. Harding arrived in 1954 when, admittedly, the peak of the emergency was past, to replace an officer who had been killed in an ambush. He tells of sweeps on Sundays and Wednesdays, run by the local regiments of the King's African Rifles, when it was usual for the K.A.R. (who had some 'fabulous shots') to kill half a dozen Mau Mau, but he adds that '. . . in all the dozens and dozens of beats my troops did we only made contact twice'. Major J. D. Brotchie, who took over from Huth in 1954, remarks: 'Any contacts were usually made in thick forest and targets were fleeting. . . . The enemy was not aggressive, at least against troops, and he was a complete master of field-craft. A favourite ploy was to put a herd of buffalo or elephant between themselves and the security forces; they would cover themselves in the appropriate animal excrement so that the herd would accept their presence.'

The wild life was, as Brotchie recalls, 'troublesome'. Since the ambush patterns had to cover all the game trails in a given area, the animals became frustrated and alarmed. 'Rhino, buffalo and elephants in particular were given to showing their displeasure, so some of us became adept at climbing thorny trees very quickly in the dark.'

By 1955, the Mau Mau had been broken, and the squadron was to spend the remainder of its existence, until disbanded in

1957, patrolling the northern border of Kenya to guard against the effects of a mutiny then infecting the southern part of the Sudan. The turbulence that was so much a part of the Middle Eastern scene gradually spilled over into the other regions of Africa, and brought more frontiers of the Empire into dispute. The various strains of nationalism, whipped up by dissident elements, put increased pressure on the British Army, increasing the demand for officers and senior other ranks to join units such as the East Africa Armoured Car Squadron to help shore up the bulwarks against an incipient disorderliness.

Concurrent with the involvement of R.T.R. members in Kenya, there began a far more important association in Trans-Jordan. Together with the worrying activities of an aggressively-minded State of Israel, adjacent to areas of especial importance to British strategy, and the threat to fuel supplies by outbreaks of nationalism in the oil-producing countries which were beginning to undermine Western influence in the Middle East, there was always the danger of direct Russian intervention. While Josef Stalin was alive, the Soviet threat was pronounced and it was generally believed that only the American possession of the atom bomb prevented the outbreak of a Third World War – an insurance which lost some of its credibility when, in 1949, the Russians exploded their own first atomic device. A combination of factors such as these had to be taken into account when juggling with the balance of power. In such a highly sensitive zone, where no one nation possessed military predominance, the British might be called upon at any moment to employ their attenuated forces in an effort to preserve the *status quo*. Therefore, the guaranteed loyalty and collaboration of Arab allies was essential to the British at this crossroads of the Empire, and in 1952 both the Iraqis and the Jordanians gave indications of fulfilling these requirements. Nuri es Said held the reins in Iraq and was strongly pro-British. Although King Abdullah of Jordan had been assassinated in 1951 and his immediate successor, Talal, had been deposed due to incapacity in 1952, the 17-year old King Hussein was firmly held on his throne by the celebrated Arab Legion under command of an Englishman, Glubb Pasha. Indeed, of the Arab forces which had fought against the Israelis in 1948, none had acquitted themselves better than the Legion.

The war with Israel had revealed, however, many shortcomings in the Legion's equipment and organization. Its armoured content was derisory, consisting largely of ex-South African Marmon-Herrington armoured cars (some still sporting Second World War shot holes) and these had been deployed as part of the infantry battalions. As early as 1949, Sir John Crocker, as C.-in-C. Middle

East, had asked specifically for R.T.R. officers and men to be sent to help modernize the Arab Legion. But from 1949 to 1951, the sole R.A.C. presence was in the shape of one R.T.R. officer – its A.A.G., Lieutenant-Colonel P. F. Walsh. The creation of an Arab Legion Armoured Corps was begun by grouping most of the armoured cars to form the 1st Armoured Car Regiment, with Lieutenant-Colonel D. B. Wormald, 13th/18th Hussars, to command it, and a little later, as more vehicles were made serviceable, Lieutenant-Colonel J. D. Lunt, 16th/5th Lancers, arrived to form the 2nd Armoured Car Regiment. In 1952, it was decided to equip the Legion with tanks, or at least with tracked A.F.V.s, and the first R.T.R. officer to join the embryo Divisional Armoured Regiment was Captain W. F. Woodhouse who, in February 1953, came straight from the Long Course at the School of Tank Technology as Technical Adjutant. He was to find that although the regiment was soon to have the more glamorous name of 3rd Tank Regiment, at that moment, it consisted of four broken-down 17pdr. Archer tank destroyers. He writes: 'Although there was no lack of willingness to learn on the part of the Jordanian soldiers, they were woefully ignorant of the problems involved in the maintenance and handling of A.F.V.s. The sight of an industrious Archer crew busily unscrewing the gun-lug nut of their 17 pounder which was stuck in recoil, was not untypical of the potential disasters with which we had to cope. . . . Courses had to be arranged from scratch and trade tests to examine the knowledge of often illiterate soldiers had to be specially devised.'

Within a few weeks, Lieutenant-Colonel J. J. Dingwall arrived to take command of 3rd Tank Regiment, while another R.T.R. officer, Lieutenant-Colonel A. R. Leakey, subsequently came to command 1st Armoured Car Regiment when 4th Armoured Brigade was formed from all three armoured units and first commanded by Wormald, now a full Colonel. From now on, the R.T.R. influence was to be strongly felt throughout the Arab Legion. The appointment of Colonel W. M. Hutton as Chief of Staff (Colonel G.S.) to Glubb Pasha ensured that the armoured view-point could be clearly stated at the top by an Arab linguist. He had successively commanded 5th and 40th R.T.R. in action, besides being Commandant at the R.A.C. O.C.T.U., Sandhurst, during the war and performing many other important tasks.

From a commanding officer's point of view the prospects were daunting. Dingwall found himself presented with '. . . a piece of desert, two Nissen huts and some ancient Archers. There were some soldiers, too, but not many . . . and I soon realised that most of them were hopelessly unsuitable. It transpired that the best thing to do was to recruit straight from the Desert.' Meanwhile,

Woodhouse had become Brigade Technical Adjutant, while T.Q.M.S. T. C. Quirke brought order to the tank park administration. Major K. Kidd was detached from the R.A.C. Centre to help train the Jordanian soldiers in Gunnery. Kidd's comments on teaching techniques are illuminating if not definitive. An 'imperial raspberry', he noted, would only make an Arab crewman sulk. Ridicule, on the other hand, worked. And if methods of instruction were a little unorthodox, '. . . perhaps a smart rap on the head with a hammers, ballpane 2lb might do much to improve some of our gunners'. Kidd's methods may not have been generally employed, but the speed with which the Arabs learned was described as 'gratifying' and was much to the credit of the R.T.R., which, by the end of 1954, included Lieutenant-Colonel J. M. Close, commanding the Arab Legion M.T. School, and Brigadier E. C. Mitford, who relieved Wormald as commander of the 4th Armoured Brigade.

These were the leaders who, from virtually nothing, created the armoured force which, in 1967 and 1973, in action against the Israelis, was to extract from their opponents the compliment that, of all their enemies, those of the Arab Legion were the most formidable. Nothing could have looked less likely in 1953, however, when everything hung on a shoestring. 'Apart from the technical and tactical training of my Regiment', writes Dingwall, 'I was expected to "find" all the buildings by scrounging or begging the Pasḥa or Arab Legion for the money . . . I was determined that we should be self-contained as regards food and ammunition within our own lines since the business of drawing these commodities from the Services in the Arab Legion was a long and tedious one. We achieved this eventually.'

Progress in everything was slow, but a firm step forward was made when the British Government was persuaded to part with two squadrons of Charioteers to replace the obsolete Archers. This A.F.V. was a classic example of mounting a modern gun, the 20pdr., which happened to be available in large numbers, on an obsolete vehicle, the Cromwell, when modern vehicles were in short supply. It satisfied many of the Arab Legion's needs by giving it a vehicle which was both fast and reliable and armed with a gun capable of dealing with almost any likely enemy.

The results of two years' hard and often unrewarding effort began to appear in 1955, the year in which the political skies began to darken over this, the poorest of all the Arab countries. That summer, however, the Armoured Corps took shape as a cohesive force and received, as the accolade of its graduation, a visit from King Hussein who, after spending the entire day in the barracks at Zerqa, bestowed upon it the title of Royal Armoured

Corps. But, although in 1953, in the aftermath of a raid by Israeli forces against Qibya, a West Bank village, the new corps' baptism of fire seemed imminent, its rôle remained defensive. The armoured car regiments took it in turn to deploy for frontier duty on the West Bank and in the Jordan Valley, and in this area, which was lacking even rudimentary military accommodation, Leakey and his family occupied for six months the cells of Nablus Police Station, which served as R.H.Q. and married quarters. Of fighting, however, there was none.

The chief target for hostilities, so far as the Arab nations were concerned, remained Israel, but unity among themselves was at a premium, while scattered Palestinian groups indulged in the minor guerilla activities of the kind that had provoked the cross-frontier Israeli raid. Egypt suffered from internal disputes throughout the better part of 1952, and these turned into a revolution when Army officers deposed the King that summer and replaced him by a Council under General Neguib. In parallel with the new Government's attempts at reform, this Council persisted in the long-term ambition to eject the British and, for that matter, all outwardly noticeable manifestations of foreign dominance. So it was to an atmosphere of intrigue and internal dissension that 1st R.T.R. (Lieutenant-Colonel N. E. O. Watts) was introduced when it landed at Port Said on 4 January 1954, to relieve, once more, the 5th Royal Inniskilling Dragoon Guards who, a year previously, had taken over from 4th R.T.R. A power struggle between Neguib and Colonel Nasser was in progress which left little time for the Egyptians to tackle the British in the Canal Zone. This enabled the 1st to spend the minimum of time on routine Internal Security duties and allowed it to train with the local infantry and with the Royal Marine Commando Brigade in Greece. Time was also spent in studying the latest tactical doctrine associated with future prosecution of atomic warfare, which then seemed likely. At the same time, they played their part in helping to strengthen the armoured units of the Iraqi Army, by training, on the Centurion, a detachment sent to Egypt in September, and later by sending a team of 3 officers and 25 N.C.O. instructors to Habbaniya to assist in training the Iraqis there.

The days of a British military presence in the Middle East were numbered. When Nasser finally deposed Neguib in 1954, the negotiations leading up to a British withdrawal from the Canal Zone gathered momentum and coincided with the West's efforts to weld together all the Arab nations into what was known as the Baghdad Pact. The old order was passing, and a new era of Arab strength, politically led by Egypt, was born.

In the summer of 1954, an agreement was reached with Egypt for Britain to retire from the Canal Zone. A phased withdrawal by the Services would begin. This, so far as the 1st R.T.R. was concerned, meant handing over Shandur Camp to the Egyptians in November, while the regiment moved to Geneifa prior to departing for the U.K. in September 1955. C Squadron would stay as the rearguard, while the British roar, which had greeted the belligerent Egyptian moves in 1951 and 1952, gave way to a purr of ceremonial parades and inspections – if not to a whimper of squabbles between storemen and administrators. Diplomacy was substituted for outright force. Although the final retreat from the British Middle East bastion was yet to be sounded, the shape of the future was plain to see. The negotiated withdrawal which had begun under pressure in India was being extended into a precipitate retreat from Empire. And agreement with Egypt may have convinced some that the great military installations with their vast accumulation of vehicles, equipment and stores which were to be maintained by a British civil contractor, would be made available to the British Army if the need arose.

As a rather inadequate substitute for forces in the Canal Zone there remained, of course, the 25th Armoured Brigade in Cyrenaica. It had been formed there in 1952 and, in 1954, under the command of Brigadier A. W. Brown, had become known as 25th Armoured Brigade Group. The subsequent activities of this Group will be described in Chapter VII, but so far as the R.T.R. was concerned in 1956, the presence within it of the 5th (Lieutenant-Colonel S. D. W. Seaver) provided the main opportunity to give desert experience to men of the Regiment, and at the same time play an important rôle in the trials of new equipment such as the Decca Navigator and the latest range of V.H.F. radio sets, above all the C 42.

The old hands behaved as if it were business as usual, with plenty of opportunities to demonstrate the art of living in 'the blue', combatting the effects of the giblis, taking a bath with one gallon of water and of operating in conditions of shimmering heat. For one crew of younger members from A Squadron during squadron training in September 1955, a test was provided beyond the imagination of those who sent them out on a night exercise. In the darkness, their Centurion fell into one of a number of unmarked, so-called 'pigeon holes' and plunged 90 feet to the bottom, where it landed on its turret. The commander lay injured, the wireless-operator was dead and the driver, Trooper G. Lucas, and the badly shocked gunner were trapped. Even as the tank was falling, Lucas managed to put the tank in neutral, switch off the engine and so position himself as to survive the final impact uninjured. He then took charge inside the tank, which was dripping with petrol and filled with fumes, calmly gave first aid to the survivors and then dug a hole under a turret hatch wide enough to make it possible for the living to be pulled out. In the meantime, Lance-Corporal V. C. E. Hammond, well realizing the danger of fire, insisted, with cold courage, upon being lowered down the hole in order to encourage those at the bottom and help in their rescue. It was he who strapped the commander to a stretcher and went up and down the hole on several occasions until everybody was safe, completing as fine an act of gallantry as any in the Regimental annals on, appropriately enough, ground that was hallowed in its past. This spirit augured well for the future.

CHAPTER VI

The Defence of Europe 1950-1956

Notwithstanding the drama of the activity in the Middle and Far East theatres of operations, it was to the defence of Europe that the British Army had mainly to address itself after 1950. There, the largest portion of the R.A.C. would be stationed as part of the deterrent to the Russian danger. Between 1951 and 1959, at least six of the eight units of the R.T.R. were to be found either in Britain or in Germany, and never between 1952 and 1959 were there fewer than five in Germany itself. Moreover, they were all assigned to an operational rôle as a result of the Government's decision, in August 1950, to embark upon military expansion and rearmament. Europe was to be defended by the creation of two regular armoured divisions, in addition to the 7th which was already in being, and all were to be brought up to strength. At the same time, the 3rd Infantry Division was to be re-activated and a number of infantry battalions brought back into existence. R.A.C. units would be expanded by relieving them of the Territorial Army support rôle and the Training Regiment rôle. Regular regiments would no longer be held at cadre strength; the Territorial Army R.A.C. units would be expected, with supplementary aid, to fend for themselves. So the 2nd R.T.R. (Lieutenant-Colonel E. F. Offord) and the 6th (Lieutenant-Colonel H. H. K. Rowe) would again assume the dignity of active armoured regiments in what was to be 20th Armoured Brigade (Brigadier C. W. M. Timmis) in 6th Armoured Division (Major-General E. C. Prior-Palmer, late 9th Lancers), forming in southern England. And a few months later, 8th R.T.R. (Lieutenant-Colonel R. N. Harding-Newman) would hand over at Catterick to the newly raised 66th Training Regiment (Lieutenant-Colonel E. C. Mitford) which was one of four new training regiments – 65th, 66th, 67th and 68th – raised to permit the release of regular R.A.C. units for a warlike task. The 8th began training at Tilshead in February 1951, and departed for Germany six months later to become part of 11th Armoured Division (Major-General H. R. B. Foote, V.C.), alongside 1st R.T.R. (Lieutenant-Colonel P. W. D. Sturdee) in 33rd Armoured Brigade (Brigadier R. F. K. Belchem). Meanwhile, 5th R.T.R. (Lieutenant-Colonel G. Fitz-Talbot) remained in 7th Armoured Brigade as part of 7th Armoured Division (Major-General C. P. Jones, late R.E.). The presence of Foote, Timmis and Belchem thus introduced a strong R.T.R. presence charged with the direction of armour in Germany, and demonstrated the wealth of talent the Regiment could call upon in the higher echelons of command.

The sudden promotion of the 2nd, 6th and 8th R.T.R. to full armoured regimental status after years of deprivation came as a shock, and provided a real test of their ingenuity. In August, with scarcely any notice, the 2nd and 6th were instructed to continue helping the T.A., but also to begin to absorb an influx of reinforcements, hand in the vehicles they had drawn up for T.A. training, move camp from, respectively, Crookham and Worksop to the Tidworth area and, in October, carry out regimental training with a number of new tanks manned by crews which were largely green. From the closely restricted training areas of the Long Valley, Aldershot and Scroften Airfield, the 2nd and 6th suddenly found themselves roaming in space on Salisbury Plain, and in danger of being invited to run before they could walk. Rowe solved the problem for 6th R.T.R. by handing over tactical training to squadron and troop leaders and contenting himself with regimental exercises which, as Captain A. R. Bisset puts it, '. . . were essentially non-tactical, disciplinary manoeuvres consisting of the whole regiment wheeling, forming columns of squadrons, etc'. The 8th R.T.R., when it arrived at Tilshead in February, was better off in that it had been able to fill its establishment with some of the pick of the 6,400 National Service and 2,000 regular recruits who had passed through its hands in the three years it had spent as a training regiment. But with so many units of all Arms now crowding onto Salisbury Plain, training areas were at a premium. Much W.D. land which had previously been available had, in the post-war years, been let to farmers who were naturally reluctant to see the work of the plough undone by the track. The W.D. Land Agent had to work fast to control a potentially acrimonious situation. In due course, land was divided into priority categories and prominently designated as Class I, II or III, this giving rise to the remark by the 8th in *The Tank* that 'It is popularly supposed that you can shoot farmers in a Class I area, whilst in the other areas they can shoot you.'

With the abrupt conversion of the Army from an almost exclusively training organization to a balanced operational force, the demand for leaders and, by implication, more Regulars, became paramount. To help overcome this problem among the lower ranks, the best recruits (National Service and Regular), whose Selection Grading was 2, were rated as O.R. IV, indicating that they had N.C.O. potential and, perhaps, encouraging them later to extend their engagements as Regulars. More persuasive in the Regular recruiting aspect, however, was the introduction of a new scheme of engagement in 1952, whereby a man could serve for three years with the Colours and three on the Reserve, in lieu of two years' National Service and obligatory reserve training. Basically this was a financial inducement which attracted a great many men, who were due for call-up, to opt for this sort of engagement. As Regulars, they would receive the relatively lucrative high rate of Regular pay along with other benefits, instead of the penurious emoluments paid to a National Service-man. Some three-year recruits actually planned farther ahead, intending to save the balance of the Regular pay which accrued over and above the National Service amount and use it to purchase their discharge after only two years' service. Few are on record as having maintained this intention.

For the first time since 1954, sufficient men were available and new equipment was coming forward. Yet nearly all the B vehicles were of Second World War vintage, produced by a panic programme of reconditioning which put back on the road a motley collection of trucks, some of them decrepit, many of them still of the two-wheel drive type. It was at this time that one of the benefits of a large regiment such as the R.T.R., composed of several units, became apparent. When the Adjutant-General sought ways to man an independent squadron of tanks for the Berlin Garrison, he found that, with the pressures then being exerted on the small cavalry units of the R.A.C., none could conveniently detach a squadron for the task. The R.T.R., on the other hand, could find the necessary strength from within, and it was N. W. Duncan, in his dual rôle of D.R.A.C. and Colonel Commandant of the R.T.R., who could say with confidence that the R.T.R. could meet the requirement. Thus, at short notice, the No 1 Independent Squadron Royal Tank Regiment came to be formed at Hohne under Major R. W. Campbell in 1951 and began to take over its Comets in Berlin on 3 January 1952.

So far as the Fighting Arms were concerned, the organization and training of the formation allocated to the defence of Europe remained as they had been in 1945. At Higher Establishment, each armoured division retained an armoured car regiment and an armoured brigade of four armoured regiments. The field artillery component was partly self-propelled and partly towed. The motorized infantry battalion in the armoured brigade, travelled in armoured half-track vehicles or in armoured tracked carriers, while the lorried infantry brigade moved in unarmoured wheeled vehicles. And within the infantry division, the sole armoured unit, the Divisional Regiment, whose task was that of anti-tank protection, was armed with self-propelled guns. Inevitably there was a shortage of up-to-date tanks. The Divisional Regiments would have to make do with ex-Royal Artillery M 10 tank destroyers, armed with 17pdr. guns, with the prospect of receiving, in 1952, the thinly armoured Charioteer, with its 20pdr. gun. It was hoped that the Conqueror would enter service in 1956. The armoured regiments had to continue with Comets until the trickle of Centurion 3s from the factories could be raised to a flood.

By the middle of 1952, the three British armoured divisions would form a major part of the N.A.T.O. defence forces, and would have responsibility for defending the North German Plain where the Russian armour seemed most likely to attack – if it did so at all. Although there were those who argued that tanks ought not to be spent in anti-tank defence, Duncan welcomed this rôle as an argument against reducing R.A.C. strength, and the British General Staff, influenced by leaders who were convinced of the existing dominance of armour, persisted in placing their reliance on tanks for all purposes. As a result, the provision of training areas in peace-time for so many tracked formations and units posed serious problems. In Germany these restrictions were more easily overcome than elsewhere, since the Occupation Powers retained plenary rights which enabled them to take liberties in the use of land and public roads which no democratically elected government would allow. But in Britain, the exercising of 6th Armoured Division in 1951 placed an almost intolerable strain on the few extensive training areas available. Only Salisbury Plain was suitable for large-scale manoeuvres and the major exercises – 'Corunna Packet' and 'Surprise Packet' – held that autumn – would further tax the already over-tried patience of land owners and Land Agents, besides causing damage of a quite insufferable cost. Indeed these exercises (with 3rd Infantry Division participating alongside 6th Armoured in 'Surprise Packet') and in which 7th R.T.R. (Lieutenant-Colonel M. J. Woollcombe), with one squadron of Churchills and one of Comets, with their turrets painted yellow, represented the enemy, were the last on such a scale ever to be held in England. They were also among the last in which the threat from nuclear weapons was, for all practical purposes, largely discounted. Even though the Rusians had exploded their first atomic device in 1949, there was no reason to believe that, in 1952, they were in a position to use this weapon tactically on the battlefield. In the early 1950s, therefore, much more attention was paid to countering the danger of enemy air attack (in addition to the threat posed by conventional ground weapons) than to atomic strikes. Apart from practising the battle tactics of 1945, using command and control techniques which were little different from those of the Second World War, considerably increased emphasis was placed upon concealment and in movement by small packets of vehicles, as opposed to the carelessly exposed concentrations of vehicles and long convoys which had been features of armies in the field after the Luftwaffe had been beaten.

Only in 1953, in the aftermath of the test firing of a low-yield nuclear shell from a 280mm. cannon of the U.S. Army, was a serious start made into the implementation of the systems of movement and deployment which nuclear weapons seemed to demand. This is not to say that no thought had been given to the subject during the years since the first explosion in 1945. For example, in 1946, while engaged in the work of S.A.E., Colonel Alan Jolly, in an article entitled 'Armour and the Next War', written for *The R.A.C. Journal*, suggested that strategic and tactical handling would have to be changed, and proposed the shape of organization and command structure that would be needed. At a time when small-yield atomic weapons were as yet unheard of, he dismissed their tactical use because of the dangers posed to friendly troops (no doubt the memories of Allied bombers ravaging their own troops in Normandy were fresh in his mind). Indeed, he visualized a more serious threat to unarmoured troops from V.T. (radio proximity) fuses. Dispersion, he foresaw, would be the key feature of future deployments, allied to rapid concentration for action followed by renewed dispersion in battles of even greater mobility than those of the previous war. Armour he deemed essential. These views, reflecting those of the War Office, the instructional establishments and B.A.O.R. formations, prevailed and were enhanced, as more information became available from the many field test explosions carried out by the Americans (and subsequent to the first explosion of a British bomb in 1952) which revealed that armoured fighting vehicles moving at speed through nuclear-irradiated areas provided their crews with far more effective protection than any other means, quite apart from the shielding their armour gave against the initial blast and heat effects of atomic weapons. Indeed, it was the sheer rapidity of response and movement which was thought to be necessary in an atomic environment that brought to attention (prior to the days when a Combat Development Branch had been introduced into the War Office) a suspicion that existing armoured divisions might be too unwieldy. No longer was there sufficient time to effect quick and elaborate tactical regroupings: the out-dated communication procedures and equipment alone, precluded this.

But out-moded though these formations might soon appear to be, their mere presence made it possible completely to revise the N.A.T.O. mode of defence. The original plan to align the main defence on the River Rhine – never politically popular in the light of the attempts to bring the West German Republic into N.A.T.O., and resurrect the German Armed Forces to help protect the German population – was superseded by a forward deployment. In the north, where B.A.O.R. stood guard, the main line of defence would be along the River Weser. By 1952, the British Army would rise to its maximum peace-time strength of 440,000 men, and nearly all the B.A.O.R. tank units would have received Centurion 3. Two years later, in 1954, the three armoured divisions would be at the peak of their strength, but, paradoxically, would be on the verge of dismemberment, after a year in which the time spent on training had reached an exceedingly high intensity.

2nd R.T.R.'s programme for 1954, as one of the armoured regiments of 20th Armoured Brigade, discloses a pattern of activity similar to that of the other armoured units in B.A.O.R. at that time. No sooner had the New Year festivities been concluded than Brigadier C. W. M. Timmis, who had raised the brigade in England, handed over to Brigadier J. W. Hackett (late 8th Hussars). While the individual training of newly-joined National Servicemen proceeded without pause, in order to replace the most recent departing group of trained crewmen, a four-day 6th Armoured Division Study period in February was followed by a two-day 20th Armoured Brigade study period in March, immediately prior to the departure of squadrons to Borkenberge for a fortnight's troop training. (The 2nd's squadrons, incidentally, had assumed names in place of letter designations in the autumn of 1953, A becoming Ajax, B–Badger, C–Cyclops and H.Q.–Nero; these names were related to those used within the unit during the Tank Brigade exercises of 1932. By 21 April, the entire regiment was at Hohne for annual range shooting, followed by training at infantry company/tank troop level in May, the Queen's Birthday Parade at Sennelager in June and then still more exercises – quite apart from social events, canoeing, athletic meetings, and Corps Week early in July. A change of command, beginning in the middle of July, when Lieutenant-Colonel R. G. S. Saunders began to take over from Offord, involved the usual administrative work, yet this was an idle month compared to August when the regiment moved again to Sennelager for training at regimental level.

Everything was leading up to 'Battle Royal', one of the largest ever B.A.O.R. exercises, involving all four of its divisions, and in which every unit of the R.T.R. in Germany (2nd, 3rd, 4th, 6th and 8th) would take part. The length and scope of 'Battle Royal' is illustrated by the 2nd's itinerary. On 18 September, with 47 tanks, it concentrated at Diepholtz and on 22 September moved to dispersal areas north of the Teutoburgerwald which it crossed next day. Not until 24 September, however, did it become heavily engaged, and even then it was not to be found in 'battle' but organizing traffic-control for an assault crossing of the River Ems, and suffering 'damage' from a nuclear strike on 25 September before incurring further casualties from a local enemy counter-attack, just prior to paratroops dropping in their rear, north of Milte at 15.24 hrs. Given the task of sealing-off the Dropping Zone, (completed by 21.35 hrs), they were ready, next day, to begin the type of rapid 'swan', so beloved of armoured regiments when let loose in the final stages of an exercise. On 27 September, they 'fought' their way south to Diestedde with the infantry of 61st Lorried Infantry Brigade riding on the tanks, and next day, provided right-flank protection for an assault crossing, and welcomed the C.I.G.S., Field Marshal Sir John Harding, when he flew in by helicopter to visit R.H.Q. All this sounds rather easy, but in fact, 'Battle Royal' took place in the most appalling wet weather which, as one participant remarks, 'made any movement across country a certain recovery operation'. The same report, which appeared in *The Tank*, says that 'Although the high-level aspect of atomic warfare was somewhat above the individual troop member, nevertheless, camouflage, immediate and deep digging and dispersion were carried out with care and skill, indicating that Jolly was on the right lines in 1946 and that the soldiers were taking the business seriously.' Indeed, for Corporal Waterhouse, a R.E.M.E. fitter attached to Badger, things turned out a little too realistically when he went to repair a tank and was greeted upon arrival by an internal explosion which blew him unconscious into the road and set the tank alight. Recovering quickly, it was Waterhouse who, single-handed, pulled out the trapped and seriously injured crew members and extinguished the fire, thus saving two lives and preventing the destruction of the tank, before relapsing into unconsciousness.

Despite the defects from which the three B.A.O.R. armoured divisions suffered – notably their inability to react or re-group swiftly enough to cope with rapidly changing situations – they did manage to satisfy, to some considerable extent, Jolly's demands for 'Mobility, dispersion, armoured protection and sustained endurance'. The 2nd had kept moving and had come home with 45 out of its 47 tanks running, a performance which few other regiments managed to emulate. The Jolly requirement which, at that time, was least likely to be met was that of producing 'the greatest possible weight of concentrated fire-power', but the resolution of this lay elsewhere and had been in the process of examination for over a decade.

Even before the Germans had first mounted an 88mm. gun in their Tiger tank in 1942, it had been realized that the existing system of fire and correction could not be employed by the tank commander. To see round obscuration, a flank observer was needed. As mentioned in Chapter III, various attempts to improve fire-control systems had been made during the past decade. For example, during the war, Offord had been engaged in devising techniques for shooting with high-explosive shells and developing simple training aids and miniature field ranges for the instruction of crews in bracketing as well as in shooting with shot. In 1950, fresh impetus was given to gunnery development by Major A. Cooper, one of the R.T.R.'s mathematicians who, before the war, had obtained a B.Sc. Honours degree and, incidentally had played soccer as an amateur. As a G.S.O. 2 at the Royal Military College of Science in 1947, Cooper found 'the opportunity, for the first time, to study in detail the technical aspects of armoured warfare'. He had been fortunate then that, under the guidance of the Commandant of the F.V. Wing, Colonel F. W. Gordon-Hall (late R.T.R.), he had been encouraged to think freely, an experience which was repeated when, in October 1950, he took over the Investigation Wing at the Gunnery School, which was then commanded by Colonel H. J. B. Cracroft, and was given a completely free hand. Again to quote Cooper: 'After a few months I had proven the gross errors in Centurion's Gun Control Equipment and the irrational performance of the 20 pr ammunition. In the presence of the obscuration problem I questioned the true fightability of Centurion without a flank observation technique. I wrote a report proving my points to Johnnie French (Colonel J. French, ex-R.T.R.) of the Ordnance Board who published an OB Proceeding on my findings and this put the cat among the pigeons. Bernard Cracroft backed me as did Colonel J. B. Robertson. . . . During these investigations the concept of the rapid rate of killing with the High Velocity gun was conceived and proved to a limited degree with specially prepared tanks and the few rounds of accurate ammunition we came across.'

In April 1952, the D.R.A.C., Duncan, made Cooper G.S.O. 1 of R.A.C. 2 because he wanted an officer there with a scientific background who could match the F.V.R.D.E. and A.R.D.E. design staffs on his requirements for an acceptable fighting capability in the tanks. But upon taking up the post, Cooper realized that this was about the last thing he could concentrate upon. At that crucial moment in the rearmament programme, all the emphasis had to be placed upon producing the Charioteer and the Conqueror for the Divisional Regiment R.A.C., while raising the anti-tank capability of the armoured regiments by giving them each four S.P. versions of the Centurion – the FV 4004 with a 120mm. gun – at the same time as experimenting with the FV 215 which was to mount an enormous 183mm. gun. But when the C.I.G.S., Field Marshal Sir William Slim, saw the prototypes of these latter two monsters, he turned them down out of hand on grounds of size. As a result, the armoured regiments had, in due course, to be given the Conqueror. Probably Duncan was over-reaching a little at this time, for he was also pressing his staff to obtain finance for Anti-tank Guided Weapon studies which had been stimulated by knowledge of what the Germans had achieved during the war with glider bombs and the X–7 wire-guided missile. But although, between 1952 and 1956, Cooper was to write the specifications for the first British A.T.G.W.s – 'Malkara' and 'Orange William' – finance was initially denied and attention was focussed almost exclusively on development of the gun.

The central problem was how to hit the target with the minimum expenditure of ammunition, without resort to fire and correction by the commander from the turret (as Gunnery School methods dictated) or by employment of an observer in a flank tank (which Offord, quite irregularly, was teaching 2nd R.T.R. in the realization that this was the only existing way to overcome obscuration). In his initial experiments (probably after reference to an F.V.R.D.E. report suggesting feasibility) Cooper had arrived at a procedure for engaging targets at less than 1,000 yards – the distance at which the shot's flat trajectory began to fall significantly below the line of sight. Taking an initial point of aim, the gunner was told to fire using the 800-yard aiming mark, add 200 and fire and then drop 400 and fire again. In this way, a hit was virtually assured by the height of the target – providing the ammunition was reliable and the gun accurately zeroed to the sighting equipment. At ranges in excess of 1,000 yards, the commander ordered the gunner to fire a high-explosive round to establish the range and, from the observation gained, ordered a correction prior to the gunner firing three rounds of shot by the same procedure as that used below 1,000 yards. This technique, promoted by Offord, worked well even if it could be a little costly in ammunition. It was also adopted by Cooper and C. J. Wieland (late R.T.R.) of F.V.R.D.E. to achieve a high rate of kill against the massed targets which a potential enemy could be expected to present – simply, it was a matter of finding the range by the three-round method of a central target within the group under attack and then aiming centre, bottom or top edge of the other targets, dependant upon the location of each in relation to the first target. Wieland and Cooper were rehearsing a crew in the drill one day and heard one member remark to another: 'You know what these two want, don't you? They want the . . . ing gun to fire like a . . . ing machine-gun!' Indeed, a well-practised crew (given time for preparation) could fire 20 rounds in a minute and score one hit per round, once the first target had been struck. In 1956, R. E. Ward's 3rd R.T.R. crews were doing this consistently, and it was he and H. E. Pyman who strongly backed Cooper in B.A.O.R.

Unfortunately, these techniques failed dramatically if the gun were incorrectly zeroed to the line of sight. Offord forcefully pointed out this anomaly when he came to Bovington at the end of 1954 to form the Equipment Trials Wing of the R.A.C. Centre, taking under central control the existing Driving and Maintenance Investigation Wing and the Gunnery Investigation Wing, and later adding a new Radio and Miscellaneous Section. He demanded a tightening-up of zeroing procedures allied to far more stringent design and manufacturing standards of all the gunnery components and assemblies. By demonstration, he showed that a precisely zeroed 20 pdr. gun in a Centurion could drift off zero by 5′ within two hours and that, therefore, some form of zeroing check was needed by crews in the field to compensate this without resorting to the standard method of shooting-in against screen targets. During the coming years, Offord and Cooper were to collaborate with Wieland in efforts to achieve an ideal. It was Wieland who applied the principle of an existing 'bore-sight', designed by R.S.M.(I) Robinson, R.T.R., to a modified German sight, to enable crews to carry out what became known as silent zeroing, using a bore-sight of original design – a practice which was officially adopted, but which declined in favour because crews were averse to making full use of the rather complicated method which evolved. A series of experiments and trials made steady progress until the day would arrive when the new Mark 3 20pdr. ammunition came into service; when silent zeroing and the Gunner's 'Eight Point Check' for accuracy became law; and the Battle Sight Technique was officially adopted and taught at the Gunnery School, where Offord took command in 1957.

This of course was not the end of the story. Indeed, before 1957, further improvements to the gun's performance had been made by the scientists and designers, and are described in Chapter IX. But a distinct revolution in gunnery had taken place in a comparatively short space of time. Scepticism there had been from the guardians of traditional methods, and disagreements had not been unknown among the revolutionaries themselves. Occasionally, change had been resisted and frustrations introduced, but, overall, there had been generated a unity of purpose in raising the standards of shooting to unprecedented efficiency in order to compensate the numerical inferiority of the N.A.T.O. Powers. No longer was rank conservatism, as suffered by the pre-war tank pioneers, allowed to halt the creation of advanced techniques. Yet the irony of it is that 'The Battle Range Technique', as Offord christened the new procedures, and which were to represent the most important postwar contribution to the art of tank warfare, has yet to be used in anger by the British Royal Armoured Corps. It has been used by Pakistani and Indian tanks in battle against each other and, above all, by the Israelis, who, engaging massed Egyptian, Jordanian and Syrian tanks in the Six Days War of 1967 and the Yom Kippur War of 1973, have seen their out-numbered tanks armed with British-designed guns slaughter a mass of Russian-designed (and some British) tanks by employing the techniques created by the R.T.R. team of Offord, Cooper and Wieland. (These three had done for tank gunnery, in terms of accuracy and technique, what Captain Percy Scott had done for naval gunnery at the turn of the century.)

The beauty of the new gunnery techniques lay in their relative simplicity. They contributed to the production of the greatest possible weight of concentrated fire-power insisted upon by Jolly in his 1946 paper. By these methods it was relatively easy to bring short-serving National Servicemen to the desired standard of proficiency. Nevertheless, by 1954, the Army and the nation were beginning to feel the pinch of so high an allotment of material and manpower resources to defence. Moreover, in the more relaxed political climate which followed the death of Stalin in 1953, and with the re-creation of the German Army in 1955, a reduction in effort became possible. Those who recognized the damage which a high turnover of partially uninterested men could do to the genuinely professional element of the Army, began to search more diligently than hitherto for ways to increase the Regular element so as to reduce the need of National

Servicemen, and as part of general economy measures aimed at retaining fewer men in uniform. So, while the statement by the Minister of War, Mr. Anthony Head, which accompanied the Army Estimates for 1954–55, referred to, 'A disturbing feature is the declining number of Regulars with over six years' service', and 'The strain on Territorial Army volunteer officers and other ranks in training and administration at the peak of the training season . . .', the principal incentive adopted to raise the recruiting of Regulars was an increase in pay, while for the T.A. it was merely the expressed hope that '. . . a larger proportion of National Service officers and men, now doing part-time duty . . . would re-engage for further periods and so help their volunteer comrades to bear the burden'. Some T.A. units imposed no such burden of course, the Westminster Dragoons being one of them. Trooper B. Perrett recalls a visit by the Honorary Colonel, H. E. Pyman, and his speech, shouted to all ranks: 'I'm told you're all volunteers [nearly accurate], I'm glad! Because when it happens you'll all be dead in three weeks!'

The new rates of pay gave some encouragement to Regulars – an unmarried captain received an extra 4s per day, bringing his annual income to £675 after four years in the rank, while a lance-corporal received another 2s, bringing his weekly pay, if he had three stars, to £4 4s, and £4 7s 6d if he had four stars. But these improvements helped only to stabilize the situation. There was but a scanty rise in re-engagements beyond the three-years mark, at which point the bulk of three-year pseudo-Regulars left the service. For this, a number of traditional factors, such as the lure of higher civilian wages, freedom of choice, separation from families, inferior accommodation were responsible – in addition to those associated with the discouraging effects upon senior ranks of seeing trained men depart as soon as they had reached a reasonable level of proficiency. Efforts aimed at stimulating recruiting lacked inspiration and were thwarted in a nation blessed by full employment and in which the popular Press tended to magnify the Army's failures and play-down or ignore its achievements. Not that the attentions of the Press, natural enough in connection with a Citizen Force with all the political implications attached, was necessarily un-constructive. Although the majority of officers might spend some of their time in dread of some local contretemps which might lead to a Ministerial Inquiry and adverse comment in Parliament or in the National Papers, this fear could also act as a deterrent to inefficiency and a stimulus to the introduction of reforms. For example, a National Serviceman's complaint to his Member of Parliament that he was being made to waste his time performing unnecessary or humiliating fatigues, instead of partaking in training, could present the Army Council with an excuse for pressing the case for additional funds to employ civilians and so relieve soldiers of irrelevant tasks. But it was quite apparent that the mere presence within a unit of National Servicemen ticking-off on a calendar the days to their release was a deterrent to recruiting.

Signs of a fundamental change in Government policy were visible in 1955. The announced disbandment of Anti-Aircraft Command in 1954 had caused the loss of 14 Regiments of the Royal Artillery and their supporting units, with attendant reductions among the officers and men. It was true that the economies reflected, in part, a different emphasis in methods, when guns were shown to be out-moded by the latest technology of missile bombardment. But overall economy was in the wind and could be detected, too, in the exercises held by B.A.O.R. during 1955 to test a new kind of light armoured division. 20th Armoured Brigade (Brigadier J. W. Hackett) in 6th Armoured Division (Major-General R. W. Macleod) provided the nucleus of the experimental formation which was planned to contain four armoured regiments, a mechanized infantry battalion, a regiment of field artillery and an engineer field squadron. 2nd and 6th R.T.R. were involved in the exercises which culminated in a Corps exercise called 'Full House', in which the experimental 6th Armoured Division and 2nd Infantry Division were pitted against the old-fashioned 11th Armoured Division. Members of the 2nd were slightly sceptical of it all, and a 6th R.T.R. report said that, so far as it was concerned, '. . . the exercise consisted of three days' waiting in a concentration area near Osnabruck and then a long armoured swan up winding and indifferent roads to the Weser bridges and on again to the eastern limits of the exercise area'. The imbalance of the new armoured division was plain for all to see. Quite obviously it was short of infantry. Equally plainly, the exercise had been designed to demonstrate to somebody's satisfaction that small formations could move fast and for a sustained period, and that a brigade group was easier to handle than the existing armoured division since regrouping was cut to the minimum.

The validity of the new organizations seemed to be accepted in the Secretary of State for War's Memorandum to the Army Estimates of 1956–57, published in February 1956. This stated that the general structure of the infantry division was satisfactory for the conduct of operations in a nuclear war, but it would have to be capable of 'being split into strong, hard-hitting, self-contained groups so that, when the occasion demanded, wide decentralization was possible while retaining the command structure to concentrate the power of the division at the right moment . . . Battles of the future will be fought as battles of all arms fighting as a team and no longer shall we attempt to equip one arm with every type of weapon . . . In order to provide strong, hard hitting groups of all arms, armour is now to be integrated in the infantry brigade . . .' This would cause considerable reorganization and reshuffling of units, and not a little disruption, quite apart from the doubts it raised in the minds of those who knew what it was like to be tied to an immobile infantry's coat-tails – and, as yet, only two infantry battalions in B.A.O.R. were fully equipped with armoured personnel carriers. But it was not yet settled, because a final decision concerning armoured divisions was reserved for additional study. In doubtful mood, the War Office stated that the old armoured division must go and the new one would have to be a specialized formation, capable of performing tasks 'other than those for which it is designed. It will then be necessary to group under it additional infantry or armour or engineers, dependent on the task'. In other words, the small armoured division had been a failure. It would be at least another year before a major change could take place in B.A.O.R.

But in respect of reorganization of the Reserve Army, the Secretary of State was adamant in opinion, and swift to act in 1956. Visualizing that, in a global war, it would be impossible to transport more than a very small part of the Reserve Army overseas, he concluded that the basic T.A. infantry division would be the best formation for tasks requiring a limited fighting rôle, but well suited to administrative work and civil defence in the event of a nuclear attack upon the United Kingdom. Both T.A. armoured divisions would be converted to infantry divisions and several T.A. armoured regiments would be amalgamated with others or would change their rôle. In so far as the R.T.R. was concerned, this would mean that, before the end of the year, the 40th would be amalgamated with the 41st to form the 40th/41st R.T.R. (Lieutenant-Colonel G. V. Stephenson) and the 44th with the North Somerset Yeomanry to form the North Somerset Yeomanry/44th R.T.R., while the 42nd, 43rd and 45th would revert to the infantry rôle whence they sprang. There was great indignation in some quarters about delay in producing a plan. An Editorial in *The Tank* remarked that 'a recent bald statement about the future of the T.A., devoid of any plan for its accomplishment . . . flagrantly flouts' the principle that '. . . the human factor remains the same and is entitled to consideration garnished with courtesy from those who handle it.' The words smacked of General Sir John Crocker, and he would soon need all his diplomatic skill to save the regular R.T.R. units from mutilation.

When the time came for the T.A. amalgamations, however, feelings among the officers and men seem to have been mixed. The 43rd expressed what was probably a fairly common view when, in *The Tank*, it recorded 'the disappointment amongst the National Servicemen in the Regiment whose entire military service had been as members of the Royal Tank Regiment. However we are in the fortunate position of having a hard core of Territorial volunteers who served with us [as 6th Bn Royal Northumberland Fusiliers] before conversion to armour who are looking forward to handling a rifle once more'. The speed of the change was electric. Tanks were rapidly cleared from the drill halls, and the three converted battalions were training as infantry at annual camp that year. There was to be no looking back, in a year when the infantry waxed strongly and armour and artillery waned.

CHAPTER VII

Débâcle in
the Middle East
1956-1957

When King Hussein came to the throne in 1953, the days of a dominant British influence in Jordan were numbercd. Hussein was not anti-British, but obviously he put Arab interests first and, and as an energetic young man, felt bound in course of time to assert his own position over Glubb Pasha. Probably the age gap separating Glubb Pasha from his new master was detrimental to a close understanding, and there is no doubt that there existed within the Arab Legion, upon whose allegiance the young king heavily depended, a strong body of opinion which rejected their old commander. Of this, British officers were aware, although the actual rapid change of mood was concealed from them. Matters were brought to a head towards the end of 1955 when opposition within Jordan to becoming a signatory to the proposed Baghdad mutual defence Pact assumed the form of serious rioting in Amman and Irbid. Internal Security became the Legion's main preoccupation. B Squadron of Lieutenant-Colonel J. J. Dingwall's 3rd Tank Regiment, under Major H. A. Cobden, played a prominent part in restoring order in Amman, while the two armoured car regiments patrolled energetically in the rural areas. Captain W. F. Woodhouse, in addition to running convoys into Amman carrying supplies to the squadron there, acted as Military Liaison Officer to the municipality of Zerqa where there were some very ugly riots. Here, a British regimental commander was killed while leading his men in their attempts to restrain a stone-throwing mob, and British families were threatened in their quarters. It was Woodhouse, too, who helped to keep the families supplied from the N.A.A.F.I. The riots were quelled, but Jordan did not join the Baghdad Pact, and resentment at Britain's part and, to some extent, their presence, increased.

On the day of the coup which ousted Glubb in March 1956, Dingwall, in his office at Zerqa, was unaware of anything unusual. He gave little thought to the difficulty he was having contacting some of his officers, and not until that evening, prior to a social gathering at Glubb's house, did it become known that Glubb had been put under arrest, and Dingwall and

Lieutenant-Colonel A. R. Leakey learned that the loyalty of their own units was suspect. Leakey's unit, in fact, was not so heavily subverted as Dingwall's, nor was he to experience Dingwall's shock at having one of his own men present a rifle to his throat when he went to investigate the trouble. It was only after Dingwall had insisted on an officer being called, and had been taken to his own officers mess that he realized, with horror, that this had become the headquarters of the coup. 'I was told the Regiment was no longer under my command (although the King contradicted this during the following days), but I demanded an officer escort to the General's house where my wife had started to take a drink some seven hours previously. I then went to find my Brigadier [E. C. Mitford] to report the situation to him. He had not been out that night and was unaware of any of the arrests . . .'

Such was the thoroughness of the rebels' planning of a coup which was almost certainly aimed principally at Glubb. British dominance was at an end. All the senior officers were at once sent home, including Glubb's Chief of Staff and successor designate, Brigadier W. M. Hutton. Captain R. J. Shackleton was one of those who were allowed to remain as so-called 'technical advisers'. He had relieved Woodhouse a month before the coup in March. One of the last to leave after the final dénouement in September 1956, he played a prominent part in the final evacuation of the British staff.

The withdrawal of Jordan's support from the British meant that, when the last unit of the British Army departed from Egypt on 13 June 1956, the final vestiges of the scheme for a strategic reserve in the Middle East had evaporated. No longer could the Suez Canal, through which passed a vast quantity of vital oil supplies and trade, be assured by the presence of a concentrated force upon the spot. Not only had Britain's reputation been severely devalued, but now her power could be applied only from distant and dispersed bases, and these were anything but secure in themselves. The Colony of Cyprus, which had proved a useful staging-post for reserves sent to Egypt in 1952, was now itself unsafe, amid the turmoil of a guerilla war associated with the Greek agitation for Enosis (union of Cyprus with Greece) and of Turkish fears of harm at Greek hands. Infantry-type units of the strategic reserve sent there were automatically involved in anti-guerilla operations. Nor was all well with the theatre's armoured forces. The 25th Armoured Brigade, which had been formed in Tripolitania in 1952 and had become known as 25th Armoured Brigade Group the following year, came under the command of Brigadier A. W. Brown. But in 1956, it was absorbed within 10th Armoured Division (Major-General J. N. R. Moore (late Foot Guards)) which itself had been formed in Egypt in October 1955 prior to moving to Tripoli. This formation was organized along the same lines as the experimental type which had failed while on trial in B.A.O.R. in 1955: in other words, it was little more than a Brigade Group ruled over by a greatly inflated headquarters in which, incidentally, Brigadier A. Jolly became Deputy Commander, in succession to Brown, in November 1956. Furthermore, its units were widely dispersed. In the summer of 1956, its headquarters was in Tripoli; its single infantry battalion, 1st K.R.R.C., in Derna; its artillery regiment, 3rd R.H.A., in Homs; one armoured regiment, the Queen's Bays, in Sabratha; another, 5th R.T.R. (Lieutenant-Colonel S. D. W. Seaver) in Barce; and the third, 10th Hussars, hundreds of miles away on the other side of Egypt, maintaining a tenuous British presence at Aqaba, in accordance with the need to keep an eye on Jordan's behalf over the Israelis. A command nightmare it might have been. An element in a strategic reserve, with complete freedom of movement, 10th Armoured Division certainly was not, particularly if King Idris of Libya were to object to the idea of foreign forces, stationed by treaty within his boundaries, being used to threaten any adjacent Arab nation.

No sooner had the last British troops departed from Egypt, than Soviet Russia made a renewed offer to finance the construction of the Aswan Dam, a political move which prompted President Nasser to ask for improved financial terms in aid of that project from the U.S.A., Britain and the International Bank for Reconstruction and Development. Eventually, the U.S.A. withdrew its offer on 19 July, and was supported in this by Britain, which led Nasser, a week later, to seize control of the primarily British-owned Suez Canal Company. The opinion of the Adjutant of 5th R.T.R., Captain G. L. D. Duckworth, as recorded in his diary, perhaps summed-up the views of a great many other people when the news broke on 27 July. 'Instant flap in U.K. and France and hostile reaction the world over. Our reactions here were, "Will it mean that we go to war with Egypt?".' He then goes on, 'In the 4th Test at Old Trafford England made 464 all out and got Australia all out for 84 . . .'

The decision by the Conservative British Government of Sir Anthony Eden on 27 July to plan for military intervention in Egypt, if all else failed, caught the British Army in Britain at a bad moment. A large percentage of the Army was National Service. The state and employment of regular units precluded their mounting operations at Corps strength – the level which the situation seemed to demand. Nothing could be extracted from N.A.T.O. forces in Germany and so, in order to raise the manpower, it was necessary to mobilize reservists – with all that implied in terms of international tension and internal disruption. In fact, there were certain infantry-type units ready for action – notably the 3rd Royal Marine Commando Brigade and the 16th Parachute Brigade – but of additional infantry formations and the essential administrative services, let alone the means to move them, there was a stark deficiency. As for armour in Britain, only two regiments of the R.A.C. were immediately available, although they were quite unready for the call when it came, to make matters worse, at the August Bank Holiday week-end. Not only were the vast majority of officers and men on leave, but the sub-units were dispersed on miscellaneous tasks throughout the land.

The senior R.A.C. officer in 3rd Infantry Division, Brigadier J. C. de F. Sleeman, returned to his Headquarters at Tidworth on 4 August, to find orders awaiting him to form an armoured brigade H.Q. and to mobilize 1st R.T.R. (Lieutenant-Colonel S. I. Howard-Jones, in process of taking over) and 6th R.T.R. (Lieutenant-Colonel T. H. Gibbon). Neither the staff nor the equipment for a brigade headquarters (known as 34th) existed, so, to begin with, Sleeman used his own staff, which had other responsibilities as H.Q. R.A.C. 3rd Division, until Major J. R. Gordon (4th/7th D.G.) and Major H. B. C. Watkins arrived as, respectively, Brigade Major and D.A.A. and Q.M.G.

1st R.T.R. had its Reconnaissance Troop and a reinforced tank squadron (without tanks) working for the T.A. at Tilshead; another squadron giving demonstrations for the School of Infantry at Warminster; a troop on Conqueror training at Thetford; and the remainder of the unit on garrison duties and fatigues at Tidworth. The 6th, who had returned from B.A.O.R. in March, destined for another round of T.A. assistance in Britain prior to relieving 10th Hussars at Aqaba, were even worse off. Scattered here and there at various T.A. summer camps they, unlike the 1st, had no mobilization rôle and, therefore, no mobilization plan. Within the past twelve months, about half of 1st R.T.R.'s tank commanders, gunners and loaders had not fired the annual open range course, and in the 6th, a bare 25 per cent had done so. Holdings of tanks were below 50 per cent, and those of B vehicles lower still, and of old types. Not one of the Centurions had been changed over from the Besa machine-gun to Browning and this, together with training in their use, had to be achieved as mobilization proceeded. Making the best of a bad job, Sleeman decided that 1st R.T.R. should take priority and be the first of his units to sail and, therefore, the first ashore in the planned landing at Alexandria for what became known as Operation 'Musketeer'.

What this meant to B Squadron of the 1st at Warminster is tersely described by its Sergeant-Major, S.S.M. H. C. Starr:

'After the last demonstration, the squadron, commanded by Major Q. St. J. Carpendale, went on block leave on 31 July. Within eight hours of their departure the regiment received orders to mobilize at Tidworth . . . Telegrams were sent to all personnel of the squadron to report back by 2359 hrs on Tuesday 4 August. Meanwhile five unfortunate "married pads" (self, S.Q.M.S. J. C. Chapman, Sergeant A. J. Buckle, Sergeant D. G. Read, Corporal Hard) undertook to hand in all accommodation stores and paint 15 Centurions and six 3 ton trucks sand coloured. The painting was carried out with the help and tremendous co-operation of the civilian staff of 27 Command Workshops, R.E.M.E., at Warminster. On Tuesday evening the roll call revealed that B Squadron had 100 per cent personnel in barracks, all vehicles painted and ready to move and all accommodation stores handed over. In order to make the exit from Warminster noticed, the Squadron Leader arranged a farewell parade and marched out with the salute being taken by Brigadier Musson, Commandant of the School of Infantry . . . The days which followed were full of frustrations, rumours, orders and counter orders. B Squadron acted as the regimental fatigue party while poor A and C Squadrons cleared their signatures of all equipment at Tilshead and Thetford . . .'

Meanwhile, Howard-Jones was attempting to concoct a joint plan with the commander of 16th Parachute Brigade (Brigadier M. A. H. Butler), but was unable to do so without maps. They were advised to visit Hobo (at that time a sick man) and found on their arrival 'maps for the whole of Egypt on display and a fascinating exposition of the whys and wherefores of landing in any part of Egypt, given by the General himself'.

For the 6th all was chaos. Lacking any sort of pre-arranged plan, they realized, as the first reservists began to report on the Saturday, that, simultaneously, they would have to rid themselves of their T.A. commitments, receive unequipped reinforcements straight from their homes, and, to quote Major J. B. Jolly, '. . . scatter to the four corners of England to collect various items of equipment; some of which we could well have done without'. After that, training might begin, with the initial understanding that embarkation was planned to commence on 11 August – a date which was progressively deferred as the impossibility of its implementation became apparent, amid a barrage of protests by Sleeman on behalf of his hard-pressed units – which were at seven days' notice to move. Then R.A.C. Records compounded the confusion by failing to realize that the establishment figures should be based on the four-man Centurion tank instead of the five-man Comet, which had gone out of regular service some years previously. As a result, in a tense, domestic political situation which demanded that the call-up of reservists must be justified by sending them to the seat of war, more than 170 trained Regular and N.S. soldiers were 'shut out' and left with rear details in Britain while excess reservists (in many cases, woefully short of training) were fitted into tank crews. Sleeman summed up his feelings in two explosive sentences: 'In B.A.O.R. a whole year of concentrated training is required to train an arm'd regiment in an N.S. Army – yet in the U.K., where units are understrength, posted with ineligibles for overseas, and woefully short of stores and equipment, they are expected to spread themselves all over the countryside providing training facilities for the T.A. and yet go to war, fit to fight, as part of the Strategic Reserve at short notice. The whole system is nonsense!'

To Captain P. S. Berry of 7th R.T.R., together with one other officer and 32 men drawn from his own unit, 5th Royal Inniskilling Dragoon Guards and 65th Training Regiment at Catterick, the quite unexpected order to abandon their jobs in the R.A.C. Training Brigade, and depart, within twelve hours, for an unknown destination, came as a shock. In addition to receiving innoculations and drawing their personal kit, they had also to make arrangements for wives, dogs, cats, cars and the paraphernalia a soldier collects at a home station. Not until they arrived at the School of Amphibious Warfare in Devon was it revealed to them that they were to form No. 1 Landing Vehicle Tank Troop R.A.C. (1 L.V.T. Troop) and to learn how to operate 16 unarmoured L.V.T. Mark IIIs under the instruction of an ex-R.T.R. officer (Captain R. Butler, R.A.S.C.) who had served in 11th R.T.R., manning the similar type Buffalo on the Rhine Crossing in March 1945. Within a few days they had to master the vehicle's mechanics, learn the rudiments of seamanship and apologise for accidentally ramming the Appledore lifeboat after an L.V.T. went hard astern on both tracks. Totally without administrative backing, they arrived at Malta by air a few days later, just as their L.V.Ts were unloaded. Luckily, the 45th Royal Marine Commando, which they were destined to carry in the assault was, as Berry puts it, 'full of interest and enthusiasm. Obviously this Brigade was alert . . .' – an impression which was reinforced when his requests for assistance and stores were instantly met by action instead of delayed by the interminable wait that so often followed a requisition in England, where, as Starr had discovered, an ammunition depot was reluctant to part with its holdings even if mobilization had been authorized.

The handicaps imposed upon the home-based units seemed to grow no less as Operation 'Musketeer' wended its way towards a doubtful climax in which, at times, even the destination was uncertain. It was of minor consequence, and yet a quite unnecessary load upon the R.A.C. units' administration, that reservists arrived un-kitted, while their cousins in the infantry reached their units, via their Depots, complete with accoutrements. Far more serious was the negligible time available for training, and no deficiency was more worrying than the meagre opportunities provided to zero the guns. There was just time to allow the 1st's crews, on 15 August, to fire a few rounds on the range, with 6th R.T.R. fitting in, as best it could, with 1st R.T.R's requirement, since the latter had absolute priority. Yet already it was known that the anti-tank protection of the invading force, once it had got ashore, would depend upon the tanks, the infantry having discarded their new BAT 120mm. guns because of insufficient ammunition. Instead, the infantry were re-equipped with the old 17pdr. anti-tank guns which were known to be ineffective against the heavy Josef Stalin 3 tanks which were numbered among the estimated 300 tanks, including Centurions, fielded by the Egyptian Army. Indeed, the presence of this well-armed and armoured, Russian-designed opponent in the enemy's order of battle caused more concern than anything else, since the 20pdr. Armour Piercing Capped Ballistic Capped (A.P.C.B.C.) ammunition was known to be incapable of penetrating the JS 3's frontal plates. Lieutenant-Colonel E. F. Offord was specially sent from the Equipment Trials Wing at Bovington to instruct the tank crews in how to apply the latest fire-control techniques, and to explain the vulnerable points of the JS 3. But he also found it necessary to persuade doubters that Armour Piercing Discarding Sabot (A.P.D.S.) ammunition was far superior to A.P.C.B.C., and to initiate a last-minute change from one to the other, with all the laborious re-stowing which that entailed.

6th R.T.R. managed to fit in one day of troop training on Salisbury Plain before a weird miscellany of tank transporters of every size, shape and description, many manned by civilians in the employment of Mr. Pickford, began to arrive on the 16th to carry them to Plymouth, and 1st R.T.R. to Portland, where the latter would load into civilian L.S.T.s. Gibbon was to comment upon the relative efficiency of the different transporter crews, and concluded that those of the R.A.S.C., with their brand-new Antars, were magnificent and made the journey to Plymouth in half the time of union men in Pickfords. Despite the demands of the priority list, 6th R.T.R. were on the move but a few hours later than the 1st, a request that they should load 15 tanks simultaneously with the 1st having been complied with, despite Sleeman's protest. Indeed, from this moment, conflicting orders from above sabotaged practically everyone's plans. Units were thoroughly disabused of their concept of an orderly approach to battle. The 1st were told that they would have to waterproof some of their tanks for an assault landing (despite their loading into civilian L.S.T.s), but no kits were readily available. Additional delay and confusion at Portland for the 1st was matched by the chaos at Plymouth where the 6th learned that they were not to travel in cargo ships, but in four naval L.S.T.s, and that there was not enough waterproofing material for them – although it was still intended that they should land, 'dry-shod', behind the 1st. Their loading tables had to be re-written and some vehicles would be 'shut out' and left behind. One L.S.T., in fact, still lay in dry dock and looked, in its untidy state, a most unlikely starter, but the Royal Navy promised it would be ready on time. So the men of 6th R.T.R. turned to making the accommodation on board as comfortable as they could, while commanders and signallers carried out wireless exercises ashore in wheeled vehicles.

H.Q. 34th Armoured Brigade also began to load on the 25th, despite its deficiency of many B vehicles, its possession of 1940 vintage office trucks which were shown to be totally useless, and of Saracen Command Vehicles which were lacking the necessary control equipment, so that it had to be designed and fitted by the signallers and R.E.M.E. on the spot.

At this point, the narrative must begin to concentrate on those R.A.C. units which would eventually see action – 6th R.T.R. and 1 L.V.T. Troop. For while Sleeman still innocently believed that the 1st would spearhead the intended invasion in its civilian L.S.T.s, which were loaded and at anchor off Portland on the 25th, in point of fact, B Squadron (less one troop) of 6th R.T.R. (Major J. B. Jolly) was already on its way, having sailed on the 23rd. They had departed in compliance with a signal sent direct to the L.S.T.s, an order which Sleeman came to hear of only because the 2nd in Command of the 6th rang him up with the news. But when Sleeman challenged the order's validity, the staff of 3rd Division dismissed it as a rumour, as nothing had been heard from H.Q. II Corps which, also, was in ignorance of what had happened. Bowing to the inevitable, and to the Royal Navy's anxiety to be in on the assault (to the exclusion of the civilian L.S.T.s), the remainder of the 6th finally put to sea in the Naval L.S.T.s between 31 August and 2 September, leaving behind H.Q. 34th Armoured Brigade and the 1st, who were to follow at an as yet undecided date.

Checks had also been applied to 5th R.T.R. and 10th Armoured Division in Libya, although the reasons for their frustrations were very different from those afflicting the 1st. The 5th had been in the middle of its Annual Administrative Inspection at Barce on 2 August when a stream of signals started to arrive for the attention of the Divisional Commander and his Staff who were touring the camp. It was intended that 'a considerable British force' should exercise on the Libyan Egyptian frontier, in support of the projected landing at Alexandria and, with this in view, preparations were made immediately to draw ammunition and stores. Orders to change to Higher Establishment were received on the 7th, but three days later, a portent of what would hamper all future operations made its appearance. Anti-British, pro-Nasser demonstrations, stirred up by ringleaders from Benghazi, made it necessary to route road convoys round Barce village, and for protective measures for the families to be taken. On 14 September, the first of 152 reservists began to arrive (some surplus to requirements, and for the same reason as had afflicted the 1st and 6th). From then on, so far as the 5th and the remainder of 10th Armoured Division were concerned, it was a matter of training and waiting. The diplomatic moves gathered momentum as the British, French and Americans tried to mobilize sufficient world support through the United Nations to override Egyptian resolve, and the Arab nations rallied round Egypt and Nasser. And Nasser, determined to reopen the Suez Canal (which had been closed in August by order of the Company, at British and French insistence), stole the initiative by importing pilots from Iron Curtain countries to assist his own people on the ships – thus effectively demonstrating not only that there was nothing indispensable about the Suez Company's pilots (as was popularly supposed), but that Soviet Russian assistance in the event of an armed confrontation might be expected.

Time was running short and attitudes were hardening. In his diary note of 5 October, Duckworth again echoed a commonly-held view that 'If it [the issue before the Security Council] causes another lengthy 'Abadan'-type discussion we shall get nowhere', and then, on the 9th, refers to 'The third incident of reservists mutinying this week . . . announced on the wireless to-day . . . I can't really blame the reservists for feeling a bit fed up but there is certainly no excuse for marching on the Officers Mess as 150 did to-day in Malta . . .' Disturbances such as these were few and far between, and this incident was caused by a newspaper reporter provoking a few drunken Guardsmen reservists. R.T.R. units were immune; on one occasion the same reporter was prevented from coming into 6th R.T.R.'s lines by the Guard Commander who threatened to 'put him inside' if he entered the camp. But rioting by Arabs became widespread on 28 October, a memorable day, during which the French in Algiers arrested local rebel leaders. Duckworth's diary records a series of serious events – a General Strike called in all Arab countries; a report that Israel had mobilized as a precaution against Arab threats and the move of Iraqi troops into Jordan; the burning of the French Consulate in Jerusalem; riots in Singapore; and, in addition to unrest in Poland, a revolution in Hungary with fighting between the Soviet Russian forces and the local populace causing heavy casualties. On the 30th came the report of the Israeli invasion of Egyptian Sinai, and of Sir Anthony Eden's ultimatum to both sides to stop fighting and withdraw. Operation 'Musketeer', as Duckworth appreciated next day, was imminent, but 10th Armoured Division was neutralized, concerned as much with Internal Security in the cities (C Squadron of the 5th was engaged as infantry in Benghazi) as with a prospective confrontation with the Egyptian Army, and hearing only by way of radio news bulletins that the R.A.F. had bombed targets in Egypt on 1 November. By now, world opinion regarding an operation of war in Egypt was split. The Russians threatened to intervene, the U.S.A. stood aside and dissent was rife among the French and the British as to the wisdom of invading at all.

With vehicles and men dispersed throughout 14 different ships (though most of them were in the four L.S.T.s), 6th R.T.R. began to arrive (unannounced) at Malta. It had been a very uncomfortable voyage, lasting from 1 to 12 September. The L.S.T. carrying B Squadron (Major J. G. R. Allen) reached port minus its rudder, which fell off at sea. The unit was ordered to disembark, move to the No. 2 Polo Field and begin waterproofing C Squadron – as and when the materials and necessary technicians arrived by air from the U.K. There, meanwhile, the 1st had been sent back to Tidworth and was undertaking some serious training while waiting, once more, for the order to sail. Training was also attempted by 6th R.T.R., although, within the confines of Malta's narrow roads and small fields, the tanks could take only a limited part. C Squadron practised loading into L.C.T.s and coming ashore on a beach in Mellieha Bay, where it was the L.C.T.s which suffered the greatest difficulties, the one carrying Squadron Headquarters finishing up broadside to the beach with two feet of water on the tank deck. Jolly compares the scene on the beach to '. . . Brighton at an August Bank Holiday. All the tank crews from the other squadrons had turned up . . . and interspersed among them were all manner of Naval and Military dignitaries; not to mention the ladies, ice cream and Coca-Cola vendors and a very browned off Beach Party, Royal Marines.' The wading equipment proved to be fully effective, but the tanks were then left stationary for a month (with their fan belts rotting in the heat) while as much radio training and street fighting practice with the Royal Marines as possible was undertaken, together with sun-compass training, in preparation for a desert march on Cairo.

The R.A.C. unit which had most scope for training was, of course, 1 L.V.T. Troop. Although taken under the wing of the 6th, it spent most of its time training with the Marines, living aboard the L.S.T.s, assigned to carry them to the assault area. Half their time was spent afloat, and they took part in several landing exercises besides field firing. 'On board ship', as Berry says, 'we took turns in watches in the engine rooms and wheel-houses and carried out training in Semaphore and Morse. Very quickly "Stand easy" and "Out pipes" replaced "N.A.A.F.I. Break" and "Fall in" in our vocabulary.'

'As the time went by', wrote Jolly, 'there seemed less and less chance of C Squadron having to test its waterproofing and we even started preparing for the departure of the reservists and planning to maintain our vehicles and equipment with only half a squadron.' There was a general sense of futility as, in mid-October, the reservists were granted seven days home leave. But on 27 October, everything went into forward gear again. The assault forces were called to readiness, and C Squadron's tanks were re-waterproofed for the last time, a long and laborious job, reckoned to need 80 hours, which had to be completed in 36 hours. But this requirement was greeted, so Jolly writes, 'with roars of laughter and as a challenge rather than an impossibility'. The impossible was accomplished to Rock 'n' Roll played through a tape-recorder, with the jazz-minded members of the squadron 'doing their work to the time of the music, or performing some kind of tribal war dance as they walked across the hangar with a strip of Prestic held at arms' length'.

Briefing for the operation began on Sunday, 28 October, loading, on the 29th and the first convoy sailed on the night of the 30th – at the moment when victorious Israeli troops were already well on their way to the Suez Canal, after crossing the Sinai Desert. It would be 6 November before the ships which had sailed from Malta and (in the case of the French) from Algiers, would be off the new landing zone at Port Said – Alexandria had been the target in the initial plan made by II Corps Commander, Lieutenant-General Sir Hugh Stockwell. In outline, an airborne assault by French paratroops and the British 16th Parachute Brigade was to take place early on 5 November, the French to seize Port Fuad on the east bank of the Canal at Port Said, and bridges near the waterworks; the British, the strip of land to the west bounding the northern shore of the Manzala Lake. The seaborne landings would follow 24 hours later and, in the British sector, would be launched against the beaches to the west of the Western Breakwater. The Royal Marines, carried in L.V.T.s and helicopters, were to seize Port Said prior to dispatching 6th R.T.R. full-speed along the Canal banks to Ismailia in an attempt to dominate the waterway and forestall further serious damage to its facilities.

Egyptian opposition to the Anglo-French invasion was confined wholly to action by ground troops, their Navy lay in port out of harm's way, and their Air Force had been neutralized by the preliminary strikes. The parachute landings were accurately concentrated and without loss either to aircraft or men, although after the landing, when the Egyptians came to realize that the invasion came only from the air, and began to fire upon the landing zones, the toll of dead and wounded began to rise. All that day, unsupported, except by air strikes, the paratroops fought to hold what they had gained and to expand, where possible, to make easier the seaborne landing scheduled for the following morning. Speedy execution was becoming more important with every hour that passed. Already, on 1 November, the Egyptians had begun sinking blockships in the Canal, and the United Nations were demanding a cease-fire. By nightfall, the paratroops had taken their objectives and had dealt with some Russian-built SU 100 self-propelled guns. By then, too, the Egyptians were in flight, and the paratroops, who could have walked into Port Said that night, were pulled back so as to be clear of the naval bombardment which would support the sea landings.

At 04.15 hrs. on 6 November, while 2½ miles out to sea, the L.V.T.s of Berry's troop, partially protected by armour improvised from track links and timbers lashed to their side plates, clambered down the ramps of their L.S.T.s into a calm sea and, with the leading wave of 40th and 42nd Commandos on board, made for the shore, and the black pall of smoke rising from burning oil tanks. Nearby, the four L.C.T.s carrying B Squadron, 6th R.T.R. were approaching, and behind them, the main body of the invasion force, including the remainder of Gibbon's command in L.S.T.s – the only armoured unit within reach, to fight the entire Egyptian Army if it chose to stand. For 10th Armoured Division was out of the reckoning, King Idris having forbidden operations against an Arab sister nation from within his frontiers, and 1st R.T.R., having embarked again and sailed for the Mediterranean on 1 November, had yet to pass Gibraltar aboard the trooper *Empire Fowey*. But already the Egyptian Army, defeated in Sinai by the Israelis, was withdrawing on Cairo – all that is, save the Port Said garrison which Nasser exhorted to fight to the last.

'Any apprehension we may have felt a few moments earlier', wrote Berry, 'was immediately dispelled by the familiar scene around us.' 'Just like an exercise', remarked one trooper as the L.C.A.s led them on a course for live action, with H.M.S. *Daring*'s guns firing live ammunition on either flank of the assault beach and four Sea Hawk jet fighters strafing the ground 200 yards ahead. A few minutes later, the first troops emerged, unopposed from the water, with an R.T.R. officer in command and Royal Marine bren-gunners firing for all they were worth at anything which remotely looked as if it might conceal the enemy. Two Egyptian machine-guns opened fire, but were instantly silenced. Accelerating once they had touched down, the L.V.T.s carried their infantry inland to the first objective, their crews heaving a sigh of relief that no mines had been laid on the beaches.

'Twenty minutes after we landed we were relieved to hear the familiar noise of Centurions once more, as C Squadron 6th R.T.R. waded ashore', wrote Berry. Almost at once, Jolly's squadron was in action, moving two troops to the right flank to counter an enemy counter-attack reported by 42nd Commando, and firing their weapons at infantry and snipers in buildings to their front. At one point, even the Armoured Recovery Vehicle, coming ashore last, engaged the enemy with its single machine-gun in the vicinity of the fishing harbour. The counter-attack faded away as naval and tank gun-fire dominated the waterfront, and a stream of Royal Marine reinforcements arrived by helicopter in readiness for the pre-planned advance to the town via the golf links. This was to be a fully-mechanized assault with the men of 42nd Commando travelling in the L.V.T.s and escorted by half of C Squadron's Centurions. It started at 07.15 hrs. led by Sergeant Lumsden's tank of 9 Troop, followed by L.V.T.s and Squadron H.Q. with four more L.V.T.s and 10 Troop bringing up the rear. Moving initially at 20mph, the pace of advance slowed as it entered the built-up area, and heavy small-arms fire was directed against it from the five-storey buildings of Rue

Mohamed Ali and side streets. Casualties in the open-topped L.V.T.s began to mount, but the Marines returned fire while on the move. One sergeant of 7th R.T.R. in command of an L.V.T. was killed, some other crewmen were wounded. At one point an L.V.T. was saved by a Marine who kicked a grenade out of the rear door before it could explode. Half the L.V.T.s were crippled by small-arms fire penetrating their unarmoured engine compartments, and it was Sergeant Roberts who prevented the advance coming to a complete halt when he pulled out his wounded driver and took the controls himself.

For the Centurion crews it was safer, even though lack of a cupola-mounted machine-gun prevented them firing at the enemy on roof-tops and in upper windows. They suffered many hits, but no casualties, and were lucky enough to spot four 60mm. anti-tank guns near the gas works and knock them out before they could open fire. For the other half of the squadron, on the left, moving south under the Second in Command, Captain M. B. Davis, in support of 40th Commando, diplomacy went hand-in-hand with battle. The crew which helped rescue the British Consul was served tea on a tray, through the window, by the Consul's butler, as a pleasant interlude on their way to seize the docks and waterfront together with a number of commercial buildings. In a maze of side-streets, where the enemy could infiltrate almost at will, a confused battle full of bizarre incidents ensued. At one moment, Corporal Fowler's tank in 11 Troop was charged by two Coca-Cola lorries full of infantry. One was destroyed by a 20pdr. H.E. shell, the other, hit by Browning fire, drove, out of control, into the Canal. As the morning wore on, the Commandos became hotly embroiled in a series of mopping-up operations, and the advance to the final objective was delayed for lack of infantry. Buildings adjacent to the Navy Basin, like the police station at Ismailia in 1952, were heavily defended and finally subdued by a troop commander, 2nd Lieutenant H. R. Leach, knocking down the gates and setting fire to a timber yard which concealed ammunition.

By midday, both the town and port were virtually under British control, although mopping-up remained to be done, and C Squadron's tanks were running short of ammunition. The remainder of the 6th had begun landing from its L.S.T.s in the fishing harbour at 09.00 hrs., A Squadron (Major R. Grierson) leading, but had difficulty forcing its way through the traffic jam when attempting to exploit the initial success. Undeterred by an attack from 'friendly' aircraft, they pressed on against opposition on the golf course, but had several tanks bogged in soft ground. Meanwhile, as B Squadron (Major J. G. R. Allen) went to the

Arsenal to restore momentum there, Gibbon received orders from General Stockwell to make for El Tina Canal station ten miles farther on, but to go no further that night. At about midday, contact was made by A Squadron with the French paratroops, who had had little difficulty in seizing the area of the waterworks the previous day, and Grierson arranged with the French Airborne Commander, General G. Massu, for these redoubtable warriors to climb aboard the tanks and motor south for El Tina where they arrived in the dark, practically unopposed, at 16.30 hrs. Stockwell then issued fresh orders, at 18.00 hrs., for a combined advance next day on Ismailia by the French and by the British 16th Parachute Brigade (Brigadier M. A. H. Butler), supported by 6th R.T.R. But already the British Government had bowed to U.N. and Russian pressure to stop the fighting. An hour later came a signal, which had left London several hours before, to say that hostilities must cease at midnight and for a standstill to be imposed immediately. Meanwhile, the 2nd Parachute Battalion, urged on by Butler, had come ashore and was making its way in commandeered transport (some of it towed by the R.H.Q. tanks) through a traffic jam in Port Said to El Tina, where the leading tanks lay back behind an infantry screen, their crews trying to sleep on the engine decks. Not until 22.15 hrs. did Stockwell's revised instructions (to get as far south as possible before midnight) reach Gibbon, and even then it was decided to wait for 2nd Para before moving. Not until its leading company arrived at about 23.00 hrs. did they all move off, 15 minutes later, at breakneck speed down the Canal Road and Treaty Road.

'A simple plan was made for dealing with the Canal Stations', wrote Gibbon, who was with the leading tanks. '200 yards short of the station the tanks halted and the leading company dismounted, formed up, fired a red verey when they had taken the station and the tanks motored through and picked them up. The column did 7 miles [without lights] in 45 minutes including clearing two canal stations on foot.'

At midnight, Butler halted the advance and held an O Group. 'We were sorely tempted to make the few miles to Qantara where we could get off the road,' writes Gibbon, reflecting the wishes of those who desired to seize a key-point and ground which would enable a broad-fronted position to be taken up. But they stayed where they were, on a one-tank front 1,500 yards south of El Cap Canal Station, and waited in disconsolate frustration.

Next day, an air of unreality prevailed as the troops in Port Said, where B and C Squadron together with the Echelon were harboured, spent their time coping with snipers and trying to prevent looting of shops and factories by the local populace. At El Cap the crews replenished, washed and shaved and turned to maintenance. In the leading tanks, at 12.45 hrs., Sergeant Jachnik was assisting his radio-operator repair the wireless set, while the driver was preparing lunch and the gunner was cleaning the Browning machine-gun near a Canal bollard. Everyone in the neighbourhood saw the party of 25 Egyptian infantry approaching – everyone except Jachnik's crew. At the sound of voices, Jachnik popped his head out of the turret and saw, nearby, a man with a whip who shouted 'Hands up!' A somewhat aggrieved Jachnik, displaying that contempt for Egyptians which was by no means always appropriate, replied 'F . . . off' and was promptly nicked in the ear by a bullet as the enemy opened fire. He dived into the turret for his sten gun, but the matter was decided by Sergeant Stebbing, whose tank was in support. He fired a burst of Browning and one H.E. round close to Jachnik's tank, killing and wounding some of the Egyptians and driving the others off. These, the last shots fired by the 6th, were called 'The war of Jachnik's ear'. The cost in lives to the armoured units was two killed and two wounded, all of them R.T.R. and, to the British as a whole, 11 killed and 92 wounded.

In the 47 days to come, as diplomatic negotiations proceeded and arrangements for United Nations' forces to take over the policing of the Canal Zone went on, the 6th and 1 L.V.T. Troop made the best of unpleasant conditions in helping keep order in Port Said and preventing the infiltration of dissidents. 3rd Division began to arrive. Scout car patrols became more appropriate to the conditions than intervention by Centurions, the overcoming of boredom as important as armed action. For a fortnight the L.V.T. troop enjoyed continuous employment, carrying Marine patrols on Lake Manzala to counter enemy attempts at movement – and on one occasion fired across the bows of a boat which would not stop, and which was found to contain a party of Communist Press Correspondents.

On 10 November, a disgruntled Sleeman, together with his Headquarters and B Echelon of 1st R.T.R., sailed into Port Said in the *Empire Fowey*, but not until the 12th was she allowed to enter harbour, and in so doing got into difficulties and was holed. Sleeman and members of his staff disembarked for a few hours on the 13th, before the ship was ordered back to Malta. He had been excluded from the planning of the actual operation, there was no administrative plan and, in his report, he was to condemn roundly the manner in which mobilization had been handled and the error that had been made in not putting his H.Q. and

1st R.T.R. ashore seven hours behind the Commando Brigade, as originally planned. That way, 'they would have been at Ismailia and Abu Sueir by the cease-fire', he claimed. Arguable though this was in hindsight, there was less disputing his plea 'That the Strategic Reserve receive priority for men, stores and equipment and training . . . so that it is ready and able to fight effectively without the appalling delays which are inherent in the existing mobilization procedure'.

At a time of national disenchantment, Sleeman's protests, reflecting as they did much overall discontent at a time of bitter disappointment, were not well received in all quarters. But in the aftermath of the Suez operation, when so much else was at stake and so many other crises had to be resolved, from Government level downwards, his was but one angry voice among many. Benefits would come to the Army as the result of the lessons learnt at Suez, but for the time being, the damage done could only be patched up and the political storm ridden out. Arab dissidence and the howl of world disapproval at an old-fashioned armed intervention had to be suffered, on the eve of an era in which successful British military operations would come to be rated as those in which force was not used at all.

No sooner was it known that the United Nations would send troops, than the apathetic populace in Port Said began to give trouble, and the 6th were repeatedly placed on alert as the infantry carried out local operations. Violence flared up in Cyrenaica on 7 November, immediately the halt at El Cap was publicized, and 5th R.T.R. found itself diverted mainly to guarding depots as infantry instead of 'sorting out Nasser once and for all', as Duckworth put it. The threat to the families was rated so serious that they were put at twelve hours' notice for evacuation. On 28 November, as the reservists got ready to go home, it was announced by Jordan that she intended to abrogate her Treaty of 1946 with Britain, and rid herself of all British forces. At the same time, the Libyan Prime Minister said that he intended to negotiate a revision of the Anglo-Libyan Treaty of 1953. Everything which had been built up over the past decade slid into ruins. A new Government, formed by Mr. Harold Macmillan, after Sir Anthony Eden resigned, was faced with the need to restore confidence and to refashion the Armed Forces as part of a process of contraction. Mr. Duncan Sandys became the new Minister of Defence. The Army cuts which had long been in preparation were revised for early publication.

For the troops who had gone to war it was a matter of handing in mobilization stores and returning vehicles to depots. What had been drawn in twelve hours would take Berry 2½ months to clear from his charge. Speaking of the Reservists, Starr (1st R.T.R.) was to comment that 'they had done their duty irrespective of the conflict of political parties' and 'they honour their commitments and quickly settle into a new regiment' – adding the rider '. . . providing the Commanding Officer takes the ordinary soldier into his confidence he will not be let down by his men, and never was this more true of Lieutenant-Colonel Howard-Jones . . .' Echoing this in his diary, after seeing off 5th R.T.R.s reservists at Tobruk, Duckworth remarked how impressive it had been to see them come straight from home and take their place in a tank crew. Then he added, with unwitting foreboding of future cuts to come, 'Another chapter in the history of the regiment has closed. We lost 7 officers and 191 O.R.s to-day – a quarter of the regiment.'

CHAPTER VIII

Retrenchment and Consolidation 1957–1960

When, in the aftermath of the Second World War, Britain felt compelled to commit a large proportion of her armed strength to the defence of Europe, she began, by implication, to turn her back upon the Commonwealth. Whereas it had been her policy, prior to 1914 and for most of the time between the two World Wars, to maintain economically only a small and relatively ineffective part of her Army in the British Isles, and to send the rest to defend her possessions in the Far East, India and the Middle East, this, by 1956, was no longer the case. Despite the loss of India and a contraction of responsibility in the Middle East, the demands to police disaffected areas elsewhere, as well as playing a rôle among the United Nations and in N.A.T.O., were creating too heavy a burden. At least two years before the Suez débâcle it had become plain that Britain, with an average 10 per cent of her Gross National Product absorbed by defence, had to make a choice between protecting the outposts of Empire or concentrating upon guarding her own homeland. While the Government's 'Statement on Defence 1956' in February of that year had given notice of what was to come, the Statement for 1957, calling for 'a new approach', sounded the tune loud and clear. Heavy manpower reductions had been mooted in 1955 and 1956, together with the hope that new proposals on pay and inducements would attract additional numbers of Regular recruits and build up the 'hard-core' of men of long service and experience. But recruiting had continued to decline. Nevertheless, the Minister of Defence's 'Outline of Future Policy', published in April 1957, made it clear that within the next three years the Services would have to recruit more men or wither away: there would be no National Service call-up after the end of 1960.

Defence in its ultimate aspect was to be based upon the principle of nuclear deterrence (at the time, almost entirely dependent upon the U.S.A.s atomic warheads). Protection of outlying parts of Europe and the Commonwealth was to depend on alliances of which N.A.T.O. was by far the most effective. The South East Asia Pact of 1954 was only in its formative stages and the embryo Baghdad Pact was threatened with collapse. In implementing heavy savings in manpower, the Army's strength in B.A.O.R. would have to be cut from 77,000 to 64,000 within the next twelve months, and the progressive reduction of overseas garrisons compensated by devising a scheme to reinforce them rapidly by air in the event of an emergency. Strong garrisons would remain for the time being in the Far East, in Hong Kong and Malaya; in the Persian Gulf and Aden Protectorate in the Middle East; and in Cyprus and Malta in the Mediterranean. These would attract their share of units. At the same time, there would be room for further economies as the result of the withdrawal from Jordan and the impending rundown in Libya.

The 10th Armoured Division in Libya was to be disbanded and the existing infantry and armoured divisions in B.A.O.R. reorganized and replaced by three 'basic divisions' each of which could control a variable number of brigade groups. This abolished the well-tried, three-brigade infantry division and with it, the Divisional Regiment R.A.C. with its anti-tank rôle – a task which, until then, had been carried out by Cavalry units. It meant also the disappearance of 6th, 7th and 11th Armoured Divisions, the experimental armoured formation of 1955 having, for a variety of reasons, failed, one of them being its administrative inability to mount sustained operations. The three new basic divisions were intended to provide what the Minister of Defence called 'hard-hitting groups of all arms'. This scheme was attractive to those who saw virtue in integrating one regiment of tanks with three marching infantry battalions in an Infantry Brigade Group, and one A.P.C. mounted infantry battalion with three armoured regiments in an Armoured Brigade Group, but it was anathema to tank soldiers, who had suffered in the past from the perils of being either hamstrung when tied too tightly to the infantry in a static situation, or vulnerable from lack of them as escorts. They flatly disbelieved the Minister's exhortation that the armoured brigade would 'depend principally on the fighting capacity of skilfully used armoured regiments', since it seemed to them that, if the armoured regiments were fewer in number (as they were), and the infantry were, except for one unit in each of the two surviving armoured brigades (7th and 20th), deficient of armoured personnel-carriers, mobility in a nuclear environment was bound to be severely restricted. In a letter to *The Daily Telegraph*, General Sir John Crocker poured scorn upon the new model. The armoured brigade would be '. . . incapable of independent action in attack or counter-attack . . . Nor can it fulfil the traditional rôle of . . . the break out and pursuit, for it is quite incapable of sustained action or even of protecting itself at night . . .', he wrote, 'Thus it would seem that

the immense potential offensive power of armour is being lost . . .
A large proportion of the available armour is to be allocated
permanently to the infantry brigades of the 'standard' divisions.
Any idea it will be possible to group these allocated armoured
units during the battle and use them concentrated as an armoured
formation is fallacious. They will be tied and dissipated piece-
meal in support of local actions. The remaining armour will be
. . . hamstrung, vulnerable, ineffective.'

Thus spoke the R.T.R.'s most experienced commander on the
eve of another sort of battle he would have to fight, one in which
something of intrinsic value, besides the survival of armour as a
potent force on the battlefield, was at stake! For in line with the
emasculation of armoured formations there was about to come a
heavy reduction in the actual number of armoured units – and
that meant disbandments within the R.A.C. No doubt the weight
of responsibility bore down particularly heavily upon Crocker at
that moment; for the man to whom, in the opinion of many
members, the R.T.R. owed most – Sir Percy Hobart – had just
died.

Towards the end of April 1957, the Army Council was ready to
give confidential notice to the affected regiments of the extent
of the cuts they would be required to sustain. A special Committee
had been formed under Lieutenant-General Sir Richard Hull
(late 17th/21st Lancers) to make recommendations covering the
whole sequence of the two-phase rundown, including disbandments. The Infantry were to lose 17 battalions; the Royal Artillery
20 regiments, in addition to the 14 it had lost in 1954 when
Anti-Aircraft Command was abolished; and the Royal Engineers
4 regiments.

The Royal Armoured Corps was to lose six units in Phase 1,
and two more in Phase 2, to be shared between the two Household
Cavalry Regiments, the twenty late Cavalry of the Line Regi-
ments and the eight Royal Tank Regiments. The initial recom-
mendation for Phase 1 left the Household Cavalry untouched,
and proposed that the Cavalry be reduced by four units and the
R.T.R. by two. This suggestion was first put by the C.I.G.S.,
Field Marshal Sir Gerald Templer, to Field Marshal Lord
Montgomery (in his capacity as a Colonel Commandant of the
R.T.R. Wing in the R.A.C.).

Templer saw the proposal as giving slight priority in favour of
the older Cavalry Regiments, and to this Montgomery raised no
objection. For, according to a message Montgomery sent to
Crocker, Templer believed that '. . . the R.T.R. had begun the
armoured business long before the Cavalry, and were the pioneers
of the whole study of the use of armour in battle'. Templer's

view, therefore, was that the Cavalry must suffer the major reduction. But General Sir Richard McCreery, as head of the Cavalry Wing, disagreed and, initially, proposed that each unit of the R.A.C. be treated in strict order of inverted seniority – those that were most junior being the first to go, as had been the procedure in 1922 when the Cavalry was last reduced in size – which would abolish the R.T.R. To Hull, who no longer approached the subject as Colonel of his Regiment, but from the outlook of Deputy Chief of the Imperial General Staff, this was totally unacceptable, and (as he told the author) he said so strongly to McCreery, taking the line that he would always fight for the retention of the R.T.R. and that 'nothing less than four battalions was a viable whole'.

In fairness to all those engaged in this round of negotiations, it must be pointed out that they were propelled into a rather undignified bargaining exchange by the impulse of loyalty to the regimental system, a condition aggravated by the fact that the R.A.C. still constituted nothing more tangible than a marriage of convenience between individual cavalry units and a large, strongly-based R.T.R. In these circumstances, nobody could afford to submit a weak opening bid and McCreery, who must be seen at this juncture as representing the extreme Cavalry view of those among its die-hards who harboured old-fashioned opinions largely rejected by the younger members, can hardly have hoped to achieve his initial target. He now proposed that 'a mathematical split based on the size of the Cavalry and R.T.R. Wings is the right answer'. He suggested that four basic considerations ought to be applied – namely, the age of the two different parts of the R.A.C.; the importance, or otherwise, of the regiment or battalion as the basic fighting unit for the British soldier; the relative upheavals in the two wings caused by reductions; and the relative efficiency of the units affected. He argued that Cavalry Regiments with histories extending over 250 years should have priority over R.T.R. units which had been in existence for only 40 years, and pointed out that the 7th and 8th had been formed only in 1937–38. He thought, too, that, for R.T.R. units, amalgamation would be easier since it had developed the regimental spirit in battalions and had remained a small corps within a corps, whereas cavalry regiments, being so small, would have even greater difficulties than the infantry who at least had their territorial associations. And he reminded the C.I.G.S. of the large part cavalry officers had taken in the formation and early fighting of the Tank Corps, pleading that it would be strange to do away with the cavalry regiments, from which these officers came, in favour of the much younger Tanks Corps. Finally, and presumably to keep disruption by amalgamation to the minimum, he recommended that 'the two comparatively new battalions of the Royal Tank Regiment, the 7th and 8th, should be disbanded, and that the 'split' should then be an even one, a reduction of two Cavalry Regiments (the amalgamation of four), and a reduction of two R.T.R. Regiments'. In other words, a reversal of the C.I.G.S.'s proposal in order that the Cavalry should lose only two units out of 20 and the R.T.R. four out of 8.

It is scarcely to be supposed that McCreery was indulging in anything other than an attempt to save something from the wreck of his original scheme. Nor can the response by Crocker (who succeeded Montgomery as senior Colonel Commandant of the R.T.R. on 1 May), be regarded as anything other than a counter-bid in the trading game. In totally rejecting McCreery's arguments, he denied the implication that members of older establishments excelled those of younger ones, and he pointed out that McCreery's suggested solution (to look at the problem from the officer point of view for a moment) '. . . would entail approximately 150 R.T.R. officers becoming redundant and having to be retired or absorbed into the remaining four R.T.R. regiments as against a rather smaller number of Cavalry officers having to be similarly disposed of, with 16 Cavalry Regiments available for the purpose'. Crocker remained convinced that the original proposal served best to share the unfortunate consequences fairly between the two wings. But when the Army Council's decision came, it dealt a much heavier blow to the R.T.R. than to the Cavalry. Three regiments from each would have to go, and this would amount, as Crocker pointed out to the C.I.G.S., to a reduction of 37½ per cent for the R.T.R. as opposed to 15 per cent in the case of the Cavalry. In addition, the 1 Independent Squadron, Berlin would be disbanded almost at once (October 1957) and have its task taken over by a squadron detached from an R.A.C. regiment (to begin with the 14th/20th Hussars), that same unit assuming from R.A.S.C. companies the task of manning the two Saracen A.P.C. squadrons which transported, respectively, the infantry battalions of 7th and 20th Armoured Brigades. 'This being so', wrote Crocker, 'I would like to have some assurance that, should any further cuts in the Royal Armoured Corps become necessary in the future, full consideration will be given to the fact that the R.T.R. is bearing a far greater share of the present reductions.' Crocker said further, 'I can appreciate the difficulties which faced the Army Council in reaching a decision on this matter. We shall accept the position with regret, but loyally.' He continued, in consultation with the other two Colonels Commandant, Major-General N. W. Duncan and Major-General H. R. B.

Foote (the latter of whom had been appointed on 1 May) to work out how best to implement the decision, in a series of negotiations which seem to have generated more correspondence than those concerned with the number of units to go. In essence, the Colonels Commandant were agreed that the 1st and 2nd should remain untouched and that the other six units should be paired without sacrificing their identity. Initially, they considered that the 3rd should absorb the 7th and become 3/7th R.T.R., the 4th absorb the 6th to become 4/6th R.T.R., and the 5th absorb the 8th to become 5/8th R.T.R. They avoided recommending 4/7th in order to prevent confusion with 4/7th D.G. But this proved unacceptably awkward to the C.I.G.S. when it came to his attention that the 3rd and 7th Hussars and the 4th and 8th Hussars were to combine, and therefore would produce 3/7th Hussars and 4/8th Hussars. To begin with, the C.I.G.S. and the Colonels Commandant tried to find a workable solution while retaining the numerical combinations, but it was Templer who cut the Gordian knot in the realization that the system which was being produced would lead to endless muddles and, maybe, newspaper criticism. He came down hard on the side of calling the remaining regiments 1st, 2nd, 3rd, 4th and 5th Royal Tank Regiments, and to this the Colonels Commandant eventually agreed, after assuring themselves that legislation would be introduced to accelerate the legal processes and avoid the freezing of the funds belonging to the units concerned. It was now recommended that amalgamations should take place between the 3rd and 6th, making the 3rd R.T.R., the 4th and 7th making the 4th R.T.R., and the 5th and 8th to produce the 5th R.T.R. 'We have paired the units for good regimental reasons', wrote Crocker to the C.I.G.S. 'The 7th was originally formed on a nucleus of a Squadron of the 4th and these two Regiments were brigaded together and fought together; they have a close mutual affiliation. Similarly the 8th sprang from the 5th.'

In breaking the news to the Regiment on 24 July, Duncan stressed the need for the recollection that it was one family. He played down the desire to perpetuate the numbers inherent in each unit's title, writing: 'you will never be forgotten'. And Crocker (who took over from Montgomery as Colonel Commandant of the R.T.R. Wing of the R.A.C. on 1 September 1957) was to report that the Regiment took the cuts well, 'but they were shaken a bit' – a remark which, some would have said, bordered on understatement. In fact, he was already getting ready for the next battle, to combat the nomination of the two regiments to go in Phase 2 – but this was a matter which time and operational considerations and would take care of.

Above: 1st R.T.R. and the Band on parade in Berlin, September 1945. (1st R.T.R.)
Below: G.M.C. Fox armoured cars of 7th R.T.R. on patrol in the Punjab, July 1947. (*The Tank*)

Above: A Comet of 3rd R.T.R. in the Malayan jungle. (3rd R.T.R.)
Below: A Comet of 4th R.T.R. leaving Ramalla through a road block on the way to Jerusalem, 1949. (T. W. Gibbon)
Right: Field-Marshal Viscount Montgomery of Alamein. (R. Bingham)

Above: General Sir John Crocker (seated) with Major-General H. E. Pyman (right) and Major P. R. C. Hobart (left). (R. Bingham)

Below: Churchills of C Squadron 7th R.T.R. in Korea on Christmas Day 1950. (4th R.T.R.)

Above: Major-General Sir Percy Hobart. (*The Tank*)

Below: A Centurion of 1st R.T.R. in the front line in Korea, 1953. (1st R.T.R.)

Top of page: A Centurion of 4th R.T.R. moves into the Bureau Sanitaire in January 1952, supported by a Daimler armoured car of the Royals and infantry of 1st Bn. Lancashire Fusileers. (EMI Films)
Above: An L.V.T. of No. 1 L.V.T. Troop passes 'Woolworth's' in Port Said, November 1956. (EMI Films)
Top right: Centurions of 6th R.T.R. advance through Port Said, November 1956. (H. Leach)
Right: A Centurion of 4th R.T.R. at speed in the Canal Zone. (W. F. Woodhouse)

Left: Farewell Parade by the Comets of The Berlin Independent Squadron, R.T.R. on 12 October 1957. (Ministry of Defence)

Below left: A Centurion of 3rd R.T.R. at range practice. (Ministry of Defence)

Right: Her Majesty, Queen Elizabeth II, presenting Standards to the 1st, 2nd, 3rd, 4th, 5th Royal Tank Regiments and the 40th/41st Royal Tank Regiment (T.A.), and Guidons to the North Somerset Yeomanry/44th Royal Tank Regiment (T.A.) and The Westminster Dragoons at Buckingham Palace on 27 October 1960. (Keystone)

Below: General Sir Alan Jolly. (Ministry of Defence)

Left: Major-General N. W. Duncan. (*The Tank*)
Centre left: Major-General H. R. B. Foote, V.C. (*The Tank*)
Bottom left: Major-General H. M. Liardet.
Right: A Saladin of 4th R.T.R. goes into action in the Wadi Nakhalain, May 1963.
Below right: Road block by H Squadron, 5th R.T.R. in Sarawak, 1965. (P. Tustin)

Above: The Sovereign's Parade, 1967. (Ministry of Defence)
Below: Her Majesty the Queen meets the men of the Regiment, 1967.
(Ministry of Defence)

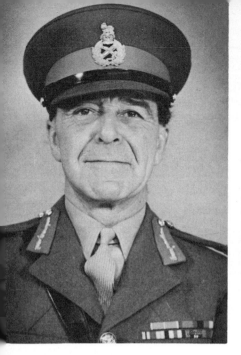

Above: Major-General J. R. Holden.
Below: General Sir Richard Ward.
(R. Ward)

Above: Lieutenant-General Sir Allan Taylor.
(Ministry of Defence)
Below: Field Marshal Lord Carver. (*The Tank*)

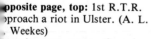

Opposite page, top: 1st R.T.R.
approach a riot in Ulster. (A. L.
P. Weekes)

Opposite page, centre: Crowd
control in Ulster by 1st R.T.R.
(A. L. P. Weekes)

Opposite page, bottom: Typical
'snap' Vehicle Control Post
(V.C.P.) in Ulster with Saracens
and Land Rovers. (1st R.T.R.)

Top: A Ferret Scout Car of 2nd
R.T.R. goes out on patrol in
Ulster, 1974. (2nd R.T.R.)

Above and right: The original
wheelbarrow and one of its more
sophisticated successors.

Above: A Fox armoured car showing its array of night fighting equipment. Note that the crew are wearing the latest type of helmet. (Ministry of Defence)

Below: A Chieftain and its crew, 1975. (Ministry of Defence)

It was fortunate that throughout most of the period in which the amalgamations were being prepared – all of them in Germany – the commander of I (British) Corps was Lieutenant-General H. E. Pyman, who took up his appointment on 1 November 1956. He would need to draw upon all his recent experience in high appointments, as Commander of 56th London Armoured Division (T.A.), as Director General Fighting Vehicles at the Ministry of Supply, as Commander 11th Armoured Division and as Director, Weapon Development, to inspire and revitalize B.A.O.R.'s main striking force during reorganization, and to do the same for his own regiment during its drastic reduction in strength. Compared to many other regiments, the R.T.R. was well provided for in numbers of officers and senior O.R.s, although in some ranks the age structure was out of balance – to some extent, the outcome of the miscalculations during the immediate post-war period, but partly as the result of promoting officers by length of service. There were 106 majors between the ages of 36 and 41 when, according to establishment, there should only have been 84, and in all units there was a surplus of majors for appropriate appointments. Not only would that surplus have to be disposed of, but many more would have to be declared redundant as the Army shrank in size – in all, 32 officers, 8 Warrant Officers and 39 senior N.C.O.s in 1958–59 and still more the following year. The threat of redundancy (welcomed by some, to whom the financial terms, when announced, were attractive) would engender a state of uncertainty which could destroy morale. Somehow the blow had to be absorbed, and one way to mitigate its worst effects was to convert the moment of amalgamation into an act of consecration.

To avoid making the mergers too abrupt, the designated units were stationed adjacent to each other during the months or weeks preceding the event. Thus, the 7th (Lieutenant-Colonel F. R. Lindsay), just a few months after being honoured at Catterick on 10 July 1957 by a visit from Her Majesty the Queen, the Colonel-in-Chief, was sent to Hohne. There, as part of 11th Infantry Brigade, it was located within a few miles of the 4th (Lieutenant-Colonel E. R. Farnell-Watson) at Fallingbostel, and Farnell-Watson would take command of the amalgamated units on 3 April 1959. The Parade to mark the occasion was held at Hohne, and the Inspecting Officer was, most appropriately, Major-General H. R. B. Foote, V.C., who had been Adjutant of the 4th in 1937, when one of its squadrons was detached to create the 7th, and who had won his Victoria Cross while commanding the 7th at Tobruk in 1942.

The 6th too would be transferred to Germany for amalgamation with the 3rd (Lieutenant-Colonel R. E. Ward). After Suez, the 6th had lived, as seemed its destiny from the moment of its formation in 1933, in a state of tension and flux. It had not long been in Barce, after taking over from the 5th in April 1957, before it was ordered to detach a squadron to Cyprus for the purpose of manning a tank element should rapid intervention prove necessary in the Middle East, the experience of Operation 'Musketeer' having shown that forces based in some Arab countries were likely to be debarred from action in others. This squadron, which was rotated at three-monthly intervals, would inevitably find itself involved in the internal security operations that were part of life in Cyprus under the persistent threat of terrorists. It dwelt in a tented camp at Dhekelia, helped guard a power-station (enlivened by bomb scares and night explosions off-stage), patrolled in the rôle of infantry and, whenever there was time, maintained and trained with its tanks. As the winter rains came there were few who did not wish for the end of their stay and a return to the comforts of Homs, where the 6th moved in November. Of action they had little, even though the B.B.C. on one occasion erroneously reported that rioting had been controlled by tanks. But it was one of the pangs of amalgamation that ,when the 6th (now commanded by Lieutenant-Colonel P. A. L. Vaux), handed over at Homs to the 2nd (Lieutenant-Colonel P. R. C. Hobart) in August 1959, it was ordered to leave 130 of its men with the incoming unit and travel to its final destination at Detmold, a shadow of its former self. If the sad, enforced transfer of so many men from the 6th to the 2nd, which was accepted with quiet dignity, underlined in itself the R.T.R.s strength in unity, the amalgamation between the 3rd and the 6th in a Parade at Sennelager on 31 October was a spectacular demonstration of its efficiency and spirit. On the airstrip, and in the shadow of a windmill painted in Regimental colours, men and tanks marched and manoeuvred with a precision that was to set the standard for still greater parades on the same ground in years to come. Here it was that Sir Harold Pyman, one-time Second-in-Command of the 6th in the desert in 1941, and Commanding Officer of the 3rd at El Alamein (who had succeeded Duncan as a Colonel Commandant in January 1959 and was now Deputy Chief of the Imperial General Staff), took the salute as the new 3rd, under Vaux, advanced on its tracks into the future.

On 1 December 1959, the 5th and 8th should have merged, but in their case Affairs of State intervened. For, at the request of the Supreme Commander of Allied Land Forces, Europe, the British Government agreed to retard the rundown of the number of units stationed in Germany by postponing some amalgamations. This caused a hiatus. Originally, it had been intended that 5th R.T.R. (Lieutenant-Colonel P. H. Hordern) should relinquish its rôle as Training Regiment at Catterick in October, and move to Fallingbostel to live alongside the 8th for some four weeks before the act of amalgamation. Instead, the 8th (Lieutenant-Colonel H. C. W. Ironside) retained its identity, and both units found themselves faced with the problem of maintaining for seven months the facade of fully-established armoured regiments without sufficient manpower to do so. Well might the 5th's reporter in *The Tank* rejoice at the prospect of 'jobs for the boys' and quote a young subaltern saying that: 'It'll be wonderful to get a major's pay after only 18 months' service', but the disruptions caused to the lives of individuals were not inconsiderable. For example, Hordern's posting upon relinquishing command of the 5th could not be delayed and therefore Lieutenant-Colonel A. McN. Taylor had to be brought in as a stop-gap at short notice to command the 5th until the revised amalgamation date of 1 July 1960, when Ironside assumed a short-lived command of the new 5th.

Throughout 1959 and 1960, it was as if the R.T.R. were undergoing a complete metamorphosis. The loss of three units, following the disbandment in October 1957 of the 1 Independent Squadron, Berlin (Major C. H. Rayment), somehow produced a closing of ranks coincident with the reduction of strength. As once it had been in the days of close infantry formation fighting, when those who survived stepped into the places of those who had fallen, the R.T.R. now acquired distinction in adversity. Many outward signs of unity were omnipresent. Increasingly, too, the centre of control converged on London. In September 1954, it had been decided to adopt St. Peter-upon-Cornhill in the City of London as the Regimental Church, one of the advantages of selecting this beautiful Wren building being that the Rector at that time, the Rev. D. A. Owen, had, from 1938 to 1941, been Padre to the 4th R.T.R. The first Regimental Service was held at St. Peter's on 21 October 1954, but it was not until the following year, in September, that the first Tank Memorial Sunday was celebrated there – an event which has been repeated annually, at a date as close as possible to that on which tanks first went into action on the Somme on 15 September 1916. On 23 October 1960, the Regiment placed its Memorial Window (a brilliant piece of work by Hugh Easton) in St. Peter-upon-Cornhill and it was there, too, that the Regimental Collect, probably composed by Owen, was first said in 1954:

'Almighty God, Whose perfect love casteth out fear, mercifully grant that Thy servants of the Royal Tank Regiment may Fear Naught but to fall from Thy favour; for His sake in whom Thou art well pleased, Thy Beloved Son, Jesus Christ, our Lord.'

It was to London, too, at dates as close as convenient to Cambrai Day, 20 November, that officers and Old Comrades came for their annual Cambrai dinners and reunions. And it was in London that the annual wives' tea party was held until it was discontinued after 1968.

Not until 1959, however, did the Regimental Office occupy its own premises, Lieutenant-Colonel R. N. Wilson, the Secretary to the Representative Colonel Commandant, continuing to work in R.A.C. 1 at the War Office until then. It was largely the dire need to place recruiting on a sound footing throughout the Royal Armoured Corps which brought about the creation of a Home Headquarters for each Cavalry Regiment and a Regimental Headquarters for the R.T.R. Close proximity to the War Office and R.A.C. Records was clearly desirable, and London the essential place to be. Part of the building containing R.H.Q. of the Westminster Dragoons at 1 Elverton Street, London SW1, proved ideal, and so it was there in April 1959 that Colonel G. Fitz R. Talbot set up an office staffed by Wilson and an additional retired officer, Major R. Thornton, and from here that Regimental policy was implemented in the years to come.

'Quite apart from carrying on with the purely domestic affairs of the Regiment', writes Talbot, 'one of the main charters given by the Colonels Commandant to the Regimental Colonel was to keep an even closer watch on the career structure of officers. Up to then many officers, either from choice or because they were in the 'unwanted' class, were spending years tucked away in E.R.E. jobs or on secondment. This had resulted in many of them being unknown to the Regiment and their annual reports gave no indication as to their potential as regimental officers . . . A second major task was to allocate all officers . . . to units . . . to give every officer, regardless as to where he was serving, a feeling that he had a 'home' or 'firm base' and, more important, for those serving at E.R.E. or in a staff appointment, the knowledge that they had a senior officer in the Regiment (ie the C.O. of the parent unit) to whom they could turn for help or guidance'. There was another reason for applying this remedy to a current defect in the Regiment, although it was not fully implemented at the time. This was to ensure that officers at regimental duty had a long-standing knowledge of the soldiers placed under their command. Under the existing system, whereby an officer might find himself serving successively in different units, it could only be to the detriment of the soldiers' career prospects, since it was all too common for their promotion to be decided by officers who knew too little about them. As it was, the initial attempt by the Regiment to rectify the present system only went so far as to allocate subalterns and captains to units through the publication by R.H.Q. of a '13 Year List' on 10 November 1959. For the time being, however, the practice of sending lieutenant-colonels and majors to command, respectively, units and sub-units was allowed to continue, with the consequence that at some unit promotion conferences, hardly any senior officers knew sufficiently well the men whose future they were deciding.

Recruiting became vital as National Service came to an end, but the need to be competitive was a new feature. Before the war, the R.T.C. rarely· had difficulty in finding the men it wanted, for then it was unique in its task and in its mechanical bent. Therefore it had had little need of a recruiting organization and had not formed one. Now it was but one of many mechanized units and was involved in the struggle to survive which affected every unit of the Army.

The main subject for discussion at the R.A.C. Conference in November 1957 centred upon recruiting, and the views of Commanders, Staff and C.O.s were freely aired in an attempt to arrive at a properly coordinated system in place of the outdated, haphazard arrangements then in operation. The cavalry regiments, for the most part, were without settled territorial affiliations, and those claimed by the R.T.R. were largely informal. As a result, those charged with finding the recruits lacked bases from which to operate, and could not build-up the long-term local contacts with the civilian communities whence the recruits came. Furthermore, all too often the man recruited was not of a sufficiently high standard. Under National Service, it had been found possible to raise the intelligence calibre of recruits, while accepting fewer untrainable Regulars and filling up the gaps with conscripts. In the all-Regular Army, this would no longer be possible and it was argued that C.O.s should have wider powers to get rid of unsuitable men. But as one Cavalry C.O. said: 'I think a lot of nonsense is talked about intelligence rating. Some of these rather basic long-term Regulars turn out much more loyal and much more regimentally-minded chaps than you expect. It is astonishing how quickly they improve when you start to train them.'

Another Cavalry C.O., Lieutenant-Colonel J. D. Lunt, 16th/5th Lancers, analysed the sort of resistance that recruiters were meeting. In addition to emphasizing the effects of 'appallingly bad publicity', he paid a handsome compliment to the Royal

Tank Regiment. Reporting the findings of a 'Gallup' poll he had carried out in his own regiment, he said that, '. . . 46 per cent did not know before actually joining up that the Royal Armoured Corps included both the Cavalry and the Royal Tank Regiment. 10 per cent still believed that the cavalry was horsed and, I am ashamed to say this, but 73 per cent had never heard of my regiment . . . There was another very interesting side-line to this; 10 per cent would have preferred to have been in the Royal Tank Regiment and that I think is not without significance. The reasons they advanced were significant; these were that the Royal Tank Regiment was more modern, that cavalry hanker too much after tradition, and they thought that in the Royal Tank Regiment they would get more opportunity to use their equipment . . .'. Lunt had asked the men what their main hates were in order of priority. The main one was 'bull' – the cleaning of web equipment and polishing boots. The second was fatigues. He added that he thought his audience would be surprised by this. The fact remains that, in the years to come, there took place a progressive elimination of 'bull' as well as a reduction in the number of fatigue duties and of petty restrictions such as Montgomery had asked for in 1947 and which still had not been fully accepted. Moreover, this was accomplished without in any way sacrificing tradition in the emotive way the Army interpreted that word. If anything, indeed, the desire for shibboleths intensified – as will be described later in this chapter.

The R.T.R.'s recruiting campaign opened in the summer of 1958 and was steered initially by a Committee set-up by the Colonels Commandant, first under J. C. de F. Sleeman and later under Major-General G. C. Hopkinson. Exhorting the entire Regiment to 'Go to It', the Committee produced a Regimental Recruiting Card describing the advantages of spending 'A Real Man's Life' in the Royal Tank Regiment. 'You can learn a useful trade . . .' it read, and 'Everyone is taught to drive. Be a Gunner, Radio Operator, Tank driver or, best of all, A TANK COMMANDER. As a Corporal you can command a tank! Be somebody – command one of Britain's latest tanks – £50,000 at your bidding!' A brochure and posters were also printed, and an organization was formed which appointed certain senior officers as Recruiting Area Organizers, covering the catchment regions which had been allocated, or which it was hoped would be allocated, throughout the British Isles, less Northern Ireland and Wales. In principle, the areas chosen coincided as closely as possible with those covered (or previously covered) by the T.A. units to which the Regular units had been affiliated. When Phase 1 of Amalgamation would be complete in 1960, the recruiting areas and their organization would be as follows:

Unit	Area	Affiliated T.A. unit
1st R.T.R.	Lancashire, Cumberland, Westmorland	40/41st R.T.R.
2nd R.T.R.	Middlesex, Hertfordshire, Essex, Kent, London, Norfolk, Suffolk, Cambridge, Huntingdonshire, Bedfordshire	Westminster Dragoons
3rd R.T.R.	Cornwall, Devonshire, Dorset, Somerset, Bristol, Cheltenham	N.S.Y./44th R.T.R.
4th R.T.R.	Scotland	Lowland Yeomanry
5th R.T.R.	Yorkshire	N.S.Y./44th R.T.R.

Permission to allow the 4th to recruit in Scotland, however, was not readily granted by H.Q. Scottish Command, and for some time activities were on an unofficial basis only because facilities to introduce recruiters into the official recruiting organization were denied. Hopkinson, who had become D.R.A.C. in 1959, says that the G.O.C.-in-C.'s argument was that, since the Household Cavalry and the Scots Greys already recruited in Scotland, an additional armoured regiment would be beyond the capacity of the region. 'I had to storm the heights of Edinburgh Castle', writes Hopkinson, 'in order to persuade him otherwise. Fortunately I had served in the 4th in Catterick pre-war and I was able to shoot a line of the close ties the 4th had with Scotland in those days.' But as Hopkinson points out, it was not until National Service was in its final throes in 1960 that the big recruiting drive got into top gear. Then 'the R.A.C. as a whole out-recruited the rest of the Army by miles; in fact after 6 months we were able to be extremely selective. The surprise of the campaign was that the southern counties won recruits much more easily than the northern ones.' He could have added that competition between regiments was, in itself, a potent incentive as part of the battle for survival, and far from unrelated to the arguments which would be advanced when further redundancies were mooted.

Undoubtedly the R.T.R.'s high reputation as a modern force played a significant part in persuading young men to join it. Undeniably the emphasis on professional involvement with machinery, to the virtual exclusion of traditional lures – '. . . this dressing up. This emotional intoxication produced by bagpipes and bearskins, and the hypnotism of rhythmical movement and mechanical drills,' as Hobo once put it – was important. And yet, at the height of its endeavours to fortify its manpower by an appeal to professionalism, those at the head of the Regiment invoked acts of homage to the Sovereign and Colonel-in-Chief to a greater extent than at any other period in its history. Frequently, after 1958, elements of the R.T.R. paraded with the ceremonial trappings of tradition, although it had begun to foster its contacts with the Queen long before that.

On 30 November 1954, two of the Colonels Commandant, accompanied by officers representing each Regular and Territorial unit, in addition to R.T.R. officers then serving at the R.A.C. Centre, the Staff College, The Royal Military Academy, Sandhurst and Mons Officer Cadet School, presented a Regimental brooch, on behalf of all the officers of the regiment, to Her Majesty Queen Elizabeth II at Buckingham Palace. In July 1957, as part of her tour of the R.A.C. Training Brigade at Catterick Camp, Her Majesty had visited the 7th, and in November of that year she had attended the Officers' Regimental Tea Party. But it was in May 1958, that there came the most significant announcement, one which was to allow the Regiment as a whole to parade before the Queen as Colonel-in-Chief. With her approval, Battle Honours were awarded together with the design of a Standard upon which selected Honours were to be emblazoned, and these were to be presented by Her Majesty as an act of consecration shared with all ranks. With the Queen's encouragement and the grant of a Standard and Battle Honours, the Regiment took its place with the other Fighting Arms.

All the Battle Honours were awarded jointly to the Regiment as a whole, so that the same honours would appear on each unit's Standard – the only difference between each Standard being that the unit's number appeared on two corners. An original design by Garter King of Arms had to be declined, however, since it included the White Horse of Hanover, and the presence of this animal was thought inappropriate. Instead, a full-faced piece of armour (normally only borne on the Royal Arms) was requested, and to this Her Majesty graciously gave permission. There was no problem in selecting the Honours for the First World War, but in the case of the Second World War, the Colonels Commandant decided to confine the list to major battles in which the Regiment had taken a particular part, to battles in which a number of units of the Regiment had been concerned or to operations which, although affecting only one or two units and, perhaps, lesser in magnitude, were historically important from the Regiment's point of view. There were 170 to choose from, but Theatre Honours were chosen in every case and, in all, 15 were chosen for the First World War and 54 for the Second, to which was added 'Korea 1951–53'. Because of lack of space, only 10 were to be emblazoned.

In fact, the 40th (The King's) Royal Tank Regiment (T.A.) had possessed Colours before it was converted from infantry to armour in 1938, but these had been burned during one of the air-raids on Liverpool. New colours had been presented to it at Bootle on 11 April 1954, by the C.I.G.S., Field Marshal Sir John Harding, when the unit was commanded by Lieutenant-Colonel I. S. Gray. These Colours, however, had to be laid up when the 40th amalgamated with the 41st in 1956. The plan to present Standards at Buckingham Palace to the five Regular units and the single T.A. unit of the R.T.R., and Guidons to the North Somerset Yeomanry/44th R.T.R. (T.A.) and the Westminster Dragoons, raised problems unlike those ever encountered before in connection with such a ceremony. It was for Talbot and his small staff to make the arrangements, such as obtaining War Office authority for the size of contingents (governed mainly by the cost of moving them to London); liaising with the Palace staff and designing the form of conglomerate parade for eight units, which were scattered from North Africa to Liverpool and Germany, and which lacked a common weapon or arms drill. This latter problem was overcome by adopting the new sub-machine-gun drill, and holding a cadre course in Fallingbostel, Germany, for the eight R.S.M.s so that they could instruct their units prior to their contingents combining at Woolwich ten days before the great day. At the same time, Talbot needed to overcome the Palace head gardener's fears that the verges would not be damaged by marching troops, and had to lay out the parade on lawns of which no map or plan existed. He also commissioned a painting of the ceremony, and the making of a film. And, last, but certainly not least, R.H.Q. organized a Regimental ball, at which the Queen and Duke of Edinburgh would be present, on the night after the parade. Talbot tells of the quite outstanding cooperation from every one concerned and mentions, in particular, the generosity of Edward Halliday who, to satisfy a personal desire, offered to paint the picture without fee, and the famous comedian, Harry Secombe, a gifted amateur 'movie' photographer, who filmed the event.

On 27 October 1960, in the presence of the Colonels Commandant of the R.T.R. and of the Honorary Colonels of the three T.A. Regiments, and watched by an audience of 2,500 past and present members of the regiments, the eight Regimental Detachments, each of 3 officers and 27 other ranks, under the command of Lieutenant-Colonel H. C. W. Ironside, were inspected by the Queen, to music provided by the combined Cambrai and Alamein Bands of the R.T.R. After the Standards and Guidons had been blessed by the Chaplain-General to the Forces, the Venerable Archdeacon I. D. Neil, and Her Majesty had presented the Standards and Guidons to each Regimental Commanding Officer and Bearer Party in turn, she spoke of her pleasure at the occasion, of her pride in the R.T.R.'s achievements over a period of only 44 years, and of the North Somerset Yeomanry and Westminster Dragoons in the wars in which they had fought. She recalled that her grandfather, King George V, had seen the first tank being demonstrated at Hatfield Park in 1916, and spoke of his part in embodying the Royal Tank Corps in the Regular Army and of being its Colonel-in-Chief. 'Your motto is "Fear Naught",' she reminded them, 'I am confident that you will be as true to it as those who served before you.' It was for Ironside, so appropriately selected for his name, to reply on behalf of the Regiments, to thank the Queen for the honour she had bestowed upon them and, speaking of the Standards and Guidons, to pledge, 'We will guard them well.'

It then remained for each unit in turn to Troop its Standard at the earliest moment to enable all the officers and men to see it and understand its meaning. The 4th R.T.R. was first to do so in a mounted parade at Hohne on 5 November.

* * * * *

The years between 1956 and 1960 may well be seen as turning-points in the R.T.R.'s history. Reduced in size, and concerned about possible further shrinkage, it was becoming aware that its rôle might also be altered. The organizational and tactical experiments which had taken place, with the possibility of nuclear war in mind, and the actual experience of small, limited wars and the latest style of internal security operation, had stimulated considerable thought about the shape of confrontations to come, and of armour's future rôle. Several members of the Regiment contributed to the debate with papers published in the military journals. Fairly typical of the ideas being discussed were those which appeared as winners of two Army Quarterly prize essays, won respectively, in 1956 by Captain K. J. Macksey and, in 1957, by Captain R. L. C. Dixon. Dealing with the subject of the George Knight Clowes Memorial Prize Essay, which questioned the form of the land campaign of the future, and how the British Army should be organized to meet it, Macksey specified two kinds of war which might be expected – guerilla warfare and nuclear warfare. He maintained that the need to achieve mobility was as imperative as ever, and that the organization needed to cope with guerilla warfare might be quite similar to that in a nuclear conflict. He visualized a requirement for combat groups able to move freely about the countryside, self-contained and comprising elements of all the fighting arms – infantry, armour, artillery and engineers. The suggested basic organization was termed 'The All Arms Battalion' and would consist of 5 companies of infantry mounted, in nuclear war, in A.P.C.s armed with an anti-tank rocket-launcher; 1 squadron of tanks, consisting of 5 troops of 4 tanks; and a battery of heavy, rifled mortars, with five troops of two mortars each. The division would remain as the basic higher formation, but its H.Q. would be invited to command nine All Arms Battalions without the interposition of a brigade headquarters. These proposals were reported by the *Daily Express* as advocating the scrapping of Army regiments and the sacking of all brigadiers and their staffs.

Dixon's winning Bertrand Stewart Prize Essay, on the more confined subject of organization for nuclear war, came closer to orthodoxy, but also recommended the abolition of brigade headquarters. He wrote of nuclear attrition followed by conventional assault, pursuit and exploitation, and demanded more fighting units and sub-units under fewer headquarters, in rather the same way as had Macksey, of whose proposals, incidentally, he was unaware when he wrote his essay. But Dixon wished to retain infantry and armoured divisions, deploring as he did the standard division then about to be officially introduced. The infantry division, he thought, should consist of 5 infantry battalions and 1 armoured regiment (as opposed to 9 to 1 previously), while the armoured division should have 3 armoured regiments and 3 infantry battalions (by comparison with the existing 4 to 4). Neither of his divisions would contain more than the indispensable minimum number of administrative units, since supply would become the responsibility of higher formations, working to a divisional bulk-breaking point. As Dixon put it, 'a more compact division with administrative appendages removed', was required.

Neither Macksey's nor Dixon's suggestions are to be found embodied in the organizations that were being adopted by the War Office, although the shift towards more closely-integrated combat groups was to be implicit in nearly all the experimental organizations tried out during the next two decades, and brigades were eventually to go. Far more closely related to the actuality of the future were the views propounded in *The Tank*, in

November 1957, by Brigadier R. M. P. Carver, as he came towards the end of the course at the Imperial Defence College. In an article entitled 'The Future of Armour', he emphasized the threat to the United Kingdom posed, on the one hand, by the ideology of Communism and, on the other, by the Powers of Asia and Africa. He then analyzed the rôle which the British Army might be expected to play in Cold War (in which he predicted a continuing involvement), Limited War (of which he believed there was little chance, with or without atomic weapons), and Global War (which he saw as being deterred by the potential contestants' fear of the consequences). Infantry, he declared, 'will always be the main need' in Cold War. 'Armoured cars and scout cars as well as light armoured personnel-carriers, probably wheeled, but also perhaps tracked, may be needed, depending on the nature of the country and the opponents. The armament of the Saladin armoured car [which, with its 76mm. gun began coming into service in 1958] should suffice as the heaviest weapon that any A.F.V. in this rôle will need.' Concerning Limited War, he saw a most difficult problem in selecting the organization and weapons needed, and went so far as to suggest that a risk might be taken of there being no such war, but he concluded that the most important techniques should be kept alive and that a reserve of units capable of fairly easy transportation should be kept in the United Kingdom. Global War, he considered a possibility, and for this he sought a highly-mobile force with the Royal Armoured Corps well to the fore and making the best use of its traditional '. . . speed of thought, decision and execution. I believe', he claimed, 'that, if necessary, we can safely afford to reduce the long-range anti-tank requirement and the degree of protection for the majority of our tanks in order to achieve the extra mobility we shall need' – and events have yet to prove him seriously wrong. In effect, Carver was sceptical about the future employment prospects of the Royal Armoured Corps: '. . . we have a small but essential part to play in the Cold War; . . . the Limited War requirement is very doubtful, but it must be insured against . . .; In the Global War deterrent we ought to have a major part to play, but we need more mobile tanks for the purpose . . .' In conclusion, he warned of the danger of others endeavouring to step into the Royal Armoured Corps' shoes. 'We are an expensive arm and an obvious target to those looking round for economies which can be justified as pruning obsolescent dead wood. We must not therefore be found fighting in the last ditch in defence of out-moded methods, but in the vanguard of the movement to reshape and reorganize the Army to perform its future tasks.'

It is unlikely that a great many people read that article at the time, but its message rang out clearly and the day was not too far removed when Carver, as Chief of the General Staff and, later, as Chief of the Defence Staff, would be at the head of those striving to keep the components of the Army adaptable and abreast of the times and conditions. In the meantime, the work of producing weapons and vehicles which would satisfy the specifications he had written was already well advanced.

CHAPTER IX

The
Frontiers of Invention
1957-1973

'It is a great pity that we are called the Royal Armoured Corps', wrote R. M. P. Carver in 1957. '. . . We should really be called the Royal Direct-fire Fighting-vehicle Corps! The criterion for the employment of the R.A.C. should be that the task to be performed demands the use of direct fire vehicles, as distinct from the use of indirect fire from vehicles, whether armoured or not, by the Royal Artillery or the use of armoured vehicles, whether tracked or wheeled, solely for the carriage of infantry.' The dictum was well enough understood among his contemporaries, although not always applied with precision when it came to the procurement of weapons by the Combat Arms for their own use. Too frequently, one Combat Arm might wish to take possession of a weapon which, within the meaning of Carver's pronouncement, belonged to another. Realizing that the R.A.C. had the vital rôle to play within the forces of the deterrent, some artillerymen and infantrymen, for example, were anxious either to operate R.A.C. weapons themselves, or somehow show that the tank, faced by the latest anti-armour weapons, lacked a future in battle. The present writer recalls Lieutenant-General Sir Kenneth Darling, as Commander I (British) Corps in 1961, relishing the prospects, before a predominantly infantry audience, of a tank eclipse brought about by the advent of infantry A.T.G.W. such as Vigilant and the proposed Inswing. His thoughts were in keeping with those of the traditional anti-tank lobby, but the effects of such prophecies merely acted as a spur to tank technologists and tacticians to prove his kind wrong.

As the prime mover in nearly all armoured developments before the Second World War, the R.T.C., by force of circumstances if no other, had produced a cadre of officers and men who were assured, both during and after the war, of places at the head of the War Office and Ministry of Supply departments associated with tank procurement, and in the crucial testing of equipment. Therefore it was no fluke that the post (or its previous equivalent) of D.R.A.C. had always been filled, until 1946, by an R.T.R. officer, and that until 1968 it was a case of 'Buggin's turn,' with Cavalry and R.T.R. officers alternating.

Nor was it remarkable that the post of Director-General of Fighting Vehicles and Engineer Equipment (within the Ministry of Supply) was shared, throughout the war, and until 1951, with officers of the Royal Artillery, or extraordinary, after Major-General H. E. Pyman was appointed D.G.F.V.E.E. in 1951, that the post became an R.A.C. preserve – and, from 1951 until 1966, a wholly R.T.R. preserve, its successive incumbents being Major-Generals H. E. Pyman (1951–53), H. R. B. Foote, V.C. (1953–55), F. W. S. Gordon-Hall (1955–58), H. M. Liardet (1958–61), W. M. Hutton (1961–64), and A. R. Leakey (1964–66) with J. G. R. Allen in office from 1973–74. It would be ridiculous to allocate all the praise for what went right and all the blame for what went wrong to these'officers alone. While one or other of them might be responsible, at the time, for a major piece of equipment's initiation, it could be many years and several successors later before the article in question, considerably modified, entered service. For example, the tank, which, in 1949, was intended to succeed Centurion in 1960, was first mooted when Duncan was D.R.A.C., but it was not until Holden held that appointment in 1966 that it began to come into service. In the meantime, successive Directors had contributed to its development, and had themselves been influenced by successive staff officers and the design staffs of the R. & D. establishments. The days when lone hands, such as Lieutenant-Colonel P. Johnson, Sir John Carden, G. le Q. Martel, or W. J. Christie, could, as individuals, dominate tank design, were past. Committees and systems engineers now ruled, and the conferences they attended grew immensely in size and frequency, while the time taken to produce a tank extended from twelve months, in 1916, to nine years in the 1960s.

Between 1930 and the outbreak of war, most young R.T.C. Officers had attended a six-months course at the Military College of Science (M.Co.S.), which was regarded by some as a scrounge or joke. Between the dispersion of that college in 1939 and even after the opening of the Fighting Vehicles Wing of the M.Co.S. in 1943, which later became the R.A.C. School of Tank Technology (S.T.T.), the supply of officers trained to think about technical subjects began to dry up, a famine which was only in part prevented when the Military College of Science re-opened at Shrivenham after the war. For the course was not popular. In 1952, for example, out of 60 vacancies available to the British Army, only 18 were filled. Some technical appointments intended for R.A.C. officers had to be given to infantry officers. Almost as of routine, those who passed the course at Shrivenham, or at the S.T.T., found themselves members of a somewhat exclusive circle, cut off to some extent from regimental duty by their rare qualifications, and therefore deprived of important contacts with troops and the machines they served. The technical officers followed each other from job to job. The same names crop up over and again among those in the key appointments at the Fighting Vehicles Department of the Ministry of Supply (as it was until 1959) and as part of the Army Department's Master General of the Ordnance's Department which, in turn, became the Procurement Executive of the Ministry of Defence in 1972. The list of those who commanded the R.A.C. School of Tank Technology (renamed the Armour School in 1966) includes many R.T.R. officers whose contribution to weapon development during the period covered by this history speaks for itself. They were Colonel O. E. Chapman (1943–46), Colonel F. W. S. Gordon-Hall (1946–48), Colonel C. B. Bouchier (1948–51), Colonel F. R. S. Mackenzie (1955–58), Colonel Sir Frederick Coates (1958–61), Colonel B. S. Heath (1961–64), Colonel R. Coombes (1964–67) and Colonel R. R. Moss (1972–74).

The S.T.T., since its formation in December 1942, at a time when British tank design was undergoing severe criticism, had taken root at Chobham where it shared ground with F.V.R.D.E. After the war, a large portion of the School was moved to the Military College of Science at Shrivenham where it formed the Fighting Vehicles Wing. But in 1951, as the result of a joint decision taken in 1949 by the Director-General of Military Training (D.G.M.T.) and the D.R.A.C., Major-General G. P. B. Roberts, it was moved to Bovington, charged with the task of producing, in a one-year course, officers capable of carrying out the duties of Regimental Technical Adjutant or any of a number of appointments in connection with, for example, Equipment Trials or Military Intelligence. The officer students, who were drawn from throughout the Army (not, by any means, from the R.A.C. only) and from Commonwealth and foreign armies, would form a cadre of technically influenced officers, many of whom would later acquire higher qualifications and make important contributions to A.F.V. development. From 1951 to 1961, it was a highly technical course, very hard work and requiring considerable application. But as Mackenzie put it, in 1958, 'Some of the most cheering remarks that have been made to [me] . . . have been those of officer students who had become somewhat bored with the routine soldiering of peacetime but who have quite changed their view of the Army as a career as a result of being able to stretch their brains'. By 1960, this view did not necessarily receive much weight in the War Office where the D.G.M.T., who had recently commanded the Military College of

Science, held that the S.T.T. Course was a wasteful duplication of the College's curriculum. Faced by a threat to close the S.T.T., the D.R.A.C., Major-General G. C. Hopkinson, had to fight hard to preserve it. At the same time, he told Coates, the School's Commandant, to 'make the course less technical and therefore attractive to the intelligent [sic] – one step up from the D. & M., Gunnery and Wireless Instructors Courses held at the R.A.C. Centre'. Hopkinson had a stiff fight with the D.G.M.T., a Sapper. 'At one stage', he recalls, 'I had to threaten to go to the C.I.G.S. and suggest the abolition of the Royal Artillery Advanced Course and the Royal Engineer's one at Chatham! I won the day.' But by 1965, the course had become 'unfashionable' and too few R.A.C. vacancies were being filled. And yet, at the R.A.C. Conference that year, commanding officers (only) voted unanimously in favour of the course, with the result that, thereafter, if they failed to fill a vacancy in their regiments, they had to submit their reasons in writing to the D.R.A.C.!

In the immediate aftermath of the rejection of FV 201 in 1949, which occurred almost simultaneously with the decision to concentrate principally upon improving Centurion, improvising Charioteer and building Conqueror, only tentative studies were made in formulating an idea of the type of tank it was thought would be needed to replace Centurion by about 1960. At the same time, work advanced on the new range of reconnaissance vehicles – the 6-wheeled armoured car would enter service in 1958 as Saladin (built by Alvis Ltd., where Major W. D. P. Sullivan, R.T.R. (retired) injected a strong regimental influence), and the 4-wheeled scout car called Ferret (built by Daimler Ltd.) a small number of which began to reach units in 1952. But the search for a suitable tracked reconnaissance vehicle – in other words, a light tank – was never entirely abandoned. Roberts had pursued the idea in 1949 by giving fresh impetus to the projected FV 301, although it was already becoming apparent that the FV 300 series of light vehicles which had been proposed in 1946, was running into serious difficulties with regard to power plant, weight and the size of armament then being demanded. By 1950, in fact, FV 301 could hardly be called a light tank at all, for the weight, at 21 tons (with a 77mm. gun and a 500hp. engine) made it heavier than the medium tanks with which most countries had started the war in 1939. Like so many of the post-war vehicles, the specifications of FV 301 tended to embody too many facilities in an attempt to satisfy all the contingencies the fighting men's experiences had suggested. Successive Directors of the R.A.C., and of other Arms, were guilty of allowing badly conceived and coordinated projects to proceed and they, in turn, were un-checked by a strong central equipment-making directorate. When pragmatism had to take precedence over theory in the rearmament drive of the early 1950s, some marginal projects had to be terminated, and in 1953 this was the fate of the entire FV 300 series at the hands of a new D.R.A.C., Major-General R. B. B. B. Cook (late 17th/21st Lancers) and of the D.G.F.V.E.E., Pyman. But in addition to lack of money there were fundamental disagreements over the requirement which affected design. FV 301 was not air-portable, while the Royal Artillery's demand that the engine be at the front to allow the fighting compartment in their self-propelled gun version to be at the rear, was difficult to reconcile with the R.A.C. require-ment for a rear-engined vehicle – quite apart from doubts which had arisen as to the chances of survival on the battlefield for such a tank, whose armour was only two inches thick.

The current state of uncertainty as to the tank's future in 1953 was to some extent reflected by the title of a committee set up that year by the Ordnance Board because, to quote the Board's history, 'the often acrimonious discussion about anti-armour performance revealed the lack of a trials authority respon-sible for the assessment and promulgation of penetration data'. The Attack of Tanks Committee was intended to consider the forms and vulnerability of existing and future A.F.V. targets, and the performance of current and projected weapons against them. In 1957, confidence returned, and it was renamed the Attack of Armour Committee, redesignated as 'a forum for the discussion of matters which have a bearing both on the defeat of armour and its performance, but which are not exclusive to either aspect'. Sponsored by D.G.F.V.E. and D.G.W.(A.) it would, after 1963, include a representative from the A.T.G.W. field, but throughout its existence it was the clearing-house for those whose technical innovations profoundly influenced the two decades of tank development under consideration here. Several R.T.R. officers served on it, including Major-General (retired) J. French, as President from 1958 to 1961, and at other times, Colonel R. R. Moss (as the representative of the Director-General of Artillery) and Major (retired) C. J. Wieland, who for many years was F.V.R.D.E.'s representative (and, after retire-ment from F.V.R.D.E., a consultant) and he, through his many contacts, was fully apprised of the R.A.C.'s opinions.

When Foote took over as D.G.F.V.E.E. in 1953, the design of the tank to replace Centurion was well advanced, as a result of the studies which had begun seriously in 1951. It was governed by the principle that it would have, to quote Foote, 'A gun armour combination which would make it superior to any known tank design in the world at that time.' At first, collaboration with the U.S.A. had led to a proposal to fit an American 105mm. gun in a 'cleft' turret, served by an externally-mounted automatic loader. But this was dropped in favour of a more conventional turret layout, and the mounting of the much larger 120mm. L 11 gun, designed at A.R.D.E., which would be essential to satisfy the penetration requirement against the Russian JS 3 and its successors. The armour basis was intended to be able to keep out all known projectiles at approximately 800 metres and, as later demanded, defeat medium artillery fire. Originally, the power plant was to have been a V-type engine, but, in due course, it was decided to abandon this and try, instead, to satisfy a N.A.T.O. requirement for an engine with multi-fuel capability. This was a fatal decision. As Foote points out, engines of this type were largely untried (there was a certain amount of German aircraft experience to call on, in addition to a small British commercial truck engine) and so Leylands, who took on the development work from F.V.R.D.E., were faced with an extensive programme of original research and development. Indeed, so unsure of success were the promoters of the multi-fuel power plant, that parallel arrangements were made to develop a conventional Continental diesel engine in one of the Ordnance factories, a scheme which, as Foote remarks, was unfortunately scuppered by the Treasury on grounds of expense. But the Treasury was not responsible for the original sad decision, and the horizontally-opposed 6-cylinder Leyland L 60 engine, which was designed to give 750hp., ran into a series of difficulties, including severe piston trouble when it was run at over 600hp. In its final form, redesign of the tank's engine compartment became necessary, which added another ton to the overall weight, and throughout its whole development, the power plant was in trouble.

Nevertheless, the 50-ton FV 4201, or Chieftain as it came to be known, incorporated many features which were a credit to British tank designers. The use of fixed ammunition (projectile and cartridge in one piece) for such a large gun as the 120mm. posed impossible problems of stowage and handling within a tank turret, and gave the loader a most arduous and complicated task. By adopting separate ammunition with a bagged charge, these difficulties were largely overcome, and to reduce the fire risk if the tank were penetrated and the charge struck, a uniquely water-jacketed stowage bin was developed. By placing the driver in a reclining position, it was possible not only to lower the hull's height, and thus save weight, but also to introduce a more refined angling of frontal armour to improve protection. The original specification (General Staff Requirement) was written by Lieutenant-Colonel A. Cooper, while he was G.S.O. 1 in R.A.C. 2 at the War Office. But it was not until 1958, by which time Foote had become D.R.A.C. (in 1955), that the final specification for Chieftain was settled, and it was 1959 before the first prototype ran – and there would be much work and many modifications ahead before it finally came into service in January 1967. Moreover, before the specification was settled, there had been a development in the gunnery sphere which raised serious doubts in some minds as to the need for the 120mm. gun, and posed the question: Was the Chieftain needed at all?

In the early 1950s, a member of A.R.D.E., Mr. L. Permutter, had carried out pure research into the characteristics of high-velocity guns. Permutter was a Belgian scientist with a none too adequate grasp of English, but he had achieved promotion through sheer merit and technical brilliance. During the Second World War he had played an important part in the development of A.P.D.S. ammunition, and it was always his contention that the crucial element was ammunition, rather than the gun. But it was gun design upon which he now concentrated in an effort to improve ballistic performance without increasing barrel length. In the course of his investigations, he experimented with a 20pdr. (83.4mm.) gun bored out to 105mm., and from the results of his analysis arrived at the conclusion, prior to 1954, that 'the gun's energy was increased by about 22 per cent with a rather greater corresponding increase in A.P. performance'. As a result of this, A.R.D.E. proposed, in 1954, to increase the gun power of the Centurion by replacing the 20pdr. with a new 105mm. gun. For practical purposes the slender 20pdr. barrel had to be increased in thickness by 12–15mm. to prevent whip. But the simple beauty of the modification lay in the fact that no major modification had to be carried out to the tank: it was simply a matter of fitting a larger calibre barrel to the original breech ring and mounting, and introducing a new range-drum skin.

In terms of effectiveness, the advent of the 105mm. in 1956 was revolutionary. It would virtually equal the performance of the only, but American, 120mm. gun then available in Conqueror and, therefore, in some respects, it made the Chieftain seem superfluous, since Centurion's life could be considerably extended by modifications to its automotive facilities, in addition to those associated with protection and striking power. But perhaps one of the most important benefits gained by Permutter's 'discovery' – as such it genuinely was – was a commercial one. In the years to come, the 105mm. gun became practically the standard tank armament of the N.A.T.O. Powers, and many other nations besides, including the strong armoured army of Israel. Large sums were earned for Britain by way of royalties and export orders, and it is noteworthy that the ready acceptance of this gun by Cook and Foote and the Army Council was matched by Treasury approval to re-arm Centurion.

In fact, slow progress with the development of Chieftain made it almost imperative to radically improve Centurion in the late 1950s and early 1960s, in order to keep pace with the appearance of Russian medium T 54 and T 55 and heavy T 10 tanks. An increase in its glacis plate thickness with the provision of extra fuel storage under armour, white light searchlights and infra-red night-vision equipment were essential. At the same time, the ammunition itself was progressively improved in quality, often at the instigation of Permutter. Many foreign purchasers of the 105mm. gun adopted the American-developed hollow-charge, High Explosive Anti-Tank warhead (H.E.A.T.) because of its undoubted penetration capability. The British retained A.P.D.S. with High Explosive Squash Head (H.E.S.H.) as an additional projectile because, while having an acceptable H.E. performance against unarmoured targets, the latter was also an armour defeating round. Each of the increasingly limited number of rounds the modern tank could stow would thus have an anti-tank capability without jeopardizing the tank's ability to engage other targets. H.E.A.T. was rejected by the British, partly because it was considered to be less effective than H.E.S.H. and partly because its performance to penetrate armour was degraded by spin induced through firing from a rifled gun.

Simultaneously, the endeavour to improve accuracy of aim together with a reduction of the amount of ammunition needed to hit the target went on unabated. Wieland persisted in his attempts to improve zeroing, and introduced a better Muzzle Bore Sight (M.B.S.) of his own design, based upon the best features of previous models (including those of German origin). Eventually, after many stages of development, he saw it accepted into service with the result that a further tightening-up of accuracy together with elimination of errors from 'barrel droop' – the bending of the barrel by anything up to 5 minutes of arc, as the result of firing or atmospheric effects – became possible. At the same time, barrel bend was kept within limits by encasing the barrel in a jacket known as a thermal shield. Wieland was among those who, in conjunction with F.V.R.D.E., R.A.R.D.E. (the latter received its 'Royal' title in 1962) and the R.A.C. Centre (which operated a so-called Gunnery Working Party) produced, in the mid-1960s, what came to be known as the

Muzzle Reference Sight – a built-in Muzzle Bore Sight. This device was intended to enable the gunner to overcome, by immediate reference during firing, any inaccuracies introduced by barrel bend.

Another approach towards solving the judgement of distance to the target was made in the mid-1950s, when scientists at A.R.D.E. and F.V.R.D.E. began looking into the use of a ranging gun – that is, the employment of a sub-calibre weapon firing tracer ammunition to establish the range to the target, before transferring the result to the sighting system of the main armament. The idea of a 'spotting rifle', firing individual rounds to establish the range, was not in itself new – it had been successfully used with the British 120mm. B.A.T. and the U.S. 106mm. R.C.L. Wieland, however, pioneered the work done at F.V.R.D.E. to modify a .50inch calibre Browning machine-gun as a ranging device for the longer range tank gun. The first trials used the 20pdr. as the main armament, but, when finally brought into service in the early 1960s, the system was mounted in the Centurion Mark 9, with its 105mm. gun. Dispersion was improved by shortening the M.G. barrel, providing a forward bearing to hold the weapon more rigidly, and by slowing down the rate of fire. A switching device in the firing gear limited the number of special tracer rounds fired to a burst of three.

After exhaustive trials, Wieland took this relatively simple system in a Centurion to Fort Knox in the U.S.A. and trained a U.S. crew in its use. This crew then proceeded, in a big demonstration, to do better with the British equipment than it could with their own 90mm. guns, for which the range was established either by optical range-finders with a hand-cranked, mechanical computor system, or by a fully automated system. In one instance, the Centurion hit six targets out of six separate target engagements, followed by five targets first time, out of six separate engagements. Yet the Americans did not adopt the ranging gun and nor, apart from its originators, has any other nation except Sweden.

The increasing complexity of tanks fitted with devices such as those engineered by the gunnery experts, began to impinge upon the ability of the average crewman to make the best use of the equipment with which he was provided. Whereas, in the early 1950s, it was the radio-operator who had need to be the deftest member of a crew, the emphasis, ten years later, had shifted towards the gunner, particularly since the new family of simpler, crystal-tuned radio sets, which began to come into service at the end of the decade, were much easier to operate. While the gunner of 1950 zeroed his gun to the sight by the use of crosswires tacked by grease across the end of the muzzle; aligned his sight using a simple graticule; and had only to manipulate a few basic controls to a simple drill in order to fire, his successor had many things to watch and a multiplicity of tasks to perform. The gunner of the 1960s (and the commander, too, for that matter) had to zero his weapons with the aid of complex gadgets, as well as having regard, during actual shooting, to a multiplicity of factors and rules which were made to appear all the more daunting by a plethora of dots and crosses within the sight, plus an array of lights, knobs, dials and levers designed to assist him fire the right round in the right direction at the right moment. There were those who believed that if longer-term Regular service had not been re-introduced, the short-term National Service soldier would have been unable to cope with the current, let alone future, turret equipment. Nor was this all. Throughout the 1960s, the number of gadgets became even more profuse, at a time when, so far as tank commanders and gunners were concerned, the cost of practising them with expensive ammunition and the shortage of adequate ranges, inhibited units from carrying out sufficient training.

In 1960, the announcement of the first working laser led to investigations into its use as an aid to range-finding until, in 1972, a laser range-finder was incorporated in the sighting system of the Chieftain tank. The adoption of a laser also made possible the invention of an important gunnery training aid in the form of a simulator, which was intended to exercise turret crews in the full range of drills and procedures without firing a single, expensive shot. In fact, the Solartron Hit Kill Simulator (later known as Simfire), which was devised in response to a specification written by R.A.C. officers in H.Q. D.R.A.C. and the Ministry of Defence in the mid-1960s, initially turned out to be more useful as a tactical aid than for gunnery training, although its adoption made it theoretically possible to keep gunners at a high state of proficiency throughout the year, instead of reaching a peak only at the time they fired their Annual Course. Far more realistic tactical exercises were made possible because a 'kill' could actually be registered against an 'enemy' vehicle, if the commander and gunner carried out the correct drill – and this facility was also invaluable in simulated tactical trials.

From the moment, in the Second World War, when it became apparent that the size of guns was certain to increase, together with a commensurate complication of most aspects of tank design and construction, the search for a smaller and more efficient weapons system to replace the ponderous high-velocity gun became urgent. After attempts in Britain had failed (in

1952) to develop a smooth-bore, low-velocity gun, called Schulman (after its inventor), which had appeared in 1947 and fired a projectile with a H.E.A.T. warhead that was dependent on air stabilization at sub-sonic speeds, attention turned to guided rockets. Towards the end of the war, the Germans had experimented with a wire-guided, rocket-propelled, anti-tank missile known as X 7, a weapon which provided a starting-point for a number of projects by various nations, notably France (where SS 10, the first practical A.T.G.W., was made in 1953), and Britain. Early in the 1950s, while he was working in R.A.C. 2, Cooper had written the specification for the first British anti-tank guided weapon. It was to have had a chemical energy warhead with a 3 inch cone and was named Project 'J' – 'but we could not get the money for even a feasibility study let alone a design study', recalls Cooper. By 1957, however, some headway had been made, and two of Cooper's specifications were under serious consideration, one of which was for an infra-red A.T.G.W., collected by a forward controller from a rearward launching site, designated 'Orange William'. It called for a maximum range of 6,000 yards, and a H.E.S.H. warhead weighing 58lb., but this was finally rejected because of valid objections to the infra-red guidance system which was considered to be too vulnerable to counter-measures.

The concept of a missile with a 50 per cent chance of a hit at long range, and with a very large warhead intended to kill from a hit on six inches of armour, was established at the R.A.C. Conference of 1952; it was accepted on the grounds that this type of weapon could only be complementary to the gun, since, at that time, it was assumed that targets up to 2,000 metres might be adequately dealt with by guns, and that at greater ranges the missile would come into its own. After taking a little more time and advice, the technicians conceded that 6,000 yards was too distant, besides being an unlikely range at which targets could be found on the battlefield. But while most nations were prepared to settle for a maximum range of only 2,000 metres for their early A.T.G.W.s, the R.A.C. demanded 3,200 metres, and this was the figure Cooper wrote into his other specification, to suit a very bulky Australian-designed wire-guided missile called Malkara. With a 60lb. H.E.S.H. warhead and a total weight of 200lb., Malkara suffered from severe limitations and could not be fitted inside a tank, or even carried satisfactorily on its exterior. Hopkinson accepted it into service in 1962, in limited numbers only, and, to gain experience, mounted it externally on a four-wheeled armoured truck known as Hornet. Its rôle was to provide long-range anti-tank support for airborne forces at the time of their landing, and the squadron given the task was Cyclops (Major J. G. R. Allen) in 2nd R.T.R. (Lieutenant-Colonel A. R. E. Davis). They were chosen by Hopkinson as the Parachute Squadron because 'they were in North Africa at that time and having a fairly peaceful time! They were also due to return to the U.K. [to Omagh in Northern Ireland] at about the same time as the production models would come into service. Their peace was somewhat disturbed by being told to start parachute training. Theirs was a very demanding task and they gave a magnificent response, providing the majority of what was to become the R.A.C. Parachute Squadron.'

'There was considerable argument within the R.A.C. on the necessity for guided missiles,' recalls Hopkinson. 'At that stage also [1960] the Infantry, for some obscure reason, also showed a lack of interest. However, Dick Simpkin [Lieutenant-Colonel R. E. Simpkin, G.S.O. 1 R.A.C. 2] and I stuck to it.' The objections to mounting an A.T.G.W. in a tank were (and remain at the time of writing) manifold. Too slow to penetrate armour by kinetic energy, the chemical energy round required a larger diameter warhead than could readily be accommodated inside a tank. Few rounds could be carried, the rate of fire was slow, the time of flight so long that the operator's composure in a hot, fast-moving engagement was bound to be affected and the cost far greater than gun ammunition. Tactical handling of this weapon was therefore very different from that of the tank gun. Nevertheless, in 1960, Hopkinson and Simpkin managed to obtain agreement to the development of a so-called, second-generation wire-guided A.T.G.W. (with a range of 4,000 yards, based on a project study by Faireys) called Swingfire, and interested the infantry in a man-portable version called Inswing. Development of both missiles was retarded by the current re-organization of the aircraft industry and the creation of the British Aircraft Corporation. The Vickers missile division which, in 1957, had produced, as a private venture, the Vigilant wire-guided A.T.G.W. (range only 1,400 yards) was incorporated in B.A.C. but, to begin with, there was poor liaison between those who had worked on Vigilant and those who were working on Swingfire. Then, in 1965, shortly after 20 Trials Unit (Lieutenant-Colonel A. A. V. Cockle, 11th Hussars) had been set up at Lulworth to evaluate both the R.A.C. and Infantry versions of the new missile, the Infantry stepped aside on the perfectly valid grounds that Inswing would be too heavy and bulky in its man-portable form. For the time being they, as well as some recon-naissance units of the R.A.C., would adopt the Vigilant as an interim weapon, to gain experience with the technique.

In any case, so far as the R.A.C. was concerned, there was no serious intention from the outset to mount A.T.G.W. inside tanks. They put Vigilants externally on the Ferret, and Swingfire on a converted and enlarged Ferret scout car, for use by the R.A.C. Parachute Squadron. And those for employment within armoured regiments would be launched from the infantry's new armoured personnel carrier, the tracked, lightly-armoured FV 432, built by J. Sankey Ltd., and designated, in its converted form, FV 438. This promised the armoured regiments the longer-range striking power they desired, at a time, in the mid-1960s, when the Conqueror tank, which had entered service in 1955, was about to be scrapped. But when, in 1964, Major-General J. A. d'Avigor-Goldsmid (late 4th/7th Royal Dragoon Guards), the D.R.A.C. at the time, came to incorporate six FV 438s within the establishment of each armoured regiment, he had to agree to a compensating reduction in the number of tanks, from 53 to 47, in order to keep within the manpower and financial ceilings then being imposed – a compromise which was by no means entirely welcomed by those who believed that, at 53, the number of tanks was barely sufficient.

The advent of 'non-tank' A.F.V.'s such as FV 432 (which entered service in 1963) did, however, open up fresh avenues for development at a time when the visions of the 1920s and 1930s of men like J. F. C. Fuller, G. le Q. Martel and P. C. S. Hobart, of all-armoured armies, were at the dawn of fulfilment. FV 432 had been specified in the late 1950s, purely as a means – or a taxi, to use the colloquial term – to carry infantry in relative safety from one place to another, before they were required to disembark and move on their feet. There was no intention on the part of the General Staff to provide facilities for the men to fight from inside their vehicle as, for example, the re-created German Army intended to do. Indeed it was not until 1960 that the officers of a new branch in the War Office (Combat Development, formed in 1959) came to appreciate that there was a significant body of opinion in the R.A.C., besides the infantry, demanding that this should be made possible. At that time, as it happened, the 1st Royal Ulster Rifles, were engaged in a trial, in conjunction with 1st R.T.R. (Lieutenant-Colonel T. D. Gregg), to see if modern infantry could do what their predecessors had done ten years before as a matter of course – man and maintain their own armoured vehicles. The R.U.R., in this case, had the rather complex and temperamental Alvis Saracen six-wheeled A.P.C. to contend with, but the fact that they managed to do so should have come as no surprise. The part played by 1st R.T.R. was significant in guiding the infantry's tactical as well as their technical footsteps, and was to hasten the day when an R.A.C. unit need no longer drive the infantry's Saracen A.P.C.s in 7th and 20th Armoured Brigade Groups (as two squadrons of the 4th R.T.R. (Lieutenant-Colonel T. S. Craig) did from 1960 to 1963). Thereafter, tank soldiers could get back to the direct fire task for which they were intended and trained.

The FV 432's arrival focussed attention on the need to develop lighter A.F.V.s, and added point to consideration of the problem of destroying their kind economically. A large number of thinly-armoured targets created a demand for rapid-fire anti-tank weapons of smaller calibre than guns of 105mm. or more. The use of expensive, slow-reaction A.T.G.W.s was largely discounted on grounds of cost effectiveness. One proposal was to mount a cannon on FV 432. But in the early 1960s, once Saladin was established in service and its inadequate cross-country performance had become evident, the need for a tracked vehicle for reconnaissance purposes and as a mount for an effective anti-A.P.C. weapon system was admitted.

In 1959, under the guidance of Hopkinson, as D.R.A.C., interest in a light tank was revived by the writing of a Policy Statement asking for a tracked or wheeled vehicle armed with a gun or an A.T.G.W. At F.V.R.D.E. and R.A.R.D.E., investigations began into the creation of a family of lightly-armoured, fast vehicles, with a cross-country performance far superior to that of existing vehicles, and capable of accepting any one of a variety of weapon systems from the existing 76mm. gun used in the Saladin, to the Swingfire A.T.G.W., or a brand-new type of 30mm. automatic cannon, the Rarden gun, which had been developed by Mr. L. Brint of the Royal Small Arms Factory at Enfield in association with R.A.R.D.E. From B.A.O.R. came a demand that this vehicle, which was known as Armoured Vehicle Reconnaissance (A.V.R.), later Combat Vehicle Reconnaissance (C.V.R.) should be tracked, since there were many places, even in that theatre, where the Saladin needed to go, but could not reach. In Southern Arabia, too, the fighting in the Radfan would have benefited from a tracked instead of a wheeled vehicle. There was agreement that C.V.R. should weigh less than 17,500lb. so that two could be carried in the Lockheed (C 130) Hercules to those many parts of the world where British influence still prevailed, particularly in Malaysia where confrontation with Indonesia was taking place.

The main disagreements over C.V.R. centred around whether it should be tracked (T.) or wheeled (W.), those who favoured the perpetuation of the traditional wheeled armoured car arguing, with some force, that silence was a virtue when engaged in reconnaissance, and that a tracked vehicle would never compete with a wheeled one in this respect. Besides, they said, wheeled vehicles are more reliable and armoured cars have often to be involved in dealing with civil disturbances, where the presence of tanks (as any tracked vehicle, for emotive reasons, would be termed) would be the antithesis of minimum force. Emotion also entered into the pleadings of many officers – and not only among the Cavalry – who regretted the likelihood of the passing of armoured cars. The present writer recalls a Cavalry colleague (who was pro-tracked C.V.R.) winning a bet that, at an R.A.C. Conference when the subject was being thrashed out, somebody would stand up and, like Douglas Haig in support of horses, argue the need for retention of the armoured car, the well-bred armoured car as developed by the British motor industry.

A special, experimental wheeled vehicle, designated TV 1000, was built by F.V.R.D.E. to discover whether a large, wheeled vehicle, steered rather in the manner of a tracked vehicle, could match a tracked vehicle in cross-country performance. By 1964, it was quite apparent that it could not, and therefore C.V.R.(T.), later developed by Alvis Ltd., became the favourite contender among the technologists. But when, at the 1964 R.A.C. Conference, an attempt was made to make a firm choice, the protagonists of wheels just about split the R.A.C. down the middle. Instead, it was proposed to produce two prototypes of each, and decide, after user trials, which should be developed, and this would take at least two years. Present at the Conference was Major-General J. R. Holden, who was to take over as D.R.A.C. in January 1965. In his own words: 'I had already concluded that we should try to get both wheeled and tracked versions. My reasons, in outline, were as follows:
  (a) Fruitless argument within the R.A.C. would cease!
  (b) Built-in delays in waiting for trials' prototypes would be avoided.
  (c) The financial climate for securing new equipment was rapidly deteriorating and it was certainly vital to come to a decision and to make the appropriate recommendation to the M.O.D. soonest.
  (d) Future rôles for the R.A.C. were difficult to envisage; however, if we opted for wheels AND tracks we would, at least, not be found wanting in armoured cars and light tanks both of which could undertake recce rôles.
  (e) The *extreme* possibilities for our requirements in the light armoured vehicle sphere were:
    (i) An Armoured Car Regiment (of the old pattern) and
    (ii) A Light Tank Regiment.

(f) We would have two basic types of brick (with variants) with which we could build mixed troops, squadrons or regiments as required . . . We could achieve MAXIMUM FLEXIBILITY.

(g) Export sales should be good.

(h) The tracked version and, to a lesser degree, the wheeled version could be adapted and varied by other arms ie R.A., R.E., Infantry.

(i) My particular reasons for including C.V.R.(W.) . . . were as follows [abbreviated here] Cheaper, silent, less provocative on I.S. duties, lighter for transport by air, easier to maintain.'

Based by F.V.R.D.E. upon the enlarged, big-wheeled Ferret (as adapted for Swingfire in the air-drop rôle), C.V.R.(W.) would be armed with the Rarden gun fitted into a specially-designed 2-man turret. Progress in producing a mock-up was swift until, in the summer of 1966 – at least a year earlier than would have been possible if the 1964 R.A.C. plan had been adhered to – both C.V.R.(W.) and C.V.R.(T.) were accepted at a meeting held at F.V.R.D.E. under the M.G.O. (General Sir Charles Jones, late R.E.). It is arguable that, had Holden failed to save it that year, the whole project might have been rejected, for in 1967 the economic crisis was to hasten the withdrawal of Britain from her overseas responsibilities and place demands upon the M.O.D. for large financial savings.

Holden's time in office as D.R.A.C., was one in which marked progress was made in the development of armour and armoured techniques, coming as it did between 1965 and 1968, when the principal projects of his predecessors were coming into service, and as the final stages for withdrawal from Empire were being undertaken, while nearly everything was being directed towards the N.A.T.O. commitment. It was Holden who, in 1965, and in agreement with D.G.F.V.E. (Major-General A. R. Leakey), insisted upon a further intensive trial of the Chieftain at Bovington, by *average* regimental crews, since so many – mainly engine – defects were apparent in the early production models – this to be followed up by remedial action before the first Mark II Chieftains were issued to the 11th Hussars in 1967.

As the first D.R.A.C. to have his headquarters out of London (as the result of the removal of all Arms Directors from Whitehall at the end of 1964), Holden was determined not to interfere with the functions of the R.A.C. Centre, within whose garrison he dwelt. From Merlincourt House in Lulworth Camp and then from Hull Down House (his choice of name) in Bovington, he encouraged the R.A.C. Centre to undertake, through various

Working Parties, numerous investigations into a host of subjects related to increasing mobility as well as the general combat effectiveness of the R.A.C. At the same time, from long range in Dorset, he attempted to keep effective touch and bring pressure to bear upon those scattered branches in the Army Department of the Ministry of Defence in London which had previously been part of D.R.A.C.'s own domain. For in 1964, the old R.A.C. 1 had been placed under the Director of Staff Duties and renamed A.S.D. 17, while R.A.C. 2 had been placed under a Director of Army Equipment Policy and renamed A.E.P. 17. Still staffed by R.A.C. officers, these branches now owed their allegiance, in the interests of a rationalized approach to equipment policy, to different masters, and looked to D.R.A.C. for advice only.

In Hopkinson's time as D.R.A.C., the project to allow R.A.C. pilots to fly helicopters within the Armoured Car Regiment had come to fruition. In Holden's time, a further step forward was taken, connected with the battlefield effectiveness of helicopters, and related to the French having first launched an SS 10 A.T.G.W. from an Alouette helicopter in 1959. Until then, a consensus consigned helicopters to reconnaissance, liaison, casualty evacuation, troop movement, and supply carrying, and this was largely a preserve of the R.A.F. Now it was obvious that the helicopter had a direct combat rôle on the battlefield, whether armed with a machine-gun or a missile, and the Army Air Corps, like the Royal Tank Corps in its early days, was eager to profit by innovations of this sort. In the early 1960s, Hopkinson had initiated a tentative examination of the helicopter's prospects as a tank killer under the auspices of the Army Air Corps, the R.A.C. Tactical School (Lieutenant-Colonel W. J. Hotblack), and the R.A.C. Gunnery School. These demonstrated the potential of the aircraft, helped focus attention on the need of anti-aircraft armament on tanks, and revealed, too, a possibility that the tank gun might pose a threat to the hovering helicopter.

There was nothing scientific about the early trials and, because they were exclusively between helicopter and tank, they fostered the impression that the one was in direct competition with the other. Indeed, it became apparent at one time that the Army Air Corps, understandably and rightly anxious to survive and expand, was attempting to acquire additional resources at the expense of the R.A.C. at the very moment when the R.A.C. was casting an acquisitive eye at the A.A.C. (see Chapter XI). One senior Army Air Corps officer made a point of comparison between the two weapon systems, with predictable bias in favour of the helicopter, before posing the seductive question, 'Wouldn't you like to trade a Scout helicopter armed with SS 11 missiles instead of a Chieftain? After all, they each cost about the same'.

In the summer of 1966, as the result of enthusiastic promotion by the Director of Land Air Warfare (Major-General N. Crookenden, late Cheshires), and with the concurrence of Holden, the Ministry of Defence called for a trial to examine the battlefield effectiveness of reconnaissance and armed helicopters. The task was allocated to the Defence Operational Analysis Establishment (D.O.A.E.), where the retired R.T.R. officer made responsible was Colonel A. Cooper who, in 1954, had tried to introduce an armoured and armed, pulse-jet helicopter for armoured car regiments, but who had left the Army in 1959 to become a scientist. The trial, Exercise 'Helltank', was originally intended to be sub-divided into three phases to examine, in Phase I, the capability of helicopters for acquiring information and targets; in Phase II, the chances of a hit being registered by various armaments (mainly tank); and in Phase III, the integration of Scout helicopters (assumed to be carrying Swingfire) with ground forces in a series of twelve, free-running exercises at combat team level. Army Aviation provided Captain N. Baldwick as its adviser to Cooper in all three phases, and D.R.A.C. sent Major M. ff Woodhead (9th/12th Lancers) for Phases I and II and Major K. J. Macksey for Phase III. The troops allocated to Phases I and II came from 16th/5th Lancers, and 19 Flt. A.A.C. (Major C. P. J. Goble) to which, in Phase III, were added some FV 432s by the School of Infantry to act in their rôle as A.P.C.s and as simulated FV 438s. It was appreciated, almost from the outset, how wrong it would be to base the study on the assumption of a simple duel between tanks and helicopters. The threat to helicopters might come from almost any element of the land forces, a danger which, as time went by, was taken to include anti-aircraft guided missiles such as Rapier and Blowpipe, then projected for service within the next decade.

It did not pass without comment on the spot that this very important study into a new dimension in warfare, took place on Salisbury Plain, centred on Tilshead and Imber, across the same ground in which the crucial experiments with armoured forces had taken place in the 1920s and 1930s under Collins, Broad and Hobart. Indeed, on one occasion, Cooper grew thoughtful, fearing the judgement of history, when he was reminded of the importance which might one day be attached to his work. Complete priority on training areas and in the supply of men and equipment was granted. The troops involved, who were kept fully informed of everything in train, and who had been heavily impressed as to the importance of introducing an atmosphere of realism into everything they did, were enthralled by the task. They excelled in their collaboration with the civilian scientists who had been attached to them as observers. For, unlike the early tank experiments, there was the minimum of hit and miss about these trials. Every event was carefully logged by observers and, in some instances, recorded on cine film and tape. Almost simultaneously, the Development Wing of the School of Army Aviation (Lieutenant-Colonel R. Parker, A.A.C.) was carrying out live firing trials with a Scout helicopter armed with French SS 11 missiles, whose controller acquired the target and guided the SS 11 through a stabilized A.P.X. sight, also of French design. These trials produced encouraging results although not, perhaps, as good as those recorded by the enthusiastic aviators, who were seen to claim, as kills, hits on a Conqueror's towing hook as well as strikes after a ricochet by an inert missile.

The first three phases of 'Helltank' seemed to confirm what had been fairly apparent prior to the trial, that helicopters had considerable difficulty in finding well-concealed targets without themselves flying too close to the enemy. Also, it was shown that any helicopter which did not hover too long might well survive, although A.A. missiles posed as sure a threat to the helicopter as did the A.T.G.W. missile to the tank. Tactically, the reconnaissance and armed helicopters took their place as part of a team, as a complementary weapon-system to those already in use. It was absorbing, as the twelve exercises of Phase III unfolded – each simulating a different aspect of war, in which the helicopters were directed to take part either in attack, defence, withdrawal or pursuit – to see how the participants on land and in the air adapted themselves to the new techniques demanded by knowledge of each other's recently-discovered capabilities and deficiencies. One preconceived notion, which, earlier, had been keenly propounded by the helicopter's supporters, that their machine was likely to be able to operate in such a way as to be unseen by the enemy, had to be abandoned. Because of their movement and noise, they were nearly always detected and often engaged. Yet when the trial was over and the results came to be analyzed, it became quite apparent that Phase III did not provide sufficient information to enable judgement to be passed on a helicopter's feasibility in a full-scale battle. It was necessary to hold a fourth phase, incorporated in an exercise at Brigade Group level in B.A.O.R. in 1967, in order to give helicopters wider scope than the restricted boundaries of Salisbury Plain allowed.

'Helltank' Phase IV, like its predecessors, was granted full priority by the Ministry of Defence, and took place, in October 1967, across typical North German plains to the north of Uelzen. The troops were provided by units of 1st Division (Major-General R. E. Ward) and control was vested in H.Q. 7th Armoured Brigade Group (Brigadier R. Worsley, late Royals), while the D.O.A.E. team, under Cooper, was changed when Major J. Cullens (A.A.C.) became his Army Air Corps' adviser; Macksey remained as the R.A.C. adviser. Once more, all the aspects of war were to be tested, but this time in a four-day exercise by battle groups of battalion size, opposed to each other. Redland would invade Blueland in the traditional manner, and launched its assault at dawn on 13 October. The order of battle was as follows:

Redland		Blueland	
2nd R.T.R. Group (Lieutenant-Colonel D. W. Ambidge)	Centurions	11th Hussars Group	Chieftains
	3 x Skeeters (Captain D. C. Crouch)		3 x Siouxs
1st Royal Anglian Group	in FV 432s	1st Black Watch Group	in FV 432s
28 Flt A.A.C. (specially raised for the exercise)	3 x Skeeters 6 x Scouts	Tp 20 Trials Unit (specially formed for the exercise)	3 x Siouxs FV 432s mocked-up as FV 438s
B Squadron 4th R.T.R. (Major L. G. Smith)	Saladins 3 x Skeeters	26 Flt A.A.C.	6 x Alouettes

In addition, several of the infantry's FV 432s were fitted with a length of piping and told to behave as if they were armed with a 30mm. gun; a proportion of the infantry were assumed to be carrying Blowpipe (a hand-held A.A. missile), and some other FV 432s were manned by members of the Royal Artillery and asked to simulate an A.A. missile system similar to Rapier.

The opening clash in the battle took the form of an all-R.T.R. confrontation, when the leading elements of the 2nd succeeded in taking H.Q. of B Squadron of the 4th by surprise and annihilating it in the first few minutes! After that, the battle progressed less dramatically, but in a highly realistic manner – which the participants enjoyed all the more because of good umpiring. It was an immense gain for realism that Redland was equipped with Centurions and helicopters with solid tail booms, while Blueland had Chieftains (whose first major exercise this was) and lattice-boom helicopters, thus making identification of friend and foe clearer. As an initial advance to contact was followed by a staged withdrawal of Blueland to a prepared defensive position, cautious probing by the recce helicopters led to a succession of strikes by the armed helicopters, corkscrewing to the attack and breaking away before retiring for their next run. Below and ahead of them, the tanks made the best of their way from bound to bound, taking maximum advantage of what cover was available, adjusting their movements to the need to avoid attention by helicopters and ground forces, including the Swingfire troop of FV 438s which also engaged helicopters. For nearly four days, this tightly umpired and impressive battle went on, culminating in its final hours in a nuclear strike by the retreating Blueland forces prior to their launching a counter-attack. But because of heavy early morning mist, this event was virtually denied the participation of helicopters – and thus emphasized one of this machine's limitations, its lack of an all-weather capability such as ground vehicles possess.

Nobody who witnessed that exercise was left in doubt that the helicopter – armed or otherwise – had a future as a complementary part of the existing system. But it was also clear that, like all other weapon systems, the helicopter needed to be integrated with other forces and could not rush, willy-nilly, about the battlefield as if possessed of an inbuilt invulnerability. By the same token, it was also appreciated that ground forces themselves could no longer behave with impunity in the face of this new threat. Not only would they have to take more care with concealment, but they needed, along the forward edge of the battlefield, improved anti-aircraft defences which would knock out unwary helicopters. For these, it was noticed, might all too easily lose their way and fall foul of ambushes at very short range.

With Chieftain's imminent arrival in service in the mid-1960s, and the knowledge that it possessed full facilities for deep wading through the fitting of a schnorkel tube, the R.A.C. Centre, together with F.V.R.D.E. and other interested organizations, began a renewed study of the means to increase mobility and, most crucial aspect of all, how to cross water-obstacles without a hold-up in movement. All manner of investigations were carried out in England and in Germany into ways and means of entering and crossing a river, as well as getting out at the other side – the latter manoeuvre usually posing the greatest difficulty. From the R.A.C. Centre's point of view, the chief difficulty lay in providing adequate training. The bridging of the narrower obstacles by the use of assault bridges launched from armoured vehicles posed few problems, and the matter of teaching crews to drive swimming vehicles, which were kept afloat by the aid of a screen, was relatively easy. But to give crews the necessary confidence to drive underwater in a schnorkelling tank demanded much time and considerable expense, because of the need to provide special training facilities, particularly those associated with underwater escape, in the manner of submariners. Gradually, it began to appear that, despite the almost universal provision of wading facilities for the new range of fighting vehicles, the art would still require specialist attention to overcome all the difficulties presented. Progress was made through a gradual approach to the subject. ,

The introduction into service in 1966 of the Alvis Stalwart High Mobility Load Carrier owed much to the initiative of R.T.R. officers, and was a step forward in mobility by giving the Army a wheeled vehicle which, by the employment of its hydro-jet propulsion, could perform to a very high standard in water as well as on land. Cooper had originally persuaded the D.R.A.C. (R. B. B. B. Cook) that there was a need of such a vehicle, but tracked, and based on the FV 400 series. This was abandoned, but the idea was taken up by Alvis as a private venture, based upon the wheeled FV 600 series (Saladin and Saracen, etc.). W. D. P. Sullivan (R.T.R., retired and on behalf of Alvis) then sold the idea in 1961 to the D.R.A.C. (G. C. Hopkinson) who arranged an unofficial trial of a prototype at the E.T.W. When this convincingly demonstrated the vehicle's potential, Hopkinson got Sullivan to write the Military Specification (!) and, in conjunction with D.G.F.V.E. (H. M. Liardet), had F.V.R.D.E. undertake the necessary final trials and modifications.

A position had been reached during Holden's time as D.R.A.C., in which sufficient new equipment became available to carry out extensive trials into new dimensions of land warfare. In the manner in which the Vickers Medium tank of the early 1920s had opened the way to a practical examination of deep strategic penetration by fast moving armoured forces, the appearance of helicopters and amphibious vehicles in larger numbers lent impetus to the demand for mobility trials in the 1960s. These were initiated or encouraged by Holden, and by his successor (Major-General G. T. Armitage, late Royals), and gradually converted to a practice which went some way to realize the mobility dreams of the early pioneers. At the same time, devices were appearing which would make possible non-stop combat by day and night. Chieftain had been fitted with a built-in searchlight equipped for white light or infra-red light. Numerous active, infra-red sources of illumination became the vogue in the late 1950s, after it became known that the Russians were equipping their vehicles in this way. But infra-red was soon regarded as a most inadequate way of seeing in the dark, besides being easily obscured by dust and smoke and too readily detectable by the enemy. Therefore it was a relief when, in the 1960s, far more efficient and, above all, 'passive', secure night vision aids began to appear, in the form of image intensifiers and low light television cameras, which enabled the observer to see without being seen; and Doppler radars such as ZB 298 to help detect moving objects in the dark or in poor visibility. It was soon realized at H.Q. D.R.A.C. and in the R.A.C. Centre (where Brigadier H. B. C. Watkins took over in 1967), as well as in the Ministry of Defence departments and branches, that there was a danger of overloading the tanks and their crews with too many gadgets. A three-man crew in a vehicle such as a C.V.R. might be asked to fight for twenty-four hours or more at a stretch – conditions that might be too much even for a four-man crew. Certainly, nobody understood what this might imply when suggestions were made to reduce crews to two.

In 1966, an experiment was undertaken by the E.T.W., R.A.C. Centre (Lieutenant-Colonel D. Hawkins, 15th/19th Hussars) to look into the problems arising out of a two-man crew, totally incarcerated in a tank for a period of 72 hours, and carrying out all the battlefield tasks which might be expected of them in action. A capsule representing a turret was mounted on an FV 431 chassis, and selected men were locked in it for the prescribed period. The trial was under the control of Major K. C. Dudley, and was conducted with Army Personnel Research Establishment, with Major J. E. Parker acting as Directing Staff officer. Dudley's recollections of this trial are mainly concerned with the amusing incidents, such as the civilian scientist who took part, but found it difficult to relax sufficiently to use the toilet tube in the company of the other crew member (Dudley); and of the loudspeaker mounted on the outside of the vehicle, through which the crew's remarks could be carried to the outside world. Dudley relishes the memory of curious day-trippers on Bovington Heath walking up to inspect an apparently unattended A.F.V. to be greeted by a deep voice inviting them to 'Take me to your leader', and of an unappreciative W.R.A.C. N.C.O. when she heard loud references to herself from the passing capsule. From this trial, a great deal of useful information was gleaned. Twenty years after the Second World War, it provided a reminder that there are limitations to the privations a man can endure while locked away for long periods in a steel box – a lesson the Israelis and Arabs were to re-learn when they used night-fighting aids for the first time on a large scale in action in 1973, and found it almost impossible to sustain operations round the clock.

To Dudley must go the credit for a number of inventions which have benefitted the R.A.C. It was he who devised a way of remotely controlling a Chieftain at the end of a cable to assist in deep wading experiments. As an electronics expert, and Project Leader, Dudley also updated the harness for Larkspur communications equipment to get it near the Clansman facilities (the next generation of communications equipment for the 1970s) and at the same time redesigned the proposed headsets and microphone boom arms attached to the Clansman helmet. With W.O. II D. Hunt (17th/21st Lancers), and financial support from a special £25,000 vote, he developed the harness which, in due course, was to be found in Scorpion (the 76mm. gun version of C.V.R.(T.)) and some of the later Chieftains, including those sold to Iran.

With all kinds of night-fighting equipment becoming available at about the same time, the need to evaluate it and decide upon the most desirable types for various tasks became urgent in the later 1960s. For this reason D.O.A.E. was asked to look into this complex problem. Almost as a matter of course, it is presumed, Cooper was put in charge of the project (Exercise 'Firefly') to examine through a series of trials the advantages and disadvantages of ZB 298 radar, the Isocon television camera, image intensifiers of all sorts, thermal imaging equipment, infra-red and white light illuminators with which, then, or one day, units of the Army and, most of all A.F.V.s, would be equipped. Naturally, too, there was a tactical aspect related to this, and in the course of these trials the counter-measures to various forms of night vision were considered and explored. 'The whole investigation was very extensive in its coverage,' recalls Cooper. 'The directing staff at D.O.A.E., I'm sure, had no idea of the diversity of information we sought. There again, an illustration of what the individual planner can do without the interference of the members of any committee!'

The many committees which characterized the system of weapon procurement in the 1960s and 1970s certainly contained their full quota of R.T.R. officers who had passed through the hands of the previous generation, who had commanded and staffed the S.T.T. and technical branches. The contributions of those such as W. A. H. Fairbairn, D. S. Squirrel, S. J. Beardsworth, A. R. Bissett, P. F. Davis, L. C. Douglass, J. G. Hind, D. R. Ivy, I. J. C. Laver, F. A. L. Samuels, D. R. Walters and W. F. Woodhouse are not to be overlooked when assessing the R.T.R.'s major contribution to A.F.V. technology through investigation, interpretation, experiment and teaching.

The proving-ground for much that had been discovered and explored in the 1960s would be on the battlefields of the Far East, in the Near East (when Israeli fought Arab) and in the urban and rural districts of Northern Ireland. Yet, so fickle was opinion with regard to the tank, and so complete the Israeli tank victory in the Six Day War of 1967, won by guns of British design and using British gunnery techniques, that the backlash of 1973 went unchallenged for a time. It is a strange comment on current reporting that because of the heavy tank losses suffered by both sides in the Yom Kippur War of 1973, responsible journals concluded that the tank's day was over. The fact that numbers of tanks had still been fighting when the war ended and that the Israelis were on top because they had won the attritional battle through a fine display of massed-tank killing with guns, received less publicity than the undeniable fact that, for the first time, A.T.G.W.s had been used in quantity and had, apparently, scored many kills. The uninformed apart, it took time to dispel this notion from the minds of intelligent people.

Yet, by an irony, of historic importance, there existed, before the Yom Kippur War, a composite material which would ensure the tank's continued existence on the battlefield, even if all other technical and tactical innovations should fail. For two decades, at F.V.R.D.E. (renamed Military Vehicles Engineering Establishment (M.V.E.E.) in 1970), Dr. Harvey had been carrying out pure research into the properties of armour, carefully measuring and analyzing the effects of all kinds of attack by kinetic and chemical energy projectiles on a wide variety of substances. From his observations in the 1960s, stemmed proposals for new kinds of protection, based on the lamination of such differing materials as steel, ceramics and plastics, which, in combination, would raise resistance to the known methods of attack without significantly increasing bulk and weight. In producing, what was announced in 1976 as Chobham Armour, Harvey did for protection what Permutter had done for attack – and extended the life of tanks for at least another generation.

But the situations in which units of the Regiment became involved from the latter 1950s until 1975 were rarely those in which high-velocity guns and heavy protection were paramount. Carver's prophecy proved valid for the British Army. This era, so far as they were concerned, was one in which under-ground subversion was occasionally enlivened by skirmishing, as the shrinking perimeter of the Empire drew closer to Home.

CHAPTER X

The
Reduction of the Outposts
1957-1967

After the Suez débâcle, and in accordance with the expressed willingness of the British Government of Mr. Harold Macmillan to stage a progressive liquidation of its colonial possessions and responsibilities, it was the rôle of the Services to secure time for a tidy and, if possible, peaceful transfer of power to the nations they were leaving behind – some of which, in 1957, were innocent of adequate government machinery, let alone armed forces of their own. Indigenous local forces, where they existed, had, more often than not, to be expanded; where none existed they had to be created. Unhappily, the mere promise of British withdrawal frequently stimulated hostile elements to make take-over attempts against a background of economic frugality. Yet these conditions were of second nature to British soldiers whose involvement in small colonial-style forces was steeped in tradition. 'Bushwhacking', as it was called, gave officers and men the opportunity to experience operational conditions in exciting countries, where their outlook would be broadened in a way that service in Europe could rarely satisfy. Its timing had merely to be arranged so as not to blight career prospects, and it was R.T.R. policy to encourage its members to apply for this kind of adventure.

In Malaya, when the Emergency was at its height, an armoured squadron was formed by General Sir Gerald Templer, the High Commissioner, officered entirely by whites (mostly from the R.A.C.), in its initial stages, and with a high percentage of British N.C.O.s, while the indigenous soldiers were under training. The first R.T.R. officer to join was Lieutenant A. E. R. Gauntlet, in 1955, but the number was increased as additional squadrons were formed, bringing the total to three by 1958, within what was called the 1st Federation Armoured Car Regiment, under Lieutenant-Colonel K. F. Robinson, 16th/5th Lancers. By then, Malaya had achieved independence, the Emergency was in its closing stages, and the British officers and N.C.O.s in the squadrons were mainly employed as instructors, allowing many more Malays to occupy posts of responsibility until the day came when they would assume complete charge. In 1959, there were five R.T.R. officers and two warrant officers in the regiment, which was split, one squadron operating against the remaining Communist terrorists in Kedah, the rest performing ceremonial duties in Kuala Lumpur. Captain W. H. Glover was in Kedah, employed on road patrols, food-denial patrols, enforcing the curfew and, not infrequently, forcing his way on foot through the jungle. He summed-up the experience when writing: 'the rates of pay are very good when married, but not so hot for the bachelors. For the gay sporting fraternity, Kuala Lumpur has almost everything to offer; for the bankrupt and less frivolous, Kedah is ideal. Whether three years out here is good for the career is a moot point, but in my own case the prospect of another three years of regular visits to the Soltau training area and freezing in a tank park 'somewhere in North Germany' far outweighed any rational career planning.'

The motivation of adventure allied to receiving higher pay somewhere other than in Germany, prompted many officers to apply for training as pilots attached to the Army Air Corps. At the same time as Glover was patrolling on the ground in Kedah, Captain D. C. Crouch, also in Malaya, was flying an Auster, hunting for terrorist camps, guiding bombers to the target, dropping messages and stores, and incidentally, surviving a crash-landing when his engine failed on take-off.

Captain G. A. Shepherd joined the Trucial Oman Scouts in 1957 because he was 'tired of inter-continental missiles and screws retaining intermediate firing needle withdrawal lever'. He discovered, as did Major A. Laing who commanded H.Q. Squadron, that the Scouts had been sadly neglected by the R.T.R., which is strange, because serving in them presented the young officer or N.C.O. with an unrivalled opportunity to enjoy the sort of soldiering beloved by Kipling and John Masters. Mounted in Landrovers and armed with infantry weapons, in squadrons consisting of two British officers, perhaps one Arab officer and 120 Arab soldiers, Shepherd found himself patrolling in the desert and deep into the mountains. Shortly before his arrival, there had been two small wars, one at Buraimi Oasis against Saudi Arabian forces, and the other against the Imam at Firq and Nizwa. In 1957, one squadron covered 4,000 miles in one month while on active service in a campaign undertaken exclusively by the Scouts. From this moment onward, with adventure promised, R.T.R. involvement with the Scouts and throughout the Gulf States would steadily increase.

Bushwhacking of a very different kind was that found by Major R. G. Lawson in the Congo, as a result of his secondment to the Royal Nigerian Army in 1962. He had not been there very long when, as a member of the staff of 3rd Nigerian

Brigade, he was sent to Kasai Province in the Congo, as part of the United Nations forces which were attempting to restore order in what had been Belgian colonial territory. After the precipitate Belgian secession from power in 1960, the Congo had relapsed into anarchy, its people subject to the depredations of undisciplined armed bands belonging to warring factions, while the remaining foreigners, notably the missionaries, remained, in circumstances of the greatest peril. It was while attempting to bring help to some missionaries that Lawson set out to land, unarmed, among the excited and dangerous populace at Sentery Here he found the sole survivor of a group of 23 missionaries, the remainder having been massacred by Congolese soldiers, and by skilful negotiation, he managed to save this man.

Lawson's commander, Brigadier J. A. Mackenzie, described him thus: 'with the nervous energy of two men . . . At times the operations room was reminiscent of some Wild West scene with Dick Lawson handling a variety of weapons and shot-guns taken off drunken soldiers of the A.N.C. [Armie Nationale Congolaise] and Gendarmerie'. Four days after the Sentery rescue he was off again to Mbulula, in the company of an equally brave Nigerian officer named Major Conrad Nwawo, to save more missionaries. By now, his fame had been spread abroad over the radio, and he was labelled by some among the Congolese as a sort of Public Enemy No. 1. Having made contact with the priests, he was suddenly set upon by suspicious and hate-ridden Katanganese soldiers, who accused him of being a spy, and beat him up severely while Nwawo was led away to a hill of execution. By somehow steering his captors towards a bungalow where some Congolese officers were standing. Lawson, in a long parley, managed to arrange for the missionaries to be evacuated, and for his companion to be spared. Even now his adventures were not over, for the car supplied for his return broke down, and he had to complete the journey on foot – a march fraught with all kinds of perils, through country which was hostile in almost every respect. To Nwawo, in recognition of his courage, there was the award of the M.C. and for Lawson the D.S.O., which made him the only R.T.R. officer to receive this decoration in times of so-called peace. Later, he was to write a successful book describing his adventures, and in it he went to the heart of the reason for bushwhacking: 'I was trying to prove to myself that it was necessary to do something that all my previous military training had taught me to be wrong, that was to do something against the trend of my instructions . . . If it did not succeed I would be in trouble; if we pulled it off I would still be given an admonishment but the work would have been done. Back in the

Regular Army in England I had never had to take such a course of action, but in the Congo things were different. Quick decisions in the bush by young officers could sometimes achieve what eluded the best intentions further back in the chain of command.'

Extremities such as Lawson had endured were unknown to the men of 2nd R.T.R. (Lieutenant-Colonel P. R. C. Hobart) during their stay in Libya between September 1959 and September 1962, and yet, for them too, there was a challenge, rare in the experience of armoured regiments. To begin with, they were rapidly converted from an armoured regiment equipped with Centurions, to an armoured car regiment with Saladins, Ferrets and Saracens when they were moved via Tidworth from B.A.O.R. to Tripolitania, with a squadron in Benghazi. Nor were they allowed much time to make so fundamental a conversion. Individual training on the brand-new vehicles had to wait until they arrived at Homs, although instructors had been previously trained in the U.K. during the unit's final months in Germany. Hobart says there were no serious problems and, indeed, within the shortest possible time, they found themselves out in the desert, coping with an unfamiliar method of operation in a totally different environment from that to which they were accustomed. Moreover, their rôle was quite different from that of the 6th, as a tank regiment, from whom they took over, reflecting, as it did, the recognition that the days when the British could use tanks without constraint in North Africa were over. During the period of protracted negotiations leading up to the eventual denial of rights for British forces to remain in Libya, the only operational rôle open to the Army was that of Internal Security, to which wheeled vehicles were far better suited than tracked vehicles.

The vast expanses of desert provided an almost unlimited training area for other units sent from Europe for short periods. Within a matter of weeks, and before they had acquired complete knowledge of desert navigation and survival techniques, the 2nd were 'out in the blue' hunting for troops of the 16th Parachute Brigade, who had been dropped as part of a mock invasion, after a flight from Cyprus. Now a dividend was paid by bushwhacking: the officer in charge of navigation was Shepherd, who had learned the art while serving in Trucial Oman. Nevertheless, it was, perhaps, fortunate that the 2nd were not immediately called upon to perform a serious operational rôle while undergoing conversion. As trail-blazers of the now accepted principle that units of the R.A.C. should be rotated from one rôle to another, it was for the 2nd to learn the lessons which future units would apply, and for the policy-makers to conclude that a period of conversion training in the United Kingdom, before assuming fresh duties in an operational theatre, was desirable. In due course, the Roulement (rotation) System would be adopted. In the meantime, the 2nd made the very best of a bad job, and it is noteworthy that, in April and May 1960, Cyclops (Major F. H. Harris) with 50 vehicles and 120 men, could motor 1,700 miles, 80 per cent over rough track or virgin desert, on a journey which took it to the borders of French West Africa in the south, and arrive home intact. Proudly, Shepherd could claim that the 2nd were the successors to the Long Range Desert Group, and could point to the fact that, even if the Saracen A.P.C.s had overheated badly and the Bedford 3-ton trucks had been a constant source of trouble, the men, and the Saladins and Ferrets had performed magnificently: with no sickness among the former and no breakdowns among the latter.

One of the joys of serving on wheels was the freedom of action accorded to squadron and troop commanders, which enabled them to operate independently at a distance from higher control. Individual initiative was thus developed in a way that was virtually impossible while serving as part of a tank establishment in Germany. This was enhanced for the 2nd (commanded by Lieutenant-Colonel A. R. E. Davis since August 1960) when, in October 1961, they were brought onto the new Armoured Reconnaissance Regiment establishment, which meant making Badger (Major R. B. C. Plowden) into an Air-portable Squadron equipped solely with Ferrets, leaving the rest of the unit much as it was. At the same time, as part of the gradual rundown of forces in Libya, R.H.Q. and one squadron were moved to Benghazi (only a few miles from Beda Fomm where the 2nd had fought so well in 1941) leaving only Cyclops (Brevet Lieutenant-Colonel J. G. R. Allen) in Tripoli, while the Libyan Army moved into the barracks at Homs. But already, Cyclops was reserved for an entirely new departure for the R.T.R., that of becoming the R.A.C.'s first Guided Weapon Squadron armed with Malkara. This was a great challenge for the R.T.R. as a whole. Men of unusual talents were required, who would volunteer for parachuting, pass the extremely stiff course of training demanded, and possess the particular qualifications demanded of guided-weapons operators. It was too much to expect that all the members of one squadron would fit this bill, and therefore it was from the rest of the 2nd, as well as from the entire R.T.R., that the requisite number of officers and men was drawn. By the summer of 1962, it was done, and for the next three years, until an R.A.C. Parachute Squadron was formed, the Parachute Squadron was an R.T.R. preserve.

The most hectic period of active service during this period was, however, reserved for the 4th. Since November 1960, the unit had been split into four segments, with R.H.Q. (Lieutenant-Colonel T. S. Craig) in Hohne; A Squadron in Lemgo and B in Celle, manning Saracen A.P.C.s for, respectively, 20th and 7th Armoured Brigades; and C with Centurions in Berlin where, in the summer of 1961, when under the command of Major G. R. Merrell, it was to witness the erection of the Berlin Wall by the East Germans, and experience the associated tensions stemming from that significant event in the Cold War. In April 1963, the 4th began to convert to the Armoured Car rôle in readiness for a year's service in Aden and the Persian Gulf, having in the meantime taught the infantry it had previously carried (1st Battalion Royal Northumberland Fusiliers and 1st Battalion Royal Irish Fusiliers) how to drive (without a single accident) and maintain Saracens, and handed over the Berlin task to a reactivated Independent Squadron R.T.R. under the command of Major R. G. Lawson.

The period of the 4th's conversion to armoured cars was intended by its new C.O., Lieutenant-Colonel H. B. C. Watkins, to serve more purposes than one. To begin with, the choice of Edinburgh as its staging-post in the United Kingdom was meant to cement the unit's association with the country whence it drew its recruits, as well as with its affiliated Lowland Yeomanry (Lieutenant-Colonel A. R. Ewing). This was to be an operation in vigorous public relations – or 'Keeping the Army in the Public Eye' (K.A.P.E.) as it was called – as well as of preparation for a testing rôle in action. Besides mounting guard at Edinburgh Castle, and indulging in a social programme, the 4th had to perform an administrative and psychological adjustment. From being a unit which had been comfortably established with its 350 families in Germany for a period of nine years, it now had to face up to a year's hardship and conjugal separation. Homes had to be found for those families that had none to go to, and a pact was made with every married man that he would be allowed one leave at home in the coming year, providing he could raise the price of the return fare. Separation from barracks and families also began in Scotland, when a five weeks' period of intensive training took troops far afield. This training placed emphasis on radio and gunnery, since drivers who were mostly accustomed to Saracens had little difficulty changing over to Saladins and Ferrets. Everyone was made to learn Morse to assist in working radio over the huge distances and difficult conditions of the Middle East, and how to shoot at targets on the hillsides of the Warcop ranges, in realistic preparation for the mountains of the Radfan. But the administrative and welfare problems consequent on, in some cases, more than a year's separation from families, was a delicate one, directly related to morale, as well as to the need of retaining men in the Service, at a time when recruiting was crucial to the new Regular Army's survival. Watkins could, with some justification, point out that the final outcome would fully justify his approach to the problem, but it cannot be ignored that there were deep feelings of concern among a high proportion of married men within the 4th, and that these were the closing days of an epoch in which this sort of exercise, in peace-time, could be permitted.

By the end of August, the redeployment to the new theatre was complete. C Squadron (Major T. S. M. Welch) arrived in Sharjah in the Persian Gulf, where it was responsible for supporting the Trucial Oman Scouts in their operational rôle and, should trouble develop, for providing the screen force in defence of the oil-rich state of Kuwait. Before being fit for action, much training had to be done in the desert during a hot, humid time of the year. Moreover, the vehicles, only 8 per cent of which were operationally fit on take-over, demanded an immense amount of work. The men's health remained good, however, and Watkins remarks that he probably devoted more time to the vehicle maintenance problem than to any other. He was proud, a year later, to hand over vehicles which were 100 per cent fit, after a year's hard operations. It justified his R.T.R. creed, as expressed to a senior officer, who had suggested that the scenery might be improved by a few more soldiers in starched K.D., that 'the first rule of the Royal Tank Regiment is 'thou shalt be on the road'.

No sooner had the remainder of the 4th begun to arrive in Aden, which was now the main British strategic base in the Middle East, and the H.Q. of Middle East Command, than it was greeted by a call to immediate action, with no time allowed for acclimatization to the intense heat or the demands of the country and the enemy. For generations, the hinterland of the Aden Protectorate had been the happy hunting-ground of tribal raiding parties, but raiding, since the announcement of British proposals in the mid 1950s, had been superseded by a deadlier kind of aggression. The Imam of Yemen, prompted by the Egyptians, who were intent upon hastening British departure from all the Arab lands, and supplied with arms from Communist and Egyptian sources, was embarked upon what amounted to war over a political disagreement. At the beginning of 1963, the separate state of Aden was included, despite strong local political objections, within the newly-created Federation of South

Arabia. The British Governor became High Commissioner, while the British forces were charged with responsibility for security to allow the new State to find its feet. The Aden Protectorate Levies were turned into an army, called the Federal Regular Army (F.R.A.), with Brigadier J. D. Lunt (late 16th/5th Lancers) as its commander, and in which Major G. A. Shepherd, now thoroughly bitten by the 'desert bug', was a squadron commander in the F.R.A. Armoured Car Squadron. Raiding from the Yemen was on the increase when the 4th arrived, and A Squadron (Major G. Forty) was immediately sent up-country to place a troop under command of each F.R.A. battalion and join J (Sidi Rezegh) Battery of 3 R.H.A. in dealing with some well-armed and persistent dissidents who infiltrated among the steep and intricately terraced peaks which dominated the wadis below. There, lurked a wily foe, and to those in the 4th with a sense of history, the task of dealing with him was reminiscent of the days, prior to 1939, when the Armoured Car and Light Tank Companies of the R.T.C. had operated so efficiently along the North-West Frontier of India.

Within 10 days of arrival, 2 Troop (Lieutenant I. J. B. Galloway) at Beihan, were invited to silence a heavy machine-gun firing from the Yemen which had defied the efforts of the Gunners with their 105mm. pieces. Instructed by Forty, who could draw on his experience in Korea, Galloway laid his Saladin's 76mm. gun on fixed lines and opened the 4th's account, on the night of 6 September, with five rounds of H.E.S.H. which scored four hits on two positions. 'It is probably quite unnecessary to say that morale is sky-high', recorded the 4th's chronicler in *The Tank*. 'For the first time in years we have a recognisable military aim!' Within a few weeks it was borne upon the F.R.A. and H.Q. Middle East Land Forces (quite apart from the dissidents) that, to quote Watkins, 'There was a new air of professionalism as far as the Armoured Car Regiment was concerned and that, as a result, very much better results were coming from local operations.' From start to finish, in fact, the 4th in the Federation of South Arabia were engaged in some sort or another of active service with the frequency of battle rising steadily throughout the latter part of 1963 and early 1964, in a mosaic of patrols, ambushes, convoy escorts and garrison duties in 'Beau Geste' desert forts. It was a troop leader's paradise, with squadron headquarters often far remote, and a visit by the C.O. dependent upon a long, well forewarned flight in a Beaver or Auster light aircraft.

Fortunate it was that the 4th's introduction to battle was progressive. The action by Lieutenant B. J. N. Coombes' troop and Sergeant A. B. Wheatley's 5 troop at Thumeir in October was one rung higher up the ladder of escalating violence. In company with infantry, they fought against well-armed tribesmen from the Yemen and repelled them after a brisk action in which Wheatley, with a snap-shot from the 76mm. gun, 'vaporized' one dissident who had had the impudence to fire at him from behind a rock. These minor aggressions from the Yemen amounted, of course, to little more than a prelude, and it was the doubtful privilege of the 4th's Captain J. A. Wright to be present when the enemy proclaimed his long-term intentions in a most dramatic way. On 10 December, he was at Aden's civil airport, performing the duties of acting A.D.C. to the High Commissioner, Sir Kennedy Trevaskis, when a bomb was thrown, killing one civilian officer and wounding 55 other people, including Wright, who was hit in the leg and had his best suit ruined. A State of Emergency was called by the Federal Government, and the British Government announced its support in aid of the suppression of dissidents in the Radfan, that crenellated and twisting area of sharp, pointed hills which lay in enemy hands, sixty miles to the north of Aden, east of Thumeir and the Dhala road.

The F.R.A.'s Operation 'Nutcracker' began on 4 January, and involved three out of its four operational battalions, with support from 3rd R.H.A., a troop of Centurions from 16th/5th Lancers, and from the 4th. Every unit concerned was stretched beyond its means, because Aden, itself, had to be secured as well as the outlying districts of the Federation. B Squadron (Major A. A. Mathieson) had relieved A up-country just before Christmas, but parts of A were sent out again to Ataq, shortly before 'Nutcracker' was due to begin. This was still not enough. 'My first task', writes Watkins, 'was to create a new squadron. This enabled us to support the operations based on Thumeir whilst doing our stuff in the rest of the Federation and maintaining an I.S. Reserve in Little Aden. Happily I remembered that D Squadron was a great feature of 7th R.T.R. I played on this and formed a D Squadron. Although it was only a very scratch affair with a tiny headquarters under Alistair Mathieson, I have never had a better sub-unit. Troops from the various squadrons rotated through it.' Most of these, it must be added, came from B and C Squadrons.

The campaign to suppress the Radfan followed roughly the same course throughout. Steady pressure from west to east was applied by the main force from the expanded base camp at Thumeir into the wadis and along the ridges, while the remainder of the Federation was kept in check by light elements. Watkins, with three, under-strength squadrons at his disposal in January, deployed A at Ataq on vigorous patrol duty, in order to relieve an entire F.R.A. battalion (less one platoon) from the Beihan area, so that it controlled two complete Sheikdoms. The remainder of B kept watch at Beihan and along the Yemen border, while D supported the infantry in the Radfan and H.Q. stood guard over Little Aden.

The attack on the Radfan had its bad moments. For a start, the enemy were almost as well armed as the F.R.A. and the helicopters which were intended to drop cut-off parties in the enemy rear were withdrawn because of the heavy and, at times, accurate fire directed against them. The key to success, as is usual in mountain warfare, was picquetting of the heights. Throughout the month, the hilltops were taken and the Wadis Rabwa and Taym dominated at the same time as the fertile Danaba Basin was overrun. Mines were a constant source of trouble, especially since the Ferret was anything but proof against the larger ones. The enemy was also very determined, to the extent that it came as quite a surprise, for example, when 2nd Lieutenant H. B. Puren actually managed to capture three of them who had set an ambush for him in the vicinity of Dhala. Nevertheless, Lunt conducted 'Nutcracker' with cool deliberation and at a low price in casualties, suffering only five killed and twelve wounded for substantial, if temporary, gains. But the strain upon his resources, deprived as he was of sufficient help from British troops, began to tell. In February, he felt no longer able to defend the vast and complex territory he had seized and a withdrawal down the wadis was ordered. It was in this operation that Sergeant T. E. F. Silverson, commanding his troop of Ferrets as if they were light tanks, gained an enviable reputation for courage and tactical insight. On one occasion, it was largely due to his skill, under very heavy fire, that an F.R.A. company, caught in an exposed situation, was saved when he placed his troop between the enemy and the company it was supporting, to enable it to withdraw to safety without serious loss. Silverson and his cars coolly kept the enemy at bay by the judicious use of their Browning machine-guns and were the last to leave.

The withdrawal of the F.R.A. from the Radfan was portrayed in propaganda by the dissidents and their Egyptian promoters as a crushing defeat for the British. As a result, the depredations multiplied until, in accordance with its Treaty rights, the Federation Government, informed that Egyptian troops were in the Radfan, applied to Britain for large-scale support. This request arrived at the very moment when the Army was stretched to the limit. For, while the operations in the Radfan had been going on, the extent of Britain's commitments had been widely increased. To the deployment of forces in Eastern Malaysia, to counter the Indonesian aggressions which had commenced in 1962, had been added, in January, the need to dispatch H.Q. 3rd Division (Major-General R. M. P. Carver) and a sizeable portion of the Strategic Reserve, to Cyprus. Carver's formation, which included three armoured car squadrons flown in by R.A.F. Transport Command, would, in March, become part of the United Nations Force whose rôle would be to maintain peace between the antagonistic Greek and Turkish communities. But that was not all. To strip the forces of their last reserves there came, early in January, urgent requests from the Kenya Government to put down a mutiny within its own army, and from the Government of Tanganyika came a similar call for help. Not until the 22nd S.A.S. had arrived from England in February and 45th Royal Marine Commando had returned from East Africa by the end of March, and 3rd Battalion The Parachute Regiment had flown down from Bahrein to join 1st Battalion East Anglian Regiment and 1st Battalion Kings Own Scottish Borderers, would a force of sufficient size be ready to supplement the F.R.A. Even then only an improvised Force Headquarters, commanded by Brigadier R. L. Hargroves, the Aden Garrison Commander, could be assembled. But its orders were firm – to end the opposition by the dissidents, and this Hargroves intended to do by methods similar to those applied by Lunt, except that this time better equipped and trained British troops were available, in addition to two battalions of the F.R.A.

Prior to the operation there was a programme of stock-piling of the Thumeir base by convoys from little Aden, escorted by Ferrets of C Squadron which arrived from Sharjah under its acting Squadron Commander, Captain D. D. A. Linaker, after its relief by A Squadron on 11 April. To Linaker, the order of priorities was at once made apparent: of the 16 Ferrets available, 10 were given to the Adjutant (Captain N. H. Cocking), for use on the Queen's Birthday Parade on 21 April, and the rest were his. There were just enough. In 15 days he ran 9 convoys over the 140-mile route, 80 miles of which was unmetalled rough ground. 'The drill we used', recalls Linaker, 'was to have 2nd Lieutenant S. Hunter-Cox out about a mile in front making sure that the route was free from mines and was passable. I led the main body with two cars and Sergeant Ford brought up the rear with two . . . When breakdowns occurred we would leave a Ferret with them to escort them back to the convoy after repair . . . one day we had so many stragglers that I was the only Ferret left for the last five miles into Thumeir.'

In Thumeir itself (where Major R. G. Morris was Base Commander), Mathieson had command of D Squadron with its three troops of Saladins and Ferrets, plus J Battery 3 R.H.A. and a platoon of the East Anglians with a mortar section. As the main force of Commandos and Parachutists penetrated into the hills and seized the peaks, it was D Squadron's task to create a diversion by establishing a fire-base in the Wadi Rabwa. But mines and road-blocks were encountered and had to be cleared under fire from the enemy on the heights, an operation which cost six wounded, including one of Mathieson's officers. It was well into the afternoon before the head of the wadi was reached. Here, the Saladins held the ring, pumping 76mm. H.E.S.H. and Browning bullets at the enemy positions, while the gunners and infantry constructed sangars from which to continue the battle throughout the following three days and two nights. It was a most uncomfortable, and yet exciting, time for everybody. Quite apart from the steady drizzle of enemy fire, there was always the danger of a sudden rainstorm falling in the hills to cause a flash-flood in the wadi which could sweep all before it and, perhaps, bog the vehicles irretrievably. Every day Mathieson himself chose to run the gauntlet of enemy fire and mines to bring up supplies, including the two gallons of water per day per man prescribed by the medical authorities, and the considerable quantities of ammunition which the R.T.R. gunners in the Saladins managed to use. Nearly 300 rounds of 76mm. and 60,000 rounds of Browning were fired, in addition to many shells from the Royal Artillery. And when the time came to withdraw, this most difficult operation was performed, bound by bound, without loss.

This was only the first phase. No sooner had Hargroves handed over operations, early on 11 May, to the newly-arrived H.Q. 39th Infantry Brigade (Brigadier C. H. Blacker, late 5th Inniskilling Dragoon Guards), than Watkins received orders to make a one-day armoured demonstration up the Wadi Misrah, due east of Thumeir, to destroy some sangars which were under construction and eliminate a threat to the base prior to more intensive operations elsewhere. He had disbanded D Squadron, so now the task was given to C, still under Linaker, who had two troops each of Saladins and 2 Ferrets, plus a Ferret troop from the F.R.A. Armoured Squadron and a troop of 3 Centurions from 16th/5th Lancers under command, with J Battery 3 R.H.A. in support. The demonstration was to take place on the 18th, and was expected to encounter strong opposition. Despite this, the Political Officer refused Proscription. This meant that very strict rules were applied to opening fire. The use of main armament was forbidden unless soldiers' lives were imperilled; and if women and children in houses were put at risk, no firing was allowed at all.

Before reaching the start-line, one of the Centurions broke down, as did Linaker's Saladin – which he described as 'an evil vehicle christened by the lads "Dysentery" '. The going was appalling. Large sharp rocks sometimes jammed the tanks' tracks and ripped holes the size of a man's fist in the tyres of the armoured cars. But, covered by the two Centurions' 105mm. guns, which took on each sangar in turn, the wheeled vehicles, led by the F.R.A. Ferrets, made slow progress while Watkins flew overhead, piloted by Lieutenant E. J. P. Hardman in his Auster from the Recce Flight. Watkins observed women at the head of the valley in the area of the fort, so this prevented it from being engaged as had been hoped. At about the same time, the troop leader's tank shed both its tracks and, shortly after-wards, the F.R.A. Ferrets, coming under fire, stopped and had to be urged on by Linaker, who dismounted to speak forcibly to their commander. No sooner had the advance started again, covered by fire from the Saladins against the sangars, than Hardman reported heavy rain falling among the hills and, a little later, great quantities of water descending the slopes. With the full approval of Brigade Headquarters, which refused Linaker's suggestion to stay out at night protected by dismounted Brown-ings, a withdrawal was ordered and (as originally had been intended) had been completed by nightfall, the broken Centurion coming back under tow from an A.R.V., but keeping its gun constantly in action on the way.

It was most unfortunate that this retreat became the subject of derogatory remarks by one of the Political Officers, an ex-cavalry man who seems to have been disappointed and to have taken the old-fashioned view that the R.T.R. was incapable of operating armoured cars – an opinion which by no means represented that of more up-to-date cavalrymen on the spot, one of whom let it be known that the 4th was the best armoured car regiment Aden had ever seen.

The next major operation was to underline this good opinion, although it came about as the result of the successes already achieved in the north of the Radfan, which had forced the dissidents to move south into the region of the Wadi Naif and Wadi Nakhalain. On the 16th, Blacker had ordered Watkins to establish a force of armoured cars and infantry (B Company, 1st Battalion East Anglians) in the Wadi Nakhalain by last light on 24 May, and to carry out an armoured reconnaissance to the head of the wadi next day, as part of 39th Brigade's intention to bring concentric pressure to bear on the dissidents in the area which was not, however, proscribed. Watkins decided to command in person, calling his group 'Watforce' and taking under command, in addition to the infantry, B Squadron (back under Mathieson's command), with two Saladin troops and two light troops, each of 4 Ferrets. Reconnaissance and planning did not quite take the full eight days (16–24 May), because Watkins managed, on 21 May, to fit in at Aden the first Arras Dinner to commemorate the battle in which the 4th and 7th had distinguished themselves in 1940.

The 40-mile approach to the wadi was made in one bound from Aden on 24 May, and 'Watforce' reached its assembly area with little time to spare, having, on the way, dispersed an innocent camel-train whose panicky riders must have had a guilty conscience, but whose mounts were easier to round-up on foot than by hot pursuit in a Ferret. Next day, the advance up the rocky floor of the wadi began, but not until midday was there an exchange of fire. A Saladin driver, Trooper Hefferman, was wounded while supporting his Troop Commander, Lieutenant M. J. Rose, on a foot patrol, but he continued to drive throughout the day with a bullet lodged in his back. The battle now became general, with the enemy firing from several sangars and caves, and the Saladins lobbing back H.E.S.H., their tracers arching into the cave mouths, with devastating effect. Yet there were still a few brave souls left on the other side who continued to shoot, and the day ended on an indecisive note as B Squadron, lacking infantry support, was pulled back to a safer night location, and the Brigadier – sensitive to the political consequences – concluded that perhaps the enemy might think this was the result of his defensive efforts. So the dose was repeated next day, the 26th, at a smarter pace and without meeting opposition. This time, it was to the accompaniment of rocket strikes by Hunter fighters, and the advance was followed up on the 27th by further patrolling, without anything of significance being found. Then the rains fell again and withdrawal was ordered for political reasons since it was judged that the use of armoured cars was piling on too much pressure in the area!

In his summary of lessons drawn from this, one of the few actions (and certainly the last) in the period covered by this volume, in which a unit commander of the R.T.R. actually commanded his sub-units in direct action, Watkins emphasized the special problems associated with operating armour unsupported by infantry in mountainous terrain, and the need to make it clear that, when withdrawal took place for security reasons, the enemy must not be allowed to draw false conclusions. The reasons for withdrawal, he added, 'should be recognizable to the enemy'. This seems to have been clearly understood by Linaker a few days later on 3 June when, once more, he forayed with the East Anglians and a Saladin troop (2nd Lieutenant P. A. Nelson) into the Wadi Misra and had the satisfaction of seeing a round of 76mm. from the first shot fired by Trooper Walker, enter a cave mouth and blow away half the hillside. Driving ahead of the infantry and coming under fire he applied what he rated as a rough test of target location. 'After a few minutes intensive fire one would stop to see if the enemy had stopped. If they did one knew one had been in the right area.' Unfortunately, on this occasion the infantry were not prepared to come too far forward until 'an ugly looking fort at the junction of the wadis had been destroyed' – a task which was allocated to the R.A.F. next day and which they failed to accomplish because they had run out of rockets. 'As soon as the aircraft went away we were told, rather patronisingly, that 'we could have a try now'. Paul Nelson and Corporal Leslie took their Saladins forward. Ten minutes and 8 H.E.S.H. rounds later, there was just a pile of smoking rubble where the fort had been.'

Fighting would continue, but with diminishing intensity, in the weeks to come now that the Radfan, for the time being, was suppressed. The record of the weeks gone by and those to come appear among the brightest in terms of achievement of the R.T.R.'s post-1945 history, subsidiary as they were to the major assaults undertaken by the F.R.A., Royal Marines, the Parachute Regiment and the Infantry. Once again, the undeniable advantage of going to war behind armour was revealed. The only casualties from enemy action were two wounded, despite the thousands of shots (and one anti-tank missile) which had been aimed in their direction, a minute proportion of the total casualties suffered by the aggregate British and F.R.A. forces involved. Many were the acts of bravery; such as Corporal Levesconte entering a burning Saladin, removing all the ammunition and so averting a serious accident; Lieutenant J. G. Rawlins driving his Ferret forward under fire, to dismount and haul a wounded infantry officer on to the engine deck and bring him back to safety; 2nd Lieutenant Stuart-Cox bearing with fortitude the burns he received when he fell into a concealed pit of hot ashes at the time when C Squadron, alone, was patrolling and holding down the Danaba Basin; Corporal Britton, his Troop Sergeant away on a course, commanding a troop in the Danaba Basin after Stuart-Cox had been injured; and Hardman at Thumeir in acute agony after he had been struck in the face by a bird (an injury which cost him an eye), bringing his Auster in to land to save his own life and that of his passenger.

The final stages of the operation were also marked by the last appearance of an R.T.R. Territorial Army unit in action, when a party of 23 Territorial Army Emergency Reservists from 40th/41st R.T.R. (volunteers known as 'Ever Readies' who engaged under a special part-time scheme to serve at short notice within Regular units) arrived at Aden for training under the command of Lieutenant B. Perret. Some of their battle-hardened veterans found themselves in the convoy to Thumeir, and under fire, with Perret affirming that they were coolness itself – although the notes submitted by the party after they returned home confessed that, at the time, they did not realize that there had been any shooting! Sadly, this unit would soon disappear in the latest round of economies imposed as Britain's armed forces contracted in line with her diminishing commitments.

The 4th would begin to depart from the Middle East at the end of August to join in another confrontation in the Far East, but the R.T.R. presence and spirit would remain, its reputation further enhanced by Major D. C. Crouch when he was commanding 13 Flight Army Air Corps and leading 3 Scout helicopters carrying a party of 22nd S.A.S. at low level to a position in enemy territory. Rounding a corner in a wadi at low level, he flew into an ambush at close range and his Scout was hit. Quick evasive action brought him to cover where he landed, dropped his passengers and took-off again to take command of his other helicopters as they approached, directing them to a safer landing place than his own, while remaining under constant fire from the enemy. Again his helicopter was hit, but still he carried on until the drop was complete. Finally, shortly before dusk, he went in once more to pick up those among the S.A.S. who had already been wounded.

* * * * *

By comparison with the experiences of the 4th, those of Ajax, the 2nd (Major G. L. D. Duckworth) were extremely mild, though none the less exacting. When, in November 1964, this squadron, equipped with Ferrets and wearing the light-blue beret of the United Nations Forces in Cyprus (U.N.F.I.C.Y.P.), assumed the task of helping to keep the peace in that troubled island, opening fire was the last thing it wanted to do. The communal fighting of earlier that year had been superseded by an uneasy peace, which was maintained by diplomacy backed up by the presence of U.N.F.I.C.Y.P. forces whose members, even the lowliest of troopers, had need to be ambassadors. Demarcation lines, which had been negotiated previously, divided the Turkish and Greek communities, sometimes cutting through a village where the factions grimly declined to speak to each other.

Intensive patrolling along narrow roads, visiting once a week each of the 52 villages for which it was responsible, kept the squadron fully occupied, quite apart from escorting convoys and indulging in social activities and training. Frequently they were called out to investigate suspicious activities, but the measure of their success in a six-months' (unaccompanied by family) tour was the absence of outbreaks of violence. Indeed, Duckworth records examples of positive achievements in improving relationships between the two sides. At one Turkish village, where the telephone was out of action – allegedly its wire had been cut by the Greeks – an investigation showed that there was a technical fault, but that the Turks had refused to allow Greek engineers to enter and put it right. Prolonged discussions with both sides by Duckworth, over the traditional cups of coffee, at last resulted in engineers being permitted to enter the Turkish village (under escort) for the first time in 12 months, and the blown fuse was replaced in thirty seconds. After that, it was a relatively simple matter to restore to this village the postal service which had been discontinued for a long time. Duckworth commented on the go-between rôle that was needed, and on the results achieved by tact and firmness, plus a touch of humour: 'It was useless to order either side to do anything – we had to persuade them with logical argument and commonsense,' and went on to delineate the requirements of a United Nations' soldier: 'he must be well-disciplined and well turned-out; he must be well-briefed on the political as well as the military situation; he must have an understanding of what the United Nations is trying to do in that situation; he must get to know the people and study their problems; he must be sympathetic and unbiassed so that they will trust him . . . .' It was Ajax's happy and rewarding lot that it was not called upon to fight during its six-months' tour.

* * * * *

4th R.T.R. (Lieutenant-Colonel J. A. Cowgill) timed its transfer from one active service theatre to another with precision, leaving the Middle East when, for the time being, the pressure was slack, and arriving in the Far East early in September 1964, at the moment when operations there entered a new phase of intensity and where, as it happened, Lieutenant-General Sir Alan Jolly was Commander Land Forces Far East. For many years there had been the threat of trouble for Malaysia with the adjoining Communist-orientated state of Indonesia under Dr. Soekarno. Its most dangerous manifestations came to the surface on 8 December 1962, as the outcome of an uprising in Brunei, which had been suppressed by Malaysian and British troops, mainly battalions of the Gurkha Regiments. At the root of Confrontation, as the oncoming struggle came to be called, were Indonesian objections to the creation of a state of Malaysia which would include Malaya, Singapore and the states and erstwhile British colonies in North Borneo. The first attacks in Borneo by Indonesian partisans, aided to some extent by the local Clandestine Communist Organisation (C.C.O.), took place on 12 April 1963, some months before the Federation of Malaysia was proclaimed. Thereafter, the escalation of guerilla warfare was gradual, but purposeful as the Indonesians slowly constructed tenuous lines of communication through thick jungle and complex terrain to supply the bases they had established at various points on their side of the North Borneo frontier. On 3 May 1964, Soekarno announced his intention to crush Malaysia. From that moment, jungle fighting and small-scale, urban guerilla combat assumed a much more aggressive form. The 4th entered a campaign in which, initially, irregular Indonesian bands had infiltrated the country to ambush and destroy their enemies, but in which, recently, regular Indonesian soldiers had been committed in larger numbers. As counter-measures, small jungle bases had been established, supplied by helicopters, from which British and Malaysian forces moved against each Indonesian incursion, while scout car patrols kept the main roads and tracks free of enemy parties. Some of the fighting had been heavy but the British and Malaysian troops had prevailed in nearly all cases.

The 4th's arrival, however, practically coincided with the first Indonesian assault upon the mainland of Malaya, an ineffectual landing by a small party on Singapore Island on 17 August, followed, on 2 September, by a much larger invasion by 96 paratroops in the region of Malacca. The Queen's Royal Irish Hussars, whose rôle of Armoured Reconnaissance Regiment the 4th took over, had been called out to help round-up the Indonesians and so, as each R.T.R. squadron arrived by air, it was put on 'alert' as it took over its vehicles – Saladins and Ferrets which were handed over by the Q.R.I.H. in impeccable order, with the 4th's squadron signs already painted on them.

For the squadrons taking over the operational commitment at Kuching and the patrolling in Brunei, could be added the anti-invasion task allocated to the half-squadron in Singapore, and the remaining squadron based on Seremban in Malaya. The latter at once found themselves keeping watch over the seaboard and roads and partaking in the search for the survivors of the first, ill-starred Indonesian adventure. They had plenty of time to become accustomed to the terrain before the next landing, by 60 men on 29 October, which fared no better than the first. Between Malacca and Johore, a combined force under Brigadier P. A. L. Vaux (Commander Malaya Area) consisting of Malayan, Gurkha and Australian and New Zealand troops from 28th Commonwealth Brigade (with whom the 4th would work should the brigade be committed to a S.E.A.T.O. operational rôle in Thailand) and C Squadron, penned in and destroyed the invaders within 36 hours. But what good the 4th would have done had they actually met the enemy is problematical, because they had been forbidden to fire their main armament and, for a while, until proving its impracticability, allowed to fire only single shots from their machine-guns! This was so very different from the Radfan, and might have been still more frustrating had it not been that the families were beginning to arrive by air in dribs and drabs – to a schedule which was so mismanaged by the Staff in the United Kingdom that, as late as March 1965, some families, whose tempers rose high, had been separated for over 18 months.

The daily round in North Borneo did possess a certain amount of atmosphere which was reminiscent of Arabia. Here, squadrons (or half-squadrons) undertook a six-months' tour, with the troops holding small fortified posts and sometimes being allowed to fire their guns at caves in the hillsides. But, as the 4th's historian points out: 'Maintaining a presence in the rear areas and "Hearts and Minds" operations [such as had been in a low key in the Radfan] were very much one and the same thing, the main tasks being fire support and escorts – of the latter anything from the Duke of Edinburgh to C.S.E. Shows . . . a Company of the 1st/10th Gurkhas, however, relied on one of our [Saladin] troops for some months to give it cover when they moved south for border operations, as Indos could pick them off from the ridge. The troop would move up and put down prophylactic fire along the ridge line at absolute maximum elevation.'

Rarely was contact made, and the experience of Sergeant K. B. Brown, when patrolling at night, ahead of a convoy, in the vicinity of the 18th Mile Police Station, south of Kuching, was all too typical of the negative results experienced when dealing with guerillas who, unlike the Yemenis, did not stay to fight. When he found suspicious objects on the road within a mile or two of the Station, he was unable to report them because, as a result of static interference, the High Frequency C 13 radio sets were quite ineffectual after dark in the tropics; nor, a few minutes later, could he report the explosion which slightly damaged a bridge. As a result, the guerillas, who at that very moment were shooting policemen, women and children near the Station, managed to escape, because there was no way to swiftly summon a road-block and search parties. Two of the armoured cars, which did at last race to the scene, skidded off the road where an oil-slick had been laid for that very purpose.

Much time was spent on dismounted tasks, and Corporal L. Kew was among those who decided, to his apparent surprise, that foot patrols could be 'very interesting and often very amusing'. But he imparts a sense of uneasiness when he describes leading his men 'away into the "ulu". The footpath was well defined but, because of recent rain, very muddy, and a few minutes later we had lost the sound of traffic and could well have been 20 miles from the road . . .': and a feeling of relief, after five hours' absence from the natural surroundings of a vehicle, when he records rounding the last bend of the track on the way home '. . . and found our trusty Saracen awaiting with open doors'. Even he, as a junior patrol commander, could find himself playing a key-rôle consulting a kampong headman or the local magistrate, while playing his part in the "Hearts and Minds" campaign. To tank men, who, over the years, had become accustomed from their duties in relatively independent squadrons and troops to working at a remote distance from their immediate superiors, the problems of making decisions and comporting themselves with assurance when deep in the jungle and miles from an officer, came easily. Indeed, it was partly at the suggestion of the C.O.'s driver, Corporal Young, an ex U.S. Army paratrooper, that a Support Troop was formed by him to act as full-time infantry, and he would have commanded it if it had not been for the fact that he was too far down the seniority list to be made sergeant, and some local police and army units preferred to deal only with commissioned officers.' And yet, when Sergeant M. Lines was detached in 1966 for a year's service with the Sabah Police Border Scouts, he so quickly adapted himself to the conditions while on patrol along the Indonesian Border, that he became a by-word in the country for his outstanding zeal and ability to organize the Scouts. So highly valued was he, that the local police authorities placed him in charge of local operations in a post which would have been filled by an Assistant Superintendant of Police had one been available.

Pointing to the lines of A Squadron of the 4th, the C.O. of 42nd Royal Marine Commando once said to a visitor: 'They drive, march, boat and helicopter in, and there's nothing they won't try.' His words high-lighted the efforts that were being made by a unit, whose equipment was intended to impart high mobility, but which was defeated by the environment in which it found itself. When all was said and done, much of the 4th's work could have been performed by the Artillery and Infantry, and as Major R. M. H. Vickers, the 4th's Second-in-Command, put it: 'In three years of active operations in Borneo . . . the armoured squadrons there have the following . . . results: Not one single shell or machine-gun bullet of the many thousands fired . . . was aimed at an enemy target. It is doubtful if a single casualty was caused. There was not one ambush, encounter or incident . . . A number of arrests, much useful information and an incalculable amount of 'Hearts and Minds' support was achieved, but 95 per cent of this work was done *dismounted*. To be brutally honest, the armoured reconnaissance squadrons . . . were odd-job men carrying out rear-area tasks to relieve infantry manpower for its main task of dominating the border.'

When the last of the regular troopships went out of service at the end of 1962, and nearly all long-range trooping took place in chartered or R.A.F. aircraft at a fraction of the cost and time, the rapid and flexible re-deployment of sub-units on a world-wide basis became a reality. But the complexity of such operations could also be daunting, and few more so than those which took place in February 1966, during the closing stages of Confrontation in the aftermath of an abortive Communist coup in Indonesia. A re-deployment took place in North Borneo at the same time as H Squadron (Major P. J. Tustin) 5th R.T.R. (then commanded by Lieutenant-Colonel P. E. Dey), began to arrive from the U.K. In the process, C Squadron of the 4th came out from Malaya to relieve a squadron of the Queen's Dragoon Guards (Q.D.G.) in the Second Division of Sarawak, while H Squadron took the place of A Squadron 4th R.T.R. in Kuching, who then returned to Malaya. Throughout this time, two different Brigade H.Q.s had to be kept informed, and at least a squadron's worth of troops ready for instant action. The hand-over of stores (supervized by Captain H. J. Murrell, the 4th's Quartermaster) involved the following exchanges:

Ammunition and Accommodation:	C Squadron 4th R.T.R. took over the Q.D.G. squadron's.
	H Squadron 5th R.T.R. took over A Squadron 4th R.T.R.'s.
Technical:	C Squadron 4th R.T.R. took over A Squadron 4th R.T.R.'s.
Stores:	H Squadron 5th R.T.R. took over the Q.D.G. squadron's.

At the same time, each 4th R.T.R. squadron retained its own vehicles and moved them to and from their locations by road and sea, while the 5th took over those belonging to the Q.D.G.

To a commanding officer, the dispersion of his regiment in this manner could be frustrating, and, possibly, it was detrimental to the regiment's welfare. Hardly ever could he exercise it as a whole, and while squadron loyalties were enhanced, some members of a unit might spend protracted periods in its service without getting to know each other. As a result, assessments of personality and prowess were much harder to obtain by those whose job it was to steer careers in the right direction.

Such matters were of little consequence to the members of H Squadron 5th R.T.R., projected, as they were, straight into action upon their arrival. New troops sent to isolated locations had to acquire, within hours, the experience that the 4th had learnt over years. Within 45 minutes of taking over, 4 Troop (2nd Lieutenant J. S. Crawshaw) was called out on escort, and within a few days the rest had found out what it was like to lie in ambush for 40 hours in the rain, without making contact; to race at high speed, to help seal-off an incursion and meet nothing; and to observe areas where targets were suspected, and yet be forbidden to fire for fear of hitting friendly forces or civilians. But if these men had been asked if they would rather be back at Tidworth, where families and girl-friends continued to reside, few would have readily accepted that option. This squadron of the 5th, like its predecessors, had its successes and moments of glory – the occasional opportunity to fire its 76mm. guns at caves in distant hillsides, the arrest of curfew-breakers and of a fish-poisoner, wanted by the police, were typical opportunities that came their way. Little wars rarely produce grand climaxes; it was the sum total of minor victorious incidents which added up to the defeat by quite small forces of the major effort by the Indonesian Army and the C.C.O. And finally, when Confrontation formally came to an end on 11 August, it was for H Squadron to wind up the R.T.R.'s presence in Borneo (the 4th had already departed in June 1966) – by helping to round-up, ten days after the 'end', a suspected party of infiltrators (to whom the word had not yet passed) before loading its vehicles into landing-craft for transhipment and handing them in at Singapore.

* * * * *

The 1st R.T.R. (Lieutenant-Colonel R. E. Simpkin) was transferred from B.A.O.R. in November and was split, after a short spell in the United Kingdom, among several destinations. C

Squadron (Major M. G. Farmer), in fact, moved to Bahrein three months ahead of the rest, to take over from a squadron of 5th Inniskilling Dragoon Guards the task of providing an L.S.T.-borne armoured squadron in the Persian Gulf, to counter any threats to Kuwait, whose oil was so important to the West. It would stay there for three months before rejoining the rest of the unit (less B Squadron) when it arrived (unaccompanied by families) in Aden in January. B Squadron (Major R. G. L. Osborne) went straight to Hong Kong, accompanied by its families, and there encountered a very different sort of service from that endured by the rest of the unit, and which will be described later.

The Aden in which the 1st arrived, was torn by a terrorism which endangered its environs and spread to the neighbouring villages of Sheik Othman and Al Mansoura, at a time when the Radfan was a much quieter region than it had been in 1964. The out-going British Conservative Government had promised independence to Aden in 1968, but when the incoming Labour Government of Mr. Harold Wilson gave every impression, under the pressures of a serious economic crisis, of being prepared to bring forward that date, the chances of a tranquil hand-over of power diminished. The local National Liberation Front (N.L.F.), with Egyptian support, had declared war against the British in October 1963. By 1965, however, an alliance of the South Arabian League (S.A.L.) and the People's Socialist Party (P.S.P.) in Aden formed the Organisation for Liberation of Occupied South (O.L.O.S.) and in January 1966 O.L.O.S. joined with N.L.F. to form the Front for the Liberation of Occupied South Yemen (F.L.O.S.Y.). S.A.L. then broke away because it was anti-Egyptian and pro-Saudi Arabian and, in December 1966, N.L.F. too broke off, leaving F.L.O.S.Y. as, basically, just the P.S.P. Egypt then switched its support from N.L.F. to F.L.O.S.Y. which vied with the N.L.F. for power, as well as in its efforts to out-do everybody else in extremes of terrorism. The appointment in March, by democratic processes, of Abdul Mackaweee as Chief Minister did nothing to relax the tension, for he was a declared supporter of Gemal Nasser, President of Egypt, and eager to hasten the British departure by every possible political manoeuvre and propaganda device.

Throughout its stay, 1st R.T.R., despite its primary rôle as the armoured regiment of the local strategic reserve, was incessantly involved in Internal Security operations, but, unlike the 4th before it, was compelled by the enemy to concentrate on the defence of the urban areas instead of the desert and hills. War was waged by the sniper, the bomber and the mine placer – and the latter was now provided with far more powerful weapons than those of the year before, many of them British Mark VI mines taken from stocks once held in Egypt. The crews of Ferret scout cars (which, as usual, acted as mine 'bumpers') were particularly vulnerable, despite the fitting of thicker armour to the floors, but it was in a mineplated Landrover that the 1st suffered its first loss on 15 January. Among the unit's tasks was that of sending out patrols to follow up information of suspicious activities. The officer in command of this particular patrol was Captain D. E. N. Robertson-Fox, who had recently spent two years on secondment to the Aden Protectorate Levies, and who was an experienced desert navigator, and fluent in Arabic. A mine exploded under the rear wheels of his Landrover, near to the petrol tank, and Robertson-Fox, strapped in as he was, was knocked unconscious as the vehicle caught fire. His driver, Trooper Clitheroe, made heroic efforts to cut him free and was himself badly burned, while Robertson-Fox, in the short time before he died, refused morphine and confined himself to ensuring that his orders to picquet the heights and make the area secure against the enemy were obeyed.

By the time Lieutenant-Colonel L. W. A. Gingell took command in March, the 1st had come to regard up-country visits as a form of relaxation, and duties in the urban areas as a strain. They were compelled to maintain a constant state of alert against a foe who threw bombs through windows and came to close range among the narrow alleys and noisy streets of the city and the villages. Cordon and search operations; check point duties, with the occasional lucky arrest of a wanted man or the discovery of arms, ammunition and contraband on camels or concealed in lorries and cars, were the interminable occupation of tank crews who were given little opportunity for tanking. There was time to train with tanks, and to go to sea for amphibious exercises, but these were regarded as a respite from the job of policing, as was the task of putting two of the new pre-production Chieftain tanks through hot-weather trials just before returning to Catterick Camp in December 1966, to take up the rôle of Armoured Basic Training Unit. Indeed it was one of these Chieftains which, uninvited, injected a symbolic gesture into the 'Farewell Parade' by tanks in Aden as the rundown, which was now to be completed by November 1967, got under way. The Quartermaster, Captain P. H. Tocock, was bringing up the rear of the Parade and his tank was in the act of dipping its weapon in salute to the C.-in-C., Admiral Sir Michael Le Fanu, when, to quote Gingell, '. . . the gun went on the 'blink' and dipped up and down. However, the C.-in-C. and the many spectators were delighted to see

the Chieftain waving farewell, and waved back enthusiastically.'
So ended the 30-years presence of British armour in the deserts
of the Middle East!

The final appearance of the R.T.R. on the Aden stages, however, was reserved for B Squadron (reinforced by men from C)
of the 5th (Major M. J. Evans). Its rôle in a three-month
(unaccompanied) tour from April to July 1967, gave a foretaste of
the infantry rôle with which all units of the Regiment were to
become so familiar in the 1970s. Heaving a sigh of relief that
some of their equipment would be Ferrets and Landrovers, they
plunged into three weeks' intensive infantry training, learning
fast, as the squadron's record shows, '. . . to fire accurately with
the S.L.R. and to augment vehicle skills with some of the more
pedestrian arts'; coping, too, with the problem of selecting those
who would go, because 'Everyone is trying to climb aboard the
buggy and it is getting a bit crowded.'

The 5th's time in Aden coincided with some of the bitterest
incidents of the British stay, when heavy casualties were inflicted
on the infantry and the subsequent counter-action led to considerable world comment, not all of it complimentary. It was
this fear of adverse comment on the part of the British which
encouraged the N.L.F. and F.L.O.S.Y. to behave as they did.
They knew well that the troops were prohibited from taking
strong measures in retaliation. Strict observance of the rules of
Minimum Force positively encouraged an escalation of violence
in a deteriorating political situation. Men who were forbidden
to open fire until they were first fired upon found themselves
fighting with one hand tied behind their backs. There were 68
incidents during the week of B Squadron's arrival, in mid-May,
when they took over from a squadron of the 13th/18th Hussars.
'We do spooky night patrols', read one report, 'in a shanty town
at a place called Slave Island and carry out mobile and foot
patrols inside and outside the married quarter perimeter . . . Our
two Ferrets have been attached to the 5th Fusiliers for operations in Crater [where the notorious battles of June were
centred] where they had their fun, being grenaded once and
fired upon four times. Luckily the grenade never went off . . .
However, Sergeant Young did have a target indicated to him and
got off 50 rounds of Browning which brought gallons of water
cascading from tanks where the terrorist was meant to be! Our
latest report is of a success to Sergeant McCabe who wounded
a terrorist he saw firing at our Security Forces.' And still they
found time to send parties up-country by air, to play games and
to climb Sham-San, the highest peak, and occasionally to be very
bored.

The June battles found the squadron in the thick of it, both in Crater, where armoured cars of the Queen's Dragoon Guards were also heavily involved, and at 'Check Point Charlie', which controlled the isthmus into Aden. Molotov cocktails were often thrown at the cars; grenades and bullets flew thick and fast, and hardly a spell of duty passed without incident. When the armed police mutinied, the Check Point troops had great difficulty in turning back F.R.A. soldiers who wanted to pass. A chaotic situation of ambush and counter-ambush culminated in a pitched street battle from which the Ferrets were rarely absent. Once again the benefits of fighting from behind armour were demonstrated; B Squadron suffered no losses at a time when the infantry were being badly hit. In the middle of July they returned intact to England with their morale high, to find awaiting them the bruising announcement that the 5th was to be disbanded in 1969, one tragic feature of the next phase of reductions in the Army, consequent upon a further contraction of its commitments at places such as Aden.

* * * * *

During the 1st R.T.R.'s original tour of duty in Hong Kong from 1957 to 1960, one of its tasks had been to hand in the Comet tanks which the 3rd had brought there in 1949, and re-equip with Centurions. But long before B Squadron arrived there in 1966, it was clear that, although China could seize the Colony as and when she chose, she was much more likely to continue to respect the *status quo*, and that even the tank squadron to which the garrison had been reduced was perhaps unnecessary. Indeed, it was the experience of B Squadron that this was the case, when, between April and November, the place was gripped by a series of Communist-inspired riots. There was nothing that tanks could do except stand idly by in case of a border incursion. When the trouble started in April and there was an initial four days Emergency, it was the only unit in the Colony not turned out: the use of tanks in such a situation was obviously unsuitable and strengthened the case for replacing them with wheeled A.F.V.s. Instead, it was officers of the few R.T.R. men then serving in the Hong Kong Regiment (Lieutenant-Colonel J. Laurence-Smith) who, as things got worse, became the most heavily involved, while the 1st did little more than contribute a few guards and scout car patrols – their most effective employment was to provide rescue teams and give assistance to the civil populace in the aftermath of a typhoon which, in June, caused some of the most damaging floods in the Colony's history.

With a certain irony, the first advance parties of the 1st flew out from Hong Kong on Cambrai Day – the Golden Jubilee of the Battle – prior to the Farewell Parade, two days later, which symbolized the end of an era. It· was not simply a matter of replacement of tanks by the incoming armoured cars of the Life Guards, but a final mark of surrender from the old concept of British Power linked to Empire. Remorselessly, circumstances were compelling the R.A.C., and the R.T.R. with it, to perform, almost exclusively, duties for which they had not bargained in the immediate post-war years. Gradually the Cold War was imposing the need to adapt, on foot if necessary, to the demands of police-style duties, as a sort of rehearsal for the more testing experiences in the 1970s, adjacent to the inner keep of Home.

CHAPTER XI

Reconstruction and Contraction 1960-1970

In the interests of sheer survival, the all-consuming occupation of the Regiment was recruiting, once National Service was pronounced as approaching its end. From the Colonels Commandant, through R.H.Q., exhortations to exert every effort flowed forth, and in every issue of *The Tank* appeared a report on the current situation with descriptions of innovations applied by units and individuals, expanded by tables showing the month by month achievements in the number of men signed on or who had been persuaded to remain with the Colours. The initial hopes of persuading National Servicemen to convert to Regular engagements were, however, mostly confounded. Indeed, so long as National Servicemen remained on unit strength (and perhaps acted as a vocal deterrent) the recruiting campaign was slow to bear fruit. In November 1959, *The Tank* complained that '. . . our Recruiting figures have fallen below the 'Target' of 50 new recruits a month. In September the Regiment only obtained 40 recruits from civil life plus one re-enlistment from National Service. There is no reasonable explanation for this drop in numbers except the increasing prosperity of the country as a whole . . . The number of recruits purchasing their discharge after only a few weeks' training is still a cause of the gravest concern . . .'

The exertions of individual regiments were, of course, only a fraction of the total effort being applied by the War Office to overcome the resistance of prospective Regulars. The Editor of *The Tank* hit one nail on the head when he referred to the prosperity of the country as a possible reason for failing to meet the target. In 1958, an independent Advisory Committee on Recruiting under a previous Secretary of State for War, Sir James Grigg, had put forward the view that 'taken as a whole, people in the Services are, if anything, a little better off than they would have been in civil life.' Corporals and below, it should be added, could no more afford to purchase a motor car than their equivalent in status in civil life, and could easily run themselves into debt in trying to do so. Grigg recommended that, in future, pay and pensions should be reviewed regularly at intervals of not more than two years, and this the Government accepted in February 1959, when it announced its intention of implementing the first such review in April 1960. Indeed, for the next decade, at least, successive reviews would go some way to satisfy the requirements of parity in pay with civilian counterparts. Likewise, there was a keen awareness that some of the new Regular recruits would bring wives with them, and far more homes would be required than had been the case during National Service when conscripts were not entitled to married quarters. In Britain the perennial housing shortage persisted. It was dismaying, therefore, for unit commanders to discover, as recruiting figures began to rise at the latter end of 1960 when the number of National Servicemen diminished, that a proportion of new recruits had been given the impression that they might soon (if not immediately) be allocated a quarter when no such promise could be satisfied. Moreover, the larger number of families loaded units with welfare problems which could not be ignored. A dissatisfied wife was frequently the reason for a dedicated soldier prematurely leaving the Colours, and so the wives had to be kept happy, and their influence rated among the important factors when evaluating the operational efficiency and deployment of units – as 1st and 4th R.T.R. discovered during their unaccompanied tours in the Middle East.

The Secretary of State for War, Mr. Christopher Soames, spoke in March 1960, of a record rate of building in the Army estimate, and in 1962, completions of quarters were 1,500, together with many new barrack blocks. Even so, it had to be admitted that 6,000 furnished hirings were needed in the United Kingdom to make a contribution to the Army's housing needs, while overseas, the requirement was no less exacting and demanded great outlay to provide accommodation in the key-stations such as Malta, Aden, Cyprus, the Persian Gulf, Malaysia and Hong Kong – garrisons which, within the decade, would either be reduced in size or totally surrendered as Britain gave up her overseas responsibilities.

The publicity generated by announcements of improved pay and accommodation contributed convincingly to the improvements in recruiting which ensued until, in 1961, the R.A.C. target was being regularly hit, month after month. Essential to recruiting was personal contact by members of the Regiment with the local population and with the Press, in endeavours to overcome the traditional hostility reserved for the Army in peace-time. For example, the 2nd R.T.R. appointed all its officers at E.R.E. and on Staff Duties in the United Kingdom to make contact with one or more of the various Army Information

Offices in their area, and in the mid 1960s developed a spectacular Musical Ride by its Ferret scout cars which performed at the Military Tournament at Earls Court, and beguiled large crowds at other outdoor public events. Detachments of soldiers from each unit toured their recruiting areas to reinforce the work of their N.C.O. Special Recruiters who were permanently located there. The local Press was wooed and reacted in diverse ways of its own, not all of them favourable, but some of them useful, if only for the publicity generated. A story in the *Glasgow Herald* in 1960 may not have been typical, but it said something about what was going on besides underlining the need for character in those engaged upon this work.

'Captain A. K. McIntosh of the 4th Royal Tank Regiment has a tongue so persuasive that it is almost subversive. He claims for his Regiment superiority over even the cosseted and corseted cavalry on a point of tradition. Who actually had tanks first? he asks. That is a nicety of argument unlikely to attract the 100 recruits [a gross exaggeration] he hopes to find in the West of Scotland during a three weeks' tour. Their signatures are expected to be cajoled more by the travelling exhibition of vehicles, weapons and model tanks. At 50 tons and £38,000 the real thing is too heavy on the roads and pocket. Captain McIntosh is himself a good argument for Army life after nine years as a regular. His only fault (if it can be so called) is that he looks too like a cavalryman . . .'

As time went by, the exploitation of such publicity as this would forge a lasting rapport with the local Press and, through them, filter through to the public which, when added to a widespread national campaign to Keep the Army in the Public Eye (K.A.P.E.) would bring lasting success in finding enough men of the right quality.

Naturally, longer time spent by Regulars in acquiring and expanding their knowledge resulted in a far higher level of efficiency in operating the more complex equipment being brought into service. Greater complexity of equipment, however, had already complicated the original diffuse Star System of pay to such an extent that it was almost unworkable, besides needing skilled specialists to administer it. From April 1960, the Pay Code was simplified by reducing the number of Pay Groups from five to four – to those of technicians, skilled tradesmen, less skilled tradesmen and, fourthly, fighting soldiers – with only three grades in each group (except technicians, of which the R.A.C. had none) below the rank of corporal. As Mr. Soames claimed during the Committee stage of the Army Estimates for 1960–61, 'The unmarried soldier on a nine-year engagement will receive seven guineas a week after recruit stage. The platoon sergeant committed to serve for nine years who is married and living in quarters, will draw in pay and allowances just over £16 a week, or £870 a year ... I honestly do not think that with these figures anyone can argue that, in future, pay will be a bar to recruitment.' And this was so. Recruiting did improve at this time while, simultaneously, the new system of bringing the rates of pay for senior N.C.O.s and W.O.s into line with those of Group B. tradesmen acted as an incentive. It also was hoped that some National Servicemen would rise to the bait; in some cases their rates of pay remained substantially less than those of the Regulars. For example, a Group B. tradesman (the average tank crewman) trooper received 7s 6d per day compared to 17s. At the same time, the administration of pay was made more effective not only because of the simplification but because, since 1954, all pay clerk vacancies on unit establishments had been filled by members of the Royal Army Pay Corps and, gradually since the time of the Korean War, all major unit paymasters had become specialist R.A.P.C. officers, many of whom had transferred from other Arms and who otherwise would have been declared redundant. The value of these mature officers was immense because of the experienced advice they could contribute. Many stayed with the same unit for years and became institutions in their own right, quite aside from the routine services they rendered.

Paradoxically, when most items of A.F.V. equipment were demanding enhanced skill from tank crewmen, the intellectual requirement for what had previously been, arguably, the most skilful crewman of all, was reduced. The introduction in 1959 of the new range of radio sets – above all, the C 42 in lieu of the 19 Set and the B 47 in lieu of the 88 or 31 Sets – made it much easier to establish and maintain communications. Tuning was now simpler and very accurate through the introduction of in-built calibration. No longer was the manipulation of an accurate net a prolonged and difficult business dependent upon the operator's skill, although the new set's propensity for screening did cause problems of siting in some locations. Nevertheless, in so far as tactics were concerned, these sets not only provided a clarity and reliability of communication (similar to telephone conversations, which until then had been impossible) but they permitted an appreciable simplification of command and control procedures, allied to almost instant changes of frequency when required. Since calibration was in-built, each set was always on net with the others and there was no need for out-stations to check net constantly with control, as had been the case before;

from now on, the control set could be the one the officer commanding happened to be using. Moreover, it was now possible during tactical regrouping, even at the lowest level of tank squadron/infantry company, or even troop/platoon level, to re-net within a few seconds. Thus the restoration of organizational flexibility through juggling with different permutations within Battle Groups became a practical proposition.

In B.A.O.R. the employment of regimental-level battle groups within the brigade groups, which formed the major portion of the three standard divisions, was an empirical product. The demands of nuclear warfare had suggested the need for a more rigid, semi-permanent grouping of armoured, infantry and artillery units and sub-units in order to dispense with regrouping to satisfy changing tactical situations. Previously, rigidity had been unavoidable because of the limitations of the old radio sets, but after 1961, the affiliations (in particular between armour and infantry) became much easier to arrange. For example, in 1961, in 1st Division (Major-General A. Jolly) and within 20th Armoured Brigade (Brigadier P. R. C. Hobart), 3rd R.T.R. (Lieutenant-Colonel A. McN. Taylor) would have a semi-permanent association with C Company, 1st Argyll and Sutherland Highlanders in A.P.C.s driven by A Squadron 4th R.T.R. (Major K. J. Macksey) and, within 5th Infantry Brigade Group, each squadron of 1st R.T.R. (Lieutenant-Colonel T. D. Gregg) would work for much of the time with the same infantry battalion. But in the years to come, the degree of permanency of affiliation would begin to be abandoned.

The influence of senior R.T.R. officers upon the B.A.O.R. divisions and their brigade groups at command level in the years between 1958 and 1970 can be judged from the table on the page opposite.

Also throughout this period, outside B.A.O.R., Major-General R. M. P. Carver commanded 3rd Division from 1962 to 1964, Major-General J. R. Holden commanded 43rd (Wessex) Division (T.A.) from 1963 to 1965 and Major-General A. R. Leakey was G.O.C. British Troops Malta and Libya from 1967 to 1968.

From time to time, the activities of the Army in B.A.O.R. became the subject for a major political debate related to its ability to carry out a specific rôle within N.A.T.O. I (British) Corps' Exercise 'Spearpoint' in the autumn of 1961 was, for example, exploited by the Opposition Labour Party to focus attention on such deficiencies as it was felt the Army might have, and to register the current concern that defence of the West depended too much on the use of tactical nuclear weapons (of which a sufficiency by then existed) instead of upon troops on the ground. To the troops taking part in this high-level exercise,

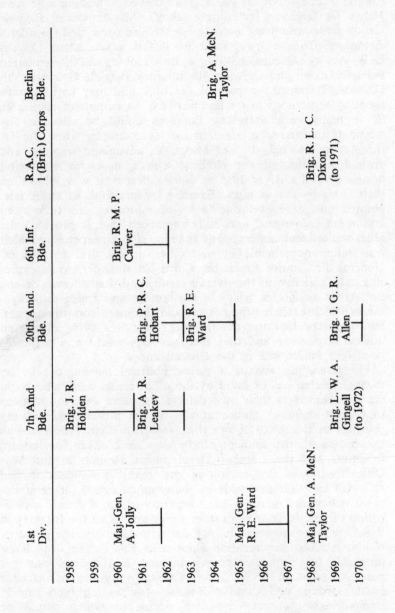

as with most others of its kind, it was rather more a matter of routine – one in which the R.T.R. played a leading rôle with Jolly's 1st Division, including Leakey's 7th Armoured Brigade Group under command (containing 1st, 3rd (detached from 20th Armoured Brigade Group) and 5th R.T.R.'s (Lieutenant-Colonel E. W. Anstey) Groups) battling against Hobart's 20th Armoured Brigade Group and Carver's 6th Infantry Brigade Group in 4th Division. It rained for part of the time and long periods were spent by some units in sterile inactivity – a complaint applicable to so many such exercises. Boredom could be alleviated by moments of intense excitement as, for example, when the 1st (Lieutenant-Colonel J. D. Masters), advancing rapidly and dramatically through the Wiehen Gebirge, nearly seized a vital bridge over the River Else at Bunde before it was 'blown' in their faces by the umpires. Exercise 'Spearpoint', as 1st R.T.R. pointed out, gave everyone 'a lot of motoring, too little sleep and some enjoyment' and Jolly remarked that it provided the other senior commanders, staffs and himself with experience which was quite unobtainable by any other means. But Lieutenant-General Sir Charles Jones, the Corps Commander, while expresing satisfaction with the overall result, had then to help defend the Army against criticism in Parliament and Press, disparagements which excluded the officers and the men from the dispute, but suggested that too much dependence was being placed on nuclear fire-power and that methods, equipment and organization were inadequate in the circumstances.

The wrangling was of a classic political nature, but by no means rejected out of hand by the officers and men, who could see for themselves their own defects and were only too anxious to correct them. A glance at any of the professional military journals in the 1960s shows that, far from being content with the out-dated, the soldiers of the day were eager for modern facilities, and the Combat Development Branch at the War Office responded by exploiting the many new ideas it had collected from far and wide in giving guidance on future equipment policy and, perhaps most urgently of all, a drastic modification of field-force organization. Once nearly all the Infantry in B.A.O.R. were mounted in A.P.C.s (FV 432s) and the potential of the latest communication equipment was evident, the latest proposals for refinements in command and control made it possible to adopt a far more ambitious system of variable Battle Groups and Combat Teams of changing (and rapidly implemented) content, the composition of which would be adjusted to suit the local tactical situation. The first official sign of the change to come was indicated by an amendment of title: in

November 1965, Brigade Groups became known as Brigades, and the implication was that they were now self-contained formations. The following October, a trial called Exercise 'Eternal Triangle 66' was carried out by 1st Division (Major-General R. E. Ward) of the practical application of so-called 'Square Brigades' – a formation which, it proposed, should comprise two armoured and two infantry units.

For 'Eternal Triangle' Ward was given 7th Armoured Brigade (Brigadier R. E. Worsley) and 11th Infantry Brigade (Brigadier J. Harmon). These he regrouped, sending 3rd R.T.R. (Lieutenant-Colonel M. A. Sanders) to join the Scots Greys in 11th Brigade and replacing it in 7th Brigade (2nd R.T.R. and 11th Hussars) with one of the infantry battalions from 11th Brigade. In addition, 11th Brigade acquired a Danish infantry battalion (1st King's Fodregiment) and a Dutch infantry battalion. The German 31 Panzer Grenadier Brigade, which also took part, changed sides at crucial moments as Ward dictated. The Tank and Infantry Order of Battle of the two British brigades, which were pitted against each other, thus stood as:

7th Armoured Brigade	11th Infantry Brigade
11th Hussars	Scots Greys
2nd R.T.R.	3rd R.T.R.
1st Battalion Royal Anglian Regiment	1st Battalion Duke of Edinburgh's Royal Regiment
1st King's Fodregiment	Dutch Battalion

The H.Q. of each unit was nominated as that of a Battle Group capable of commanding Combat Teams, which were based on existing H.Q.s of tank squadrons and infantry companies, and had an Artillery Forward Observation Officer permanently attached. A squadron commander, for example, might find himself with three of his organic tank troops plus an attached infantry platoon in its FV 432s, while his fourth troop was detached to a Combat Team commanded by an infantry-man – a permutation which could be switched sometimes twice, but on average once a day – creating complex variations which, some thought, might not withstand the strain of war.

The 7th Brigade concentrated between Soest and Hamm and, in good weather, advanced rapidly eastward on 24 September, crossing the River Alme, the Helmern/Haaren feature, the Eggegebirge and the River Weser until it was in sight of Gottingen. Then the 11th Brigade was given the initiative and pushed the 7th back. Notes by those taking part give the impression of an extremely fast-moving exercise packed with surprise situations in which the new system was tried to the limit. The 3rd R.T.R. describing the initial stages of 11th Brigade's counter-offensive in crossing the River Diemel, catches the spirit of the exercise, as well as the interweaving of elements from the Battle Groups:

'Our sappers laid their bridge with great skill in an un-guarded point of the enemy southern flank. The D.E.R.R. [Duke of Edinburgh's Royal Regiment] established a firm bridgehead and were supported by the Scots Greys who swept over the bridge in the shortest possible time. C Squadron followed and was soon established on their first objective. A Squadron moved forward gingerly . . . B Squadron and C Company [of the Dutch battalion] were united in a reserve position north of the river and were ready to go . . .'

Major G. L. D. Duckworth, commanding Ajax of the 2nd R.T.R. on the other side, became convinced that the Battle Group system would work, but he was among those who had reservations about flexible Combat Teams. 'The infantry never quite kept up with the switches of platoons from one combat team to the next', he wrote, 'and the logistic tail had perma-nent problems'. He could have concluded that the system was too complicated and that in war, only the simple plans work. But he noted in his diary, 'Plenty of fast moves, changes of plan and "the fog of war" kept us confused and on the hop through-out. None of us was ever in reserve. The soldiers greatly enjoyed it and had a good run [250 miles] in their Centurions.'

This exercise, in fact, was Ward's masterpiece, and extremely testing for the officers who, from brigadiers downwards, got little sleep. Typically, towards the end, he suddenly introduced 31 Panzer Grenadier Brigade in support of 11th Brigade from an angle, from outside the 'agreed' exercise area – a surprise move which promoted heated arguments with the umpires, but which had the effect of keeping the pot on the boil when every-body was on the verge of exhaustion. Of real shot and shell there was none, but the fear of failure under the gaze of a stern taskmaster to some extent compensated for that.

To those who interpreted the spirit of the time as one that encouraged radical rationalization were added those of a cynical inclination who did not agree with the setting-up, by Sir Alec Douglas Home's Conservative Government, of a unified Ministry of Defence on 1 April 1964. This monster, it was claimed by its advocates, 'will greatly help the achievement of a unified defence policy and the efficient and economical pro-vision of our military forces'. It also provided a stimulus to bureaucracy and a starting-block for further reduction in the numerical strength of the Armed Forces. Yet in fairness to the

Government of the day and its successor, the cloth had to be cut to suit the circumstances. Force levels were bound to be settled at the behest of operational requirements and not, in the final analysis, at the bidding of emotional cries from hard-line defenders of the Regimental System – no matter how vital that appeared to be to vested interests and those who argued that the Army's morale would collapse if the existing system were abandoned. In 1963 and 1964, as shown in the previous Chapter, the Army was at full stretch, and it was to the R.T.R.'s benefit, for example, that the temporary need actually to expand was reflected in a cessation, for the time being (1963), of talk of further amalgamations and saw instead the re-formation of the Independent Squadron, Berlin, under Major R. G. Lawson.

A dire shortage of training areas in Europe, as Germany's forces expanded at a time when it might soon be politically impossible to exercise in Libya, promoted the initial use of land in Canada for mobility training across wide expanses of country. In 1964, Hale Force was formed – a composite R.A.C. squadron consisting of one crew from each armoured regiment in B.A.O.R. to be known as C Squadron Lord Strathcona's Horse and commanded by Major J. W. Turner, 17th/21st Lancers – and was flown to the Wainright Training Area in Alberta, Canada. Here they manned Centurion Mark 3 tanks of 1953 vintage, with 9,000 miles already on their clocks. 5th R.T.R. provided a crew under Corporal Gee, and in due course they found themselves involved in a month's training which took them into territory where space seemed boundless, and which produced many new problems. A temperature of 105°F. was trying. To Gee, it was an education: 'To read a map in the area was tedious, the terrain undulating and riddled with small spurs and re-entrants with little or no vegetation other than prairie grass . . . On 23rd July we started on the big brigade Exercise "Lashback" and it was a fantastic change to actually see Honest Johns flying about and napalm bombs being dropped by aircraft of the R.C.A.F.' He goes on to tell of hiring a car to visit more distant parts of the country in what amounted to a new approach to the sort of Adventure Training (as successor to earlier so-called Initiative Training) which all unit commanders were endeavouring to promote for their men, no matter in which part of the world they were serving.

The need to develop a man's physical and psychological stamina and his resourcefulness for nuclear war had been pointed out by Major R. E. Simpkin in his prize-winning Bertrand Stewart Essay of 1960. 'Tactical training', he wrote, 'must introduce an element of stress and physical hardship.

Expedition training and the practice of dangerous sports must be regarded as training rather than recreation and given appropriate moral and material backing.' This theme had already been taken very much to heart by Lieutenant C. J. S. Bonnington when, in that same year, as a member of the British Indian Nepalese Services Himalayan Expedition, he had, as one of the final assault party, flown a Regimental pennant from the peak of Annapurna II (26,041 feet). The R.T.R. had made a donation to the expedition, which had received no Treasury support, and the experience gained by Bonnington was to stand him in good stead in the years to come and lead him eventually to the peak of Everest by the most difficult route. This individual triumph was, of course, a prestige venture and outside the sort of thing Simpkin was considering. Lieutenant-Colonel P. E. Dey went to the hub of the problem of arranging Adventure Training at unit level, in an article in *The Tank* in March 1965, when he described the difficulties of running this sort of programme in B.A.O.R., where the German Government was quite naturally anxious that the adventurers' venture should be kept within bounds, to avoid the abuse which had been introduced by earlier, over-zealous Initiative Training exercises. The capture of trophies from unwilling members of the public had to be forbidden, as one chorus girl would have agreed when, it seems, she put up a spirited defence of her dignity – if nothing else. Dey went on to regret the changed conditions once Adventure Training was 'recognized'. Previously, he wrote, 'it was relatively easy to organize, 'but now that it is recognized . . . prior notice of intended expeditions varies from six to twelve months . . . All travel expenses and equipment have to be paid for from Adventure Training funds and the expenditure has to be approved of in advance . . . By the time the date arrives unit commitments have changed so much that one is lucky to be able to select a party and leader after tapping the resources of all Squadrons. Even a recent Escape and Evasion exercise, organized by 7th Armoured Brigade, was nearly thwarted by a belated commitment of entertaining the Royal Naval Staff College.'

Bureaucracy, as has been mentioned, was on the rampage, while other institutions fell into decay and sometimes disappeared. Students of Rome's decline and fall recognized this disease. As the Ministry of Defence burgeoned, the nearby R.T.R. Officers Club was one institution to die, unlamented, in 1965. Never· a very healthy body, it had failed to meet the needs of the younger officers to whom its atmosphere was too old-fashioned. At a time when many London clubs were suffering severe financial deprivation and higher costs, the R.T.R. Club had to be closed because a large majority of officers declined to support it. For partially related reasons, mess and club life throughout the Army was changing in order to satisfy the wishes of the young people of the affluent society of the 1960s. Officers' messes tended to become more informal and to permit the presence of ladies far more readily than had been the case in the 1940s. Sergeants' messes, on the other hand, often acquired a somewhat stiffer manner, which was exemplified by the formal dinners and guest nights they held, to a standard which was often higher than that achieved by officers' messes in the past. Regimental clubs improved their standards enormously. The old canteen atmosphere provided by N.A.A.F.I. no longer sufficed. The Corporals managed their own clubs (the standard of which rose steadily under their guidance) and the troopers demanded something much better than a beer bar in which to pass their time. Many units – and sub-units too in certain circumstances – out-flanked the N.A.A.F.I. monopoly to establish their own troopers' clubs and, in accordance with the members' wishes, did not invariably sell alcohol if tea, coffee and soft drinks were preferred. As for the wives, their clubs had official status, and in overseas garrisons they were an essential facility in helping some of the younger and home-sick women to feel at home in a foreign environment. A well-run wives' club was considered to be an asset to any unit as a forum in which the opinion of the wives could be made known, through which information could be exchanged which might be turned to the husbands' benefit, and as a centre for entertainment – even if, in the few less-imaginatively run, Bingo were the common pastime.

*　　*　　*　　*　　*

Over all hung the threat of further reductions in the size of the Army. Fearing the worst in 1957, ten years before the next blow fell, Crocker had written an appreciation of what the loss of another unit might do to the R.T.R. He argued that the only equitable way to effect a further reduction in the R.A.C. was by imposing cuts upon the two Wings in proportion to their existing composition, and he dreaded Phase 2, fearing the increased number to be compulsorily retired because 'it will mean cutting into the heart of the Regiment and dismissing many first class, highly qualified and experienced officers. The effect will be calamitous both on the confidence of those remaining and on the ability of the Regiment to attract high quality officers in the future . . .' To Templer, Crocker quoted a letter from Montgomery in which the Field Marshal declared:

'It is my very definite opinion that with the cut of three Regiments and the Independent Squadron, the R.T.R. has contributed fully to the reduction in the size of the armour of the Army. It should not be cut any more. Any further reduction in the R.A.C. should surely be within the Cavalry Wing – by amalgamations.'

It was the Territorial Army which received the first heavy blow, and this fell within the meaning of the originally declared purpose of reduction – as a means to 'streamline' the Service, to make it more efficient and more capable of accepting and developing new techniques and of operating modern, complex weapons' – as Crocker interpreted the original Sandys policy. But financial stringency was at the root of the matter and in 1965, the Labour Government was intent upon achieving noticeable savings in defence expenditure, in line with a policy of radical fiscal and social reform. The Director of Army Staff Duties (Major-General R. M. P. Carver) had to find a way to save a further £20 million, an almost identical sum to the one spent annually upon the T.A. and the A.E.R. But Carver, in conjunction with another ex-R.A.C. officer who understood only too well the difficulties part-time soldiers had in coping with modern techniques, the D.C.G.S. (General Sir John Hackett, late 8th Hussars), was able to convince the Army Board that, to quote Carver, the aim was 'to bring the establishment of the T.A. into some relation both to what it could recruit and to the resources that could be devoted to it, as well as relate it to the military need'. Carver, in a letter to the author in 1978, goes on:

'Not only was the concept of mobilising a number of reserve divisions out of line with our whole strategic concept, but it was wholly unrealistic to think that the resources of money and manpower could be provided to produce properly equipped and trained modern divisions in this way in time to take part in operations on the Continent. The real need, as it is to-day, is to provide individual reinforcements and logistic units to strengthen the peace-time orbit. This the A.E.R. did economically, but that was highly unpopular with the T.A. who were, and are, only interested in preserving local units. Hence the clash and the preservation of the ridiculous cadres and units with no realistic wartime rôle.'

There was opposition from the hierarchy of the T.A., and there are still those among the Regulars who maintain that the severance of a valuable contact point with the man in the street was, at £20 million, too high a price to pay. Yet many T.A. officers came to understand Carver's point of view and, as Henry Stanhope wrote in *The Times* in 1976, 'the T.A. came to acquire a grudging admiration for the D.A.S.D. [Director of Army Staff Duties], and few would now quarrel with the wisdom of his rationalisation.' As a result, only one R.A.C. T.A. unit would survive – an Armoured Car Regiment, to be known as The Royal Yeomanry Regiment, with its squadrons dispersed all over the country. The 40th/41st (Lieutenant-Colonel A. H. Parkes) would disappear on amalgamation, in April 1967, at the same time as The Queen's Own Lowland Yeomanry (Lieutenant-Colonel A. D. Monteath), became merged with what was known as the Territorial and Army Volunteer Reserve. When the ex-members of the 40th and 41st came to the funeral of their Honorary and most dedicated Colonel, Colonel J. L. Finigan, in 1975 they also, in a way, buried a symbol of the past, a staunch supporter of the Citizen Army.

In place of the T.A. another, already well-established organization grew in size to help maintain the contact with the man in the street. In 1965, there were 35 branches of the R.T.R. Association in existence, of which those in London and Bovington were among the largest. By 1975, there were 39 spread throughout the country, filled by men whom civilians regarded with respect when they mentioned that they had been members of the Royal Tank Regiment, and to whom prospective recruits looked for guidance and inspiration. They and their members help to keep the Regiment in the public eye, even by breeding, as did L. J. Pearce, a rose christened 'Fear Naught'.

In February 1967, Mr. Denis Healey, when presenting the Defence Estimates for 1967–68, referred ominously to a need to reduce the Armed Forces further, and already, studies were under way within the Ministry of Defence to decide ways to do so. To the forefront of the minds of several senior officers was the realization that, in the Cold War, the R.A.C. was not pulling its weight to the same extent as the Infantry, and that this failure was not only the result of inhibitions imposed by its equipment: to some extent, it was argued, there was an unwillingness to undertake new work. The fact that a large proportion of R.A.C. involvement in South Arabia and Borneo had been on foot did not pass without notice, but it was strenuously proposed by Carver's successor as D.A.S.D. (Major-General C. H. Blacker, late 5th Inniskilling Dragoon Guards) that, if the R.A.C. was to save itself from heavy cuts, it must get into fresh business and take on rôles such as 'Sky Cavalry'

– a U.S. Army concept, in which troops were moved to and about the battlefield in helicopters. In parallel with this concept emerged a revival of an insistence from the 1940s, that the R.A.C. should cease to be a loose collection of units and become 'A True R.A.C.', meaning that each unit of the R.T.R. should become an individual Regiment (in the manner of each Cavalry Regiment) and that the officers should be commissioned onto a Common Roll.

There was little disagreement that the R.A.C. should seek fresh fields in which to function, and that the existing tendency of the Royal Artillery to dominate Army Aviation should be challenged. If the R.A.C. could 'take over' the Army Air Corps, the identity of some regiments might be saved. But Exercise 'Helltank' had yet to demonstrate the extent of the helicopter's combat effectiveness (see Chapter IX), and the cost of procurement of huge numbers of these machines was, in any case, enormous. This was pointed out by the Q.M.G., General Sir Alan Jolly, who, as the R.T.R.'s senior Colonel Commandant, argued the Regiment's case in the ensuing debate. Along with Major-General H. M. Liardet, the Representative Colonel Commandant, he maintained, as had all his predecessors, that the R.T.R. must remain one Regiment. Liardet recalls how hard Jolly fought against parts of the 'True R.A.C.' proposal. 'We stuck out all along for our present organization, it was a miracle that we had Alan in high places because I was retired by then and hadn't got the same 'weight' as a serving officer'. The R.T.R. got what it wanted because Jolly was able to convince members of the Army Board that the proposal to convert the R.A.C. into more fragments than before was ludicrous, at a time when the Infantry was grouping into larger Regiments. As one non-R.A.C. member of the Army Board said: 'The one thing about the R.A.C. which makes sense is the R.T.R.' So the move towards 'A True R.A.C.' was limited to the eventual adoption of a Common Roll (but one in which officers continued to be commissioned into Regiments of their own choice) and the abolition of the Cavalry and R.T.R. Wings, leaving, from April 1968, just one R.A.C. Colonel Commandant, the first of whom was to be the Chief of Defence Staff, Field Marshal Sir Richard Hull (late 17th/21st Lancers).

It is pleasant to record that there was a total lack of animosity in the negotiations which attended the reductions of 1967. Some there were who, remembering Sir Richard McCreery's proposals in 1957, worried that, if the R.T.R. were placed on an equal footing with the Cavalry, it would automatically, on account of its low seniority, be the first to go when redundancies were arranged. But Hull and Jolly were on the best of terms, with Jolly (knowing of Hull's opposition to McCreery in the past) convinced that there was no intention on the other's part to 'do-down' the R.T.R. And, indeed, Hull did nothing to impose the independent Regiment solution.

When it came to deciding how many and which units should be lost within a Corps' percentage, it was Holden, as D.R.A.C. (apart from being the third R.T.R. Colonel Commandant), who occupied a central section of the stage. To begin with, he told the M.O.D. that none should be lost and for this, in his own words, he 'received no compliments'. Holden was determined to fight all the way to prevent as many disbandments as possible and to be 'strictly neutral as between Cavalry and R.T.R. and that I should be seen to be so. From time to time I was accused by one side of being pro the other – with which I was well satisfied.' Ordered to reduce by four units, he initially proposed the amalgamation of two R.T.R. units; the amalgamation of the 10th and 11th Hussars; the employment of one R.A.C. Regiment to run the R.A.C. Centre and to provide the Demonstration Squadron at the School of Infantry; and the amalgamation of the Life Guards and the Royal Horse Guards (the Blues) into a single R.A.C. unit which would be incorporated in the R.A.C. Order of Battle and therefore be compelled to crew tanks. He intended that the Household Cavalry should no longer enjoy what he called 'The Good Life'; that is manning *only* armoured cars abroad or in Britain. While the matter of the Household Brigade proved difficult to resolve, the other units of the R.A.C., including the R.T.R., accepted their fate with quiet resignation. But despite the support of the D.C.G.S. and D.A.S.D., Holden's scheme for the Household Cavalry was turned down by the Army Board. As a compromise, therefore, he managed, after prolonged and difficult negotiations, to arrange for the amalgamation of the Blues and the Royal Dragoons. 'My condition for agreeing to this', he wrote, 'was that BOTH Life Guards and Blues/ Royals would have to convert to Armoured Regiments in their turn, but that one or other would always be in the Armoured Car rôle for duty at Windsor.' In addition, it was agreed that neither the A.B.T.U. nor R.A.C. Centre Regiment rôle would be filled by the Household Cavalry.

It was a tribute to the respect that Holden, with his irrepressible sense of fun and india-rubber face, was held by the entire R.A.C., that he carried off this coup and strengthened the R.A.C.'s unity in the process. In 1966, Lieutenant-Colonel D. B. Wood, R.E.M.E., wrote in the *British Army Review*, 'When officers of the Royal Tank Regiment are occasionally given command of Cavalry Regiments, I will believe that the Royal Armoured Corps is a reality and that the Army as a whole seriously intends to remove restrictive practices.' A few months later, Major R. M. H. Vickers, with the full concurrence of the Colonel of the Royals (Lieutenant-General Sir Desmond Fitzpatrick) and the R.T.R. Colonels Commandant, was selected to command the amalgamated Blues and Royals in June 1968.

Nevertheless, the 5th R.T.R. was doomed, and any suggestion, in a prolonged debate, that it should be amalgamated with the 1st or the 2nd was finally rejected. In the end, it was a Regimental decision to abolish one unit rather than disrupt two, and with pangs of sadness, the Regiment approached the celebrations of its Golden Jubilee of Cambrai 1917, well knowing that the 2nd's notes, misquoting Shakespeare in *The Tank*, were all too apt when they referred to the great gathering at Reinsehlen Camp in Germany on 14 July 1967, when all five units paraded for the last time before their Colonel-in-Chief, Her Majesty the Queen: 'When shall we five meet again?' This parade was largely Ward's brain-child, and to bring so many units together was itself a wonderful feat of organization by R.H.Q. (where W. M. S. Jeffery was then Regimental Colonel) as well as by Ward's 1st Division. For although the 1st R.T.R. had its A Squadron (Major J. D. Bastick) in Berlin (while the remainder of the unit performed its tour of duty as A.B.T.U. in Catterick) and the 2nd, 3rd, 4th and Cambrai and Rhine Bands were located in B.A.O.R., many other components of the Regiment had to be gathered from the United Kingdom – including H Squadron (Major J. G. R. Dixon), 5th R.T.R., and the Mark V tank and Rolls-Royce armoured car (their crews dressed in First World War uniform) from the Tank Museum. From far and wide they came, the three Colonels Commandant (General Sir Alan Jolly and Major-Generals H. M. Liardet and J. R. Holden); the distinguished British and German guests and senior officers of the Regiment with their ladies; the representatives of the Allied Canadian Régiment de Trois Rivières and the Australian 1st Armoured Regiment; the large contingent of Old Comrades and the mass of officers and men with their families.

Before them, to the sound of the Cambrai and Rhine bands, marched the men of the Regiment to salute their Chief as she arrived, escorted by Ferrets, and greeted by a fanfare of trumpets and the command from the Parade Commander, Lieutenant-Colonel D. W. A. Ambidge, for a Royal Salute. From that moment all was movement as the Queen drove in a Landrover along the drawn-up ranks, where they stood before serried Centurions, Saladins, Ferrets, Saracens, Bridge-layers and Stalwarts. Then she saw the crews double to their vehicles, heard the engines splutter into life and registered the crescendo of power as they moved amid towering fumes and dust to thunder past in troops of four to salute her. First to reach the saluting dais were the Mark V and the Rolls-Royce. Next came the modern, armoured vehicles with drivers intent upon maintaining tight and immaculate formation, and each gunner traversing his turret and dipping the gun until the muzzle nearly touched the sand-shields of the preceding vehicle. Commanders stood in their turrets at the salute, Standards and pennants flying. Bringing up the rear came a single Chieftain, the higher-pitched note of its multi-fuel engine proclaiming that this was the fighting vehicle of the future, with which all the armoured regiments would soon be equipped in place of the ageing Centurions. Finally, above and behind, flew Sioux and Skeeter helicopters from the Air Troops of the 2nd, 3rd and 4th, trailing plumes of smoke in the Regimental colours of brown, red and green. It was at a peak of high emotion when Her Majesty addressed the Regiment and in the course of her speech said:

'Your contribution on the battlefield has been formidable and, on some occasions, decisive, but perhaps the most important task in the defence of our country has been, and to a certain extent remains, the development and teaching of the armoured conception of warfare. We live in uncertain times but it is difficult to imagine the situation arising for many years in which the technical skills and expert training of the Royal Tank Regiment would not be required by the British Army.'

Afterwards, the Queen mingled with her Regiment in both the formal and less formal moments of the reception and luncheon that had been prepared, and here it was that she met all ranks and was able to make her own assessment of their quality and poise.

Life in the Regiment went on. The 5th, from 1968, under the command of Lieutenant-Colonel R. G. Lawson, until its disbandment with due ceremonial in November 1969, made the best of its last days. Squadrons from the 3rd (Lieutenant-Colonel M. A. Sanders) moved to Tidworth early in 1968 to assume the rôle of Armoured Reconnaissance Regiment from the 5th, with the attendant duties of rotating one Ferret squadron to Cyprus in the U.N.F.I.C.Y.P. rôle, and another to Sharjah, where its Saladins and Ferrets stood ready to support the Trucial Oman Scouts and Sultanate of Muscat's Forces. Unaccompanied by families though these short tours were, they were usually regarded by those involved as a prized task now that there were so few overseas postings available, with the exception of B.A.O.R. of which, some members of the R.A.C. had had enough. For exercising in B.A.O.R. was becoming increasingly circumscribed because of the multiple restrictions being placed upon the use of training areas by the West German Government and the local authorities. After the final withdrawal of British forces from Libya in March 1970, the Persian Gulf States offered just about the only piece of desert readily available for training and, therefore, the future use of training areas in Canada became all the more desirable.

Bushwhacking continued to supply its rewards and, for several officers and men, a taste of action. Of this, Major D. Shillinglaw, when he was commanding B Company, Northern Frontier Regiment in the Gulf in 1969, had plenty, involved as he was with 25 enemy contacts, many of them ambushes, during four months of operations against well-armed dissident forces. Shillinglaw did not enjoy the benefit of armour, for his work was that of an infantry officer, with the demands placed upon him of leading his men at the front, while retaining tactical control and co-ordinating the fire of his supporting artillery, mortars, machine-guns and aircraft. At the other end of the scale, there was the mundane task of undertaking the rôle of R.A.C. Centre Regiment, which fell, in August 1970, to 2nd R.T.R. (Lieutenant-Colonel G. L. D. Duckworth) as the first unit of the Regiment to have to undertake this rather uninspiring work. But by having to provide the demonstration squadron at the School of Infantry, Warminster, and thereby preserving in one sub-unit the skills which would be required when the day came to reconvert to an armoured regiment, the task was made more bearable. Likewise, the 4th, in January 1973, while under the command of Lieutenant-Colonel L. A. W. New, would become the A.B.T.U. at Catterick and would detach A Squadron to Berlin as was, by then, the ordained routine, allowing at least a part of each regiment when engaged upon one or other of the training rôles to retain an operational element.

These were days, too, when the R.T.R. could heave a sigh of relief, in the hope that it would not forfeit more of its strength. Yet for a time in 1968, there had been fears of a further decrease in order to fulfil the decision by the Ministry of Defence that one more armoured unit must be disposed of. Only one of the cavalry regiments which had been in existence in 1922 remained untouched by some form of amalgamation, and, because it was the Scots Greys, serious consideration was given to amalgamating them with the 4th R.T.R. in view of the latter's Scottish connections through recruiting. However, this course did not find favour with the Greys – quite apart from anybody else – and there were those, such as Sir Richard Hull, who had maintained that the R.T.R. would no longer be a viable whole if it fell below four units. It was the 3rd Carabineers who were chosen for marriage with the 'Scottish Cavalry' and it was their name which disappeared from the Order of Battle. But by then, too, the whole aspect of soldiering within the British Army was changing dramatically. Just as it began to look as if the withdrawal from Empire were entering its final stages, and the future, almost wholly devoted to satisfying Britain's commitments to the defence of Europe, the fatal shots, fired in Ulster in 1969, signalled the start of what was to become a protracted fight, this time at the very gates of the nation.

CHAPTER XII

The Fight at the Gates 1968-1975

Scarcely a moment in history has passed when there has not been a problem of government among or with the Irish; they would not be the same people if this were not so. The Tank Corps first experienced the 'Troubles' in 1919, when the 17th Armoured Car Battalion was sent there and, from 1919 to 1922, there was either a battalion or at least a company there, helping with tanks or armoured cars on escorts or patrols, to cope with the vicious guerilla war which led to the division of the country into the Irish Free State and Ulster. Thereafter, during spells of militant activity by Republican forces in Ulster in the 1930s and 1950s, the R.T.R. was uninvolved and it is most unlikely that many of its members gave serious thought to what was impending when, in 1968, communal unrest began, in the shape of demonstrations and marches which, as time went by, the Royal Ulster Constabulary (R.U.C.) found almost impossible to control.

After the rioting in Londonderry on 5 October 1968, a chain of events occurred which led to the first sabotage attack in Belfast on 30 March 1969, when the Ulster Special Constabulary was called out, and widespread disturbances, from which the small army contingents in Ulster kept apart. Not until July 1969 were troops called into the principal riot areas of Londonderry and Belfast, but from then on, military involvement inexorably increased as the Irish Republican Army (I.R.A.)[1] threw down the gauntlet and embarked upon an all-out attempt to undermine the rule of law and take control of Ulster. Soon the R.U.C. could no longer perform its duties in the Catholic areas. Also, its Intelligence Service was already seriously reduced in effectiveness. It became dependent upon the Army, which was on the eve of further reductions in strength and which, faced by the need to send reinforcements, once more

[1]The I.R.A. was split into two factions; the Official I.R.A. with pro-Communist leanings, once given to force, but now committed to achieving their aims primarily by political means, and the Provisional I.R.A., bent upon capturing Northern Ireland from the British by force.

230

became over-stretched – a process which was accelerated when, in March 1970, for the first time, Catholic riots were directed specifically against the troops, as well as the local Protestants. This was a turning-point, one which prompted the C.-in-C., General Sir Ian Freeland (late Royal Norfolks) to give a public warning that people carrying or throwing petrol bombs were liable to be shot and, on another occasion, to remark that Northern Ireland must eventually solve its own problems and that the Army could not stay for ever.

By June 1970, full-scale guerilla warfare, with pitched battles in the streets, was endemic. The damage and casualties incurred were enormous. Large quantities of arms and ammunition were being uncovered in searches by the Army and Police, but the Security Forces could barely hold their own, practising minimum force only, in a situation which, to many people, seemed in need of something more drastic. The strong-arm Ulster Special Constabulary had been disbanded in April on the grounds that it had taken extreme action in dealing with rioters. At about the same time, too, the R.U.C. had been disarmed, while the formation of a part-time Ulster Defence Regiment (U.D.R.) under British Army commanders was commenced. In these circumstances, the conduct of anti-guerilla action and the enforcement of law and order could only fall to an even larger extent on the Army, so that it could no longer perform all the duties thrust upon it without drawing upon units then garrisoned in Germany.

15th/19th Hussars Group with 4th R.T.R., July–December 1971
In October 1970, Lieutenant-Colonel J. S. F. Murray (15th/19th Hussars), stationed at Fallingbostel, was ordered by the G.O.C. 1st Division to prepare his Regiment, less one squadron, for operations as infantry in Ulster in August 1971, and to take under command two squadrons of the 4th R.T.R. (then at Hohne on the other side of the ranges) to bring him up to four company strength. The squadron of each regiment left behind in B.A.O.R. was to remain fully operational and administer the barracks and the families. Already some armoured reconnaissance units of the R.A.C. were in Ulster, but Murray's Group was the first to be committed as infantry in the Operation 'Banner' rôle,[1] as well as being the first mixed R.A.C. group. Their methods would point the way for those who would follow, in a task quite unlike anything undertaken by tank

[1]Operation 'Banner' implemented the involvement in Ulster of British units from B.A.O.R.

regiments hitherto. The problems they solved while, indeed, new, were almost identical with those that would be met by their successors. Their description in this book raises fresh difficulties for the historian, because he is writing about events which took place so recently, which are related to continuing operations and which are, therefore, subject to the restrictions and distortions imposed by security. Here, therefore, it is only possible to set the scene, to highlight, within the chronology, some of the most celebrated or typical incidents which occurred as the months and years went by, and to paint in the tones and colours in an endeavour to show what these operations were intended to achieve at the time.

Murray has written that he regarded the R.T.R. as 'the modern equivalent of Cromwell's Ironsides who, in their day, were the best soldiers in Europe. My Squadron Commander when I was an Officer Cadet at Bovington was Major Jock Holden . . . I am able to say that when we, a Cavalry Regiment, found ourselves day by day working closely with an R.T.R. unit we were put on our meṭtle and I think that applied to the R.T.R. as well . . .' Murray adopted the joint motto of the two Regiments – 'Be Swift, Be Bold, Be Vigilant and Fear Naught' – and it was ideally appropriate for them in the test that was to come. From the start, it was a dangerous task, and the training he carried out was highly realistic, modelled as it was on the experiences of the infantry and engineer units which had already seen action in Ulster. After the intensive tank training, which had to last them for the next nine months, the tank crews put their Chieftains into light preservation and, in April, turned to acquiring, in three months, the infantryman's skills. This included a taste of simulated rioting in a part of Fallingbostel barracks – renamed Ballyfally – which proved far more harmful to those taking part on both sides than the injuries sustained (with a few notable and tragic exceptions) during the real thing. The 4th's contribution to 15th/19th Hussars' Group was A Squadron (Major J. A. T. Slade), re-christened D Rifle Company, and B Squadron (Major P. Hammond) which became B Rifle Company – but for the purpose of this narrative they will be called by their usual names. Each was of about 125 men armed with S.L.R.s and the .usual paraphernalia of anti-riot gear. B recorded that during training they had been subjected to crowds throwing paving-stones, bottles, logs, petrol bombs and 'to have had five hospitalised – and we have been lucky'; and that their 'Jocks' formed a mutual respect for the 'Geordies' of the 15th/19th 'based on the number of injuries inflicted on each Squadron' during their inter-squadron 'rioting'.

But Murray demanded much more besides sheer courage, physical strength and thoughtful technique; he insisted also upon outstanding behaviour and bearing. Tempers were to be kept strictly under control: 'If any one officer or soldier does lose his temper in the face of provocation from civilians while we are in Ulster, we will have failed as a Regiment,' he wrote, 'We must learn to grin and bear it'. In the middle of the rough and tumble, as he welded Jocks and Geordies into a conglomerate group, he held a Queen's Birthday Parade, a simple ceremonial parade with the officers and men dressed in combat clothing, with weapons and equipment as for I.S. operations in a deliberate attempt to achieve the standard of turnout required, and as a way of welding the sub-units together. The C.O. of the 4th – Lieutenant-Colonel M. H. Sinnatt (who had purposely stood aside from the training of his squadrons) – took the salute. And, in order to eliminate, if possible, the accidental discharge of firearms (so often a cause of death or injury in operations), Murray laid down that any man carrying out incorrect 'Make Safe' or 'Unload' drills on the range or in training would be automatically given 28 days' detention or fined seven days' pay, while officers would be 'invited' to make a contribution towards the Welfare of the Regiment.

When Murray arrived with the Advance Party in Ulster on 23 July, he observed the signs of strain in members of 21st Engineer Regiment, from whom his Group was to take over, and was taken aside by the Commander, Land Forces (Major-General A. H. Farrar-Hockley, late Glosters) who said, 'Keep it to yourself. Internment is coming – perhaps rather sooner than you think'. At the same time, he was promised ten Ferrets for the Group's Reconnaissance Troop. From the notes of both A and B Squadrons, emerges an air of suppressed excitement, an ill-concealed desire to get on with the job. At first, the Group was sent to one of the quieter areas between Belfast and the border. A Squadron shared with another unit a disused linen factory near Lurgan High Street – and made the best of poor accommodation, sleeping on double-tiered bunks. Yet here the comfort was rated superior to that of the hangar at Long Kesh where B Squadron dwelt as part of a total population of 400 men in one building, sharing three showers. Almost at once, the first members of the advanced party were out on the streets, a search party from A immediately finding two walkie-talkie radio sets and some I.R.A. leaflets, while members of B, on their first night, 'went to a riot in Lurgan as guests of 21 Engr Regt'.

No sooner had the Main Party arrived at Aldergrove airport on 3–4 August, than they were involved in the hectic routine which was to absorb every waking moment for the next four months. B Squadron was now allotted Banbridge as its operational area. Basically, each squadron was permanently on four hours' stand-by duty, with one troop at 60 minutes' notice and another at 30, with duties similar to those which had fallen to the lot of their predecessors in India, Palestine, Libya, Egypt, Southern Arabia, Cyprus, Malaya, North Borneo and Hong Kong, when dealing with racial and religious conflicts during the past 25 years. They patrolled the streets, guarded police stations and other vital points (including their own premises where a strong-point came to be known as a sangar), made searches for seditious literature and all manner of warlike materials, and stood facing the hostile crowds who hurled abuse, rocks and nail bombs, and which sometimes sheltered a hidden sniper. From the moment they left the safety of their quarters, often in the company of television crews who followed them everywhere in the hope of a scoop, they were at risk and subject to tension. And sometimes, even in their barracks, they were far from entirely safe. To pass the time when they were not in action they watched television, listened to the radio and, with the exception of A Squadron at Lurgan, paid visits to a discotheque established by Murray. Here, they could meet young women from all over the Province, in an establishment which was strictly supervised by the Army Physical Training W.O. II of the 15th/19th, who was known to the girls as 'Hitler'. Apart from this they ate, got what sleep they could and wrote letters home – or sometimes telephoned, even to Germany. Meanwhile, their families waited in fear that news reports of riots would mean that their men were in peril – as, for much of the time, they were. Discipline – the intelligent kind, backed by up-to-date information – was needed at home or in the garrisons of B.A.O.R. as much as it was in the environs of Banbridge and Lurgan. A well-produced news-sheet helped both soldiers and their dependents to understand what was going on and why they were being put at risk.

The decision on 8 August by Mr. Brian Faulkner, the Prime Minister of Northern Ireland, to arrest and intern all known members and sympathisers of the I.R.A. was recognized by the soldiers as a provocation, and none were more sure of a hot time than the members of B Squadron when they were moved into Belfast on 5 August prior to the start of internment – Operation 'Demetrius'. When guarding R.U.C. stations they automatically became the target for terrorists. Troopers Skinner

(Lisburn Road) and Warnock (Mount Pottinger) both had narrow escapes, on the 6th, from respectively, a sniper and a spray of machine-gun fire from a passing car. But when the operation began, and the troops moved in during the early hours of the 9th to arrest the wanted men in their areas, surprise was complete. Security was tight and the R.U.C. had been kept in the dark. B Squadron rounded-up five of the seven men they had been sent to collect, and then returned to their police stations as Belfast, and many other outlying towns and villages, erupted into a cacophony of dustbin lids, banged as a warning by women and children, the whine of Saracens, shooting, burning and rioting. Very soon, the streets were deserted save for military patrols and burning vehicles as the noise of battle swelled. In Old Park Station, 2nd Lieutenant J. D. Lowry witnessed a major gun battle in the Ardoyne on the 9th and 10th and became the target for intermittent sniper fire throughout the 11th. On the 12th, B Squadron returned to Long Kesh as the Province Reserve.

Meanwhile, A Squadron, detached from 15th/19th Hussars and under command of another brigade, made arrests at Lurgan and then had to stand between noisy Protestant and Catholic crowds 'looking at each other' and attempting to build barricades. Lieutenant N. B. Bovingdon's troop spent 3½ hours dispersing a crowd while under bombardment from bricks and petrol bombs, and the rest of the day breaking down the barricades as fast as the crowds could build them – thus diverting them from more destructive occupations. Often, indeed, a diplomatic word with the local community leaders, would bring peace. Sometimes there was comedy to defuse the situation – such as the occasion when Lance-Corporal Mason told a chanting crowd to 'Shut up or I fire' [rubber bullets, of course] and when, to his surprise, they did so, he fell off the wall he was standing on. A sense of humour was essential, but, as Murray remarked, 'Even though our mailed fist was kept firmly in a velvet glove, the Irish, both Protestant and Roman Catholic, knew it was there. Once they had let off steam they quickly calmed down and then the more moderate and decent folk would appear and say, with cups of tea, how ashamed they were of the whole business. And each and everyone, regardless of his behaviour, was always addressed as 'Sir' or 'Madam' by every soldier.'

When the initial wrath provoked by the internment had evaporated, the squadrons reverted to the basic tasks of dominating an area to instil confidence among the locals, to prevent inter-factional trouble, to eliminate snipers which, at the time, were a serious menace and, every now and then, to try and capture at snap road-blocks those who had evaded the internment net. A Squadron spent almost the entire four-month tour based on Lurgan, and, in September, was given an occasional break in the routine, when sent to patrol Lough Neagh in assault boats, in order to check gun-running by that route. For B, at the end of August, there came a complete change from the hurly-burly of Belfast and its outskirts, when they were put under command of 14th/20th Hussars in the border area adjacent to Newry, Crossmaglen and Forkill – a notorious zone, with Catholics and I.R.A. galore, all mixed up with traditional smugglers, whose pastime had been disrupted and, in some respects, improved by the emergency. Here the action had the flavour of border war in North Borneo, except that thick forest was replaced by agricultural land. Nightly, the I.R.A. made forays from Eire to lay ambushes and plant bombs; in the early hours of 4 September they managed to explode a home-made, Claymore mine as an armoured Landrover of 4 Troop was passing the Derrybeg housing estate, near Newry. Standing at the back while riding shot-gun and operating the searchlight, was Trooper Warnock, who died from his injuries while the other two members of the crew were injured. This was the first R.T.R. death of the campaign, the effect of which, as Hammond wrote at the time, 'the Squadron has stood extremely well and has shown . . . remarkable self control. It has made them all the more determined in their approach to operations and we now look forward to the opportunity to at least even up the score . . . The people of Bessbrook . . . are all upset and sorry for what has happened. By last night they had donated, completely off their own bats, over £40. One scarcely knows what to say in such circumstances.'

Attention was again focussed upon the border when, on 13 October, Operation 'Ashburton' began, a systematic attempt to block or crater all unapproved border crossing-points in order to hamper the movement of gun-runners and wanted men between Ulster and Eire. B Squadron provided one troop each day, under command of C Squadron Royal Scots Dragoon Guards (R.S.D.G.), to escort the demolition parties of Sappers. On the second day, it was the turn of 4 Troop (2nd Lieutenant C. P. Lavender) with 2 Saladins and 2 Ferrets of the R.S.D.G. under command, to crater roads within a few yards of the border, south of Forkill – their work being diligently reported and filmed by a B.B.C. T.V. crew. At 10.00 hrs. a Claymore mine exploded under the leading Ferret and, at the same time, heavy small-arms fire opened from three places inside Eire. A Sapper was hit, the armoured cars deployed to seek the enemy and 4

Troop dismounted as a Contact Report was sent. With that nice disrespect reserved by all 'infantrymen' for armoured soldiers, Lavender commented: 'Needless to say the armoured cars were not much help and we proceeded with clearing either side of the road. At this stage the fire was still pretty intense, not a shot having yet been fired by any of the convoy. A sound rather like that of a 'hand held' para illuminating flare being fired was then heard and on enquiring I discerned that an unidentified missile had passed between the RE 4 ton truck and the armoured Pig. . . . the fact that they had fired it was rather horrifying, especially as it had obviously been intended for the Sappers' explosives truck! . . . a fine battle then developed . . . during which 2 Section (Cpl Spalding) and Tp H.Q. fired a total of 132 7.62 rounds and a Ferret from the R.S.D.G., 190 rounds of .30 Browning . . . a good piece of infantry tank indication [after I sent Tpr Lilley to the F.S.C. to indicate the targets . . .] After half an hour of this fire battle only sporadic fire was being directed against us . . . Thereafter the decision was made to continue with the task and . . . the cratering was carried out successfully. . . . Certainly it was the first time for most of the troop that they had been under fire and the reaction was very good when bullets started flying. . . . The I.R.A. . . . fired an estimated (conservative) 600 rounds and a rocket launcher . . . We estimated there were about 20 I.R.A. gunmen opposing us.'

A note of disgust is then attached when it transpired that one of the gunmen (who had also been concerned with Warnock's death) had been arrested in the South and given a paltry 14 days' sentence for possession of firearms, leaving him free to ambush yet another convoy near Forkill a little later. And finally, the futility of these operations was exposed, when the holes were filled in each night after they were made.

On 23–24 October, came the Newry Uprising (as local terminology called a fermented riot), after A Company 2nd Light Infantry (L.I.) had shot dead three bank robbers in Hill Street. Within the hour, fierce rioting had broken out and the infantry were surrounded in the centre of the town (which was 85 per cent Catholic). B Squadron was given the task of blocking the routes from the West to prevent reinforcements reaching the rioters, and of then moving to the relief of the hard-pressed Light Infantry to prevent the riot getting out of hand. Lowry's troop was told to seize a road junction as a secure base for Lavender's to pass through and link up with the 2nd L.I., and here, a heavy battle took place with harsh, joint-action by both troops, in air thick with C.S. gas fired by the L.I. Within a

400–500 square-yard area, there were 1,000 rioters, and Hill Street was blocked by many burned-out cars and lorries which provided the best illumination after the street lights had been extinguished. Twenty-three rubber bullets were fired by the 4th. These, in addition to a certain amount of physical persuasion by the Jocks, re-established control by dawn, as reinforcements began to arrive from a distance, and what amounted to a curfew was imposed. Like so many events of its kind, the rioting died down as soon as the troops took a firm hold of the situation, and they satisfactorily prevented a further outbreak of violence on the 26th, when 10,000 people turned up for the funeral of the three robbers. From then on, in conjunction with the R.U.C., the squadron concentrated on 'low key' operations in an attempt to bring the town back to normality, with the additional result that, unlike the other predominantly Catholic areas of Londonderry and Belfast, 'no-go' areas were prevented in Newry.

Not a day was to pass without some incident or another. The diaries tell of unbroken action, changing tactics to meet a volatile situation, successes, failures, triumphs, tragedies, humour, hatred, common-sense, weariness, tension and boundless courage by all concerned – not excluding the families in Germany, who were kept briefed and cared-for by the members of the units which had remained behind. Occasionally, soldiers, always wanting something more exciting to do, were foolhardy, but discipline was strictly enforced. Of the 4th, Murray would write of the deep impression they had made: 'They won all our hearts and many of our battles.'

In their last two days in Ulster, the Group (less B Squadron) carried out two pre-dawn raids into estates where it had never been possible to catch I.R.A. because of their 'vigilante' patrols. But this time, with the practice that makes perfect, they achieved what Murray listed as 'the most successful "lift" since Internment', or as a member of A Squadron put it:

'We decided to call on some old friends who, for the past four months, had not been at home. The early-morning visits were merely a parting gesture to display our continued interest in their affairs. By five o'clock on each morning we found that our friends had returned the compliment and were, in fact, at home . . . Of the seven retained over the two days, one or two were very old friends of ours, and quiet beers were drunk in celebration . . .'

A and C Squadrons 1st R.T.R., January–May 1972
Two squadrons of 1st R.T.R. (Lieutenant-Colonel S. J. Beards-

worth) went to Ulster as part of 13th/18th Hussars Group (Lieutenant-Colonel A. C. Ansell) a month after the 15th/19th had departed, and were sent, to begin with, to places which had been familiar to their predecessors – C (known as C Company) (Major A. L. P. Weeks) to Lurgan (where it remained all the time), and A (known as D Company) (Major M. N. S. Moriarty) to Long Kesh, whence it took turns to guard vulnerable points to the south-west of Belfast, acted as a mobile reserve and watched over the internees who were imprisoned there. And as with his predecessors, Ansell insisted upon treating his group as a whole, and renamed it 'The Lilywillies', a portmanteau name incorporating his own Regiment's nickname with 'My Boy Willie'.

They were fortunate to the extent that their period in Ulster coincided with a determined attempt on the part of the Security Forces to maintain 'a low profile' in the hope that this would lead to an improvement in relations with the Army, and a gradual cessation of violence. That this was to be an unfulfilled hope was almost immediately made apparent by the Catholic community strengthening its hold on the so-called 'no-go' areas, while the Provisional I.R.A. (P.I.R.A.) perpetrated ambushes whenever possible, and maintained the level of protest through 'Civil Rights Marches'. On 30 January, the tension was heightened by a notorious confrontation at Londonderry between Catholics and the 1st Battalion, The Parachute Regiment, which led to a number of deaths, and added yet another emotive date, 'Bloody Sunday', to Irish history. And as Catholics tempers rose so, too, did those of the Protestants who interpreted any form of softness by the Security Forces as a weakening of the Government's intentions to keep the Army in Ulster. The Protestants were prepared to look to their own defences, and with this in mind, they strengthened their own para-military organizations. So, when tracing the story of the 1st R.T.R.'s stay in Ulster, conflicting themes frequently emerge to illustrate the pattern of duties which was to be theirs and that of all their successors, on each Op. 'Banner' tour in the infantry rôle, throughout the years to come.

The incidents quoted below are selected from *The Tank*, because they were written close to the events and catch the flavour of action as few other available reports do. Community relations while engaged on house search at Lurgan, just after arrival in January:

'Corporal "Yoko" Johnson's section [in C Squadron] was offered tea all round, and he reckoned that had the search gone in at about 0730 hrs [instead of 0530 hrs as it did] they would have sat down to Sugar Puffs, boiled eggs and toast. Second-Lieutenant David Lloyd-Edwards, however, was given the task of searching a house belonging to the father of the Official I.R.A.'s Chief Recruiting Officer. Predictably tea was not offered. Instead a stream of the most indelicate language, followed by an impassioned speech on the theories of Leninism and the advantages of life under the communist system.'

A Squadron when engaged in snap road-blocks (Vehicle Check Points (V.C.P.)), searching the Belfast to Dublin express and going through the internment camp with a fine toothcomb:

'The finds varied from tunnels to poteen stills, but about the most tiring part of the operation was the standing, motion-less, looking mean, tough and determined.'

After 'Bloody Sunday', the black flags came out in Lurgan, the rioting became widespread, and C Squadron was in the thick of it. Weeks and Sqn Sergeant-Major Briggs were caught in an ambush and their escort, a cook called Private Gaffy, was wounded. An orgy of arson and hijacking led to this radio conversation of interested resignation at something beyond recall:

'Hello 3, this is 31 – they've hijacked a bread van.'

'3 Roger – let them set fire to it, then there'll be toast for tea.'

And, when the rocks and bottles flew in the Kilwilkie:

'Sergeant Ken Watkin showed his soccer expertise by neatly deflecting the missile to the pavement. Trooper "Mad Mitch" Mitchell needs practice, as his attempts at deflection failed and an airborne brick felled him.'

This was followed by a comment from A Squadron, who were sometimes called down to back up C in Lurgan:

'. . . and when we do go we stand by to watch C being roughed up by 12-year-olds.'

The story of three days in the life of one troop (3 in A Squadron commanded by Lieutenant I. Stevens) between 27 and 30 March after the Prime Minister (Mr. Edward Heath) had announced a new 'Initiative' for Ulster and brought a strong Protestant reaction, is by no means unique:

'Sitting astride the Shankhill and Wakehurst estates [in Lurgan] while the stones and bottles flew . . . amid mumblings of "British Army bastards" from Protestants and "You're doing a *grand* job lads" from the Catholics . . . manning the barriers outside the Catholic estate with the local vigilantes and trying to keep the people calm . . . we had a good work-ing understanding with the Catholics who kept us awash with tea, biscuits, cake, soup etc. [Later in Obin Street, Portadown] . . . a crowd of almost 200 Protestants appeared at the tunnel hurling bricks and bottles. The Catholics replied with one quick return volley. . . . We then sat and kept the crowds apart for half an hour. The Protestants . . . returned at about 1730 hrs in greater numbers intent on burning the Catholics out. Swift intervention by Corporal Farrell's section and a section from A Squadron 13th/18th Hussars drove the Protestants back, but there were some ugly scenes. . . . All this came to an end on 30 March when we took over the close guarding of Long Kesh from A Squadron 13th/18th Hussars.' Long Kesh was the worst chore of all and it was sometimes felt necessary to give a few men a break by attaching them, informally, to infantry units in the Ardoyne where the action was hottest. Moriarty records his foremost impression of Long Kesh as 'closely resembling a Nazi Concentration Camp. The internees lived in appalling squalor and their accommodation reeked of stale food. . . . Each compound had its quota of record players and late into the evenings Irish rebel songs could be heard. Twice we searched it and on the first occasion we discovered the beginning of a tunnel and some replicas of traditional I.R.A. weaponry.'

The 1st R.T.R. would return to Germany, in their own words, '. . . some thinner, some quieter; many more have grown up; all are better and more experienced soldiers, wiser men. Militarily, the tour was a useful counter-point to the hum-drum mechanized life in B.A.O.R., but the sight of British people in bitter conflict was one that all would prefer to forget'. Unhappily the struggle could not be confined to Ulster. On 23 February, seven people were killed by a bomb at the Officers' Mess of 16th Parachute Brigade in Aldershot, as a reprisal for 'Bloody Sunday'. It began to dawn on some of those engaged in Ulster, who groped at an understanding of the destructive mentality of the enemy, that to give way there would merely advance the day when a similar struggle might break out on the other side of the Irish Sea.

In Ulster, no one tour was quite like another, because each was varied by the location to which a unit was sent, the current political situation and, to some extent, the length of stay in the province. Since action was virtually non-stop from the moment a unit arrived until the day it departed, and the number of incidents in which each was involved legion, there can be no possibility here of describing each encounter in detail. Out of a grey panorama with monotonous over-tones appear the characteristic flashes of pathos, gallantry, triumph, failure, and weariness – and it is natural that those incidents that were dramatic should figure most prominently.

3rd R.T.R. Group at Long Kesh and County Fermanagh, January–May 1973

Under the command of Lieutenant-Colonel J. G. R. Dixon, R.H.Q., the Reconnaissance Troop and A and C Squadrons in the infantry rôle, were deployed to guard H.M. Prison, Maze at Long Kesh, to patrol the country surrounding Newtownards and to detach one squadron to County Fermanagh – the former and latter locations being potentially volatile areas at any time. But Operation 'Motorman', on 31 July, 1972, had eliminated the Catholic 'no-go' areas and this, symbolizing the Army's pronounced intention of dominating the extremists in order to neutralize their capability until a political settlement could be reached, had its effect. For the time being, the I.R.A.'s offensive declined, especially since many of its best trained men were already dead or behind bars. The Reconnaissance Troop, for example, covered 30,000 miles in its Ferrets in February, but saw little action among the 'troubles' attending a three-day strike. The most dangerous locality was County Fermanagh with its long, easily crossed borderland with Eire, where many hard-core terrorists lived. From the base camp at St. Angelo (built on a disused aerodrome and once likened to a luxurious P.O.W. Camp), the squadron, whose turn it was to act as garrison, controlled an armoured car squadron of the 16th/5th Lancers, plus a battery of R.A. (also as infantry) while coming under the direct operational command of R.H.Q. 16th/5th Lancers from Omagh. Highly tempting targets were the R.U.C. Police Stations, which were frequently attacked with small-arms fire and sometimes by rockets. The station at Crosslea was first to receive some Russian-made RPG 7s on 26 March, and on one occasion the terrorists managed to smuggle a bomb right into St. Angelo Camp in a hijacked laundry van. Fermanagh, indeed, was a bombers' paradise at this time, with some very large devices being planted in road culverts with quite devastating effect upon vehicles caught in the explosion. In fact, just before the 3rd left, 6 Troop (Lieutenant W. H. Russell) found a booby-trapped bomb close to the border, and a patrol of the 16th/5th Lancers was lucky to escape serious injury when a 'giant' culvert bomb exploded between Belcoo and Garrison. This was the area where the 1st R.T.R. was about to arrive, as it took over from the 16th/5th, and the perils awaiting them were to get worse before the threat could be seriously tackled.

Badger and Ajax, 2nd R.T.R., respectively September 1973–
January 1974, and January–May 1974

Badger (Major M. G. Tweed) equipped with Saladins, Ferrets and Saracens, picked a hectic time in which to take up residence at Gosford Castle near Armagh. At the beginning, Tweed found himself beset by an old-fashioned request from the 1st Battalion, the Hampshire Regiment, that of having his troops split up into 'penny packets' to support the local infantry companies spread all over a large rural area. He resisted and, instead, was given the task of dominating, by mobility, the huge area north and west of Armagh, while the infantry controlled the towns and the border. A succession of brick throwing and sniping incidents began from the moment of their arrival, to which the riposte was a most encouraging 'lift' of four wanted men at dawn one day by Second-Lieutenant Burr. When they took over from 9th/12th Lancers it was said this was 'the-land-where-nothing-happens', but this should have been a warning in itself. The terrorists were merely recuperating prior to taking the initiative against a unit new to the Province, with bomb attacks and a so-called '6-hour Offensive'. At once, Badger joined in the counter-offensive enthusiastically, sealing the border, lifting the wanted, guarding vital points, dealing with hijacks, and searching for culvert bombs, always in the fervent hope that they would spot them before they were blown. Often there was nothing to report, but sometimes they won: 'One night two terrorists, one carrying a bomb, were crossing from the Republic by way of Clady Bridge. Suddenly there was a bang and then there were none. Second-Lieutenant P. H. Bangham's section were sent up at once to admire the bits and were immediately invited by the Garda to step back into Ulster. Next day they went up again in daylight . . . and at once came under fire from two gunmen. Some minutes and a hundred Browning rounds later, two more terrorists were bagged.'

Tweed wrote: 'Certainly our particular approach to the job – hearts and minds patrolling in 24 hour Ferret deterrent patrols, community relations efforts and simply being in the right place at the right time – seemed to pay off. . . . At times it is difficult to convince the cold, wet and weary soldier that he must go on, for as soon as the Army lets up, the rule of the I.R.A. creeps back. . . .'

With this, Major A. J. Cornwell of Ajax did not entirely agree, when he took over from Badger in January. To him, the Saladins and Saracens 'simply invited the opposition to have a poke at them' and he therefore spent two weeks getting rid of them and thereafter spending '. . . 75% of our time on our feet in the villages and towns. The main idea was to get people on the ground listening and looking. We used Landrovers for transport and communications and we banned the use of A Vehicles. We also went slow – from place to place slowly and deliberately, and we had a minimum of 100 metres between vehicles. They might get the first . . . but we didn't ever give them the chance to get two vehicles with one bomb'. As a result, the period of Ajax's tour passed off without the same feverish activity and high drama of that of their predecessors. Nevertheless, big bombs continued to be laid, indicating an unchecked source of supply somewhere near at hand. At the same time, efficiency among the Security Forces improved. Captain F. R. Geisler was master of a very slick operation in February, which caught two hooded bank robbers who held up the Postmistress of Carnagh and took £140. But for the most part, their's was a familiar story of fruitless V.C.P.s, occasional 'lifts', a plethora of bomb hoaxes and sometimes the discovery of the real thing (with the Ordnance Corps Ammunition Technical Officer (A.T.O.) called in to perform his hazardous tasks of neutralization), or of a bomb factory with its store of explosive, Cordtex and old clocks. And all the time they were anxiously watched over from a distance by their families in Germany, who were kept as fully informed as possible by the publication of a weekly news-letter produced by the squadrons.

1st R.T.R. at Omagh, May 1973–November 1974

The rôle assumed by 1st R.T.R. (Lieutenant-Colonel J. P. Maxwell) could be seen from the map as an up-scaled version of those undertaken by Ajax and Badger of the 2nd. With the complete unit based on Omagh (after taking over from the 16th/5th Lancers) the squadrons were deployed under Maxwell's command throughout Fermanagh and Tyrone engaged in the routine of patrolling and helping to garrison such hot-spots as the fortified, border R.U.C. stations at Belleek (sometimes, for clear reasons, known as the Alamo), Rosslea and the Deanery at Clogher. While the mobile patrols in their Saladins, Ferrets, Saracens and Landrovers quartered the roads, the static detachments (usually from the Assault Troops) stood watch and ward behind protective sandbags, wire mesh and corrugated-tin walls. The major difference for the 1st compared to the 2nd, lay in their committal to Ulster for 18 months which meant that they were accompanied by their families, whose quarters were in the vicinity of Lisanelly Camp – a barracks laid out on modern amenity lines, without facilities for defence. While Maxwell could publicly relish the prospect—or, as he put it, that: 'The Regiment is on its own here and everything that happens is of our own making; there is no "Them" to curse when things go wrong', he was close to the mark when he added, 'Our life will be as lively and enjoyable as we manage to make it,'—the future was not without its anxieties.

The threat to family life in Omagh was first demonstrated on the night of 20 June, when two troopers and their wives, walking from the camp to their quarters, came under fire from four mortar bombs which had been aimed at the camp and had missed by 100 yards – the I.R.A.'s home-made weapons were often highly inaccurate. Reaction to this attack was immediate, based on the use of a mobile reserve through a search by a combined force of A.A.C. helicopters equipped with the powerful Nitesun searchlight and air-lifted men of A Squadron (the Sky Cavalry) who were hot in pursuit within eight minutes of the attack. On 29 August, the attempt to intimidate the families was more direct, when a hijacked post-office van containing a .400lb. bomb was driven into the married quarters estate and detonated without warning. Sixteen quarters were extensively damaged, but fortunately none of the sixteen women and children, who had been hit by flying glass and débris, were seriously hurt. It was on an occasion such as this that so much depended upon the spontaneous good neighbourliness of everyone, allied to swift remedial action by the Quartermasters' departments, as well as the medical teams, to make good the damage. In addition, the 1st took advantage of the talents of Sergeant M. Newton, a former journalist, to launch a monthly tabloid newspaper called *First Edition*, published to professional standards, to amuse as well as keep the widely-spread unit well-informed, and sustain family morale with propaganda quotes on the lines of 'No I.R.A. will make me go home'.

Newton had plenty to write about. Action was continuous and sometimes extremely hectic. He could tell of Trooper Wallace coolly driving his Landrover to safety on 10 July, when a 200lb. mine exploded 15 feet in front of his vehicle; of the dramatic capture by Lieutenant R. N. Hine and Corporal Hepworth of two terrorists in the act of planting a bomb on 15 July, during an operation under the direct command of Major D. L. Lewis, and in which a troop detached from 4th R.T.R. took part (the 4th at that moment being non-operational in the A.B.T.U. rôle at Catterick); of the death of an A.T.O.,

Staff-Sergeant M. Beckett, R.A.O.C. (attached to the 1st) when he was tackling a bomb in Pettigo on 30 August; of a massive campaign of disruption on 25 October, when 21 minor incidents occurred within a few hours, ranging from vehicle hijackings to bomb hoaxes and some random shooting; and of the battle of Belleek at breakfast-time on 25 November – 'The nine-minute gun battle that terrorised a town', as the headline had it. The latter was, indeed, a well coordinated attack from across the nearby border, opened by a prolonged burst of machine-gun fire directed at the sentry, Trooper Brooks, and rising to a crescendo as Brooks replied with his L.M.G. until the rest of the Assault Troop, under Sergeant R. Litchfield of A Squadron joined in. RPG 7 (Russian Bazooka-type) rockets were now fired by the terrorists – two of them soaring overhead to land in the village behind, two being retarded by the wire-mesh screen surrounding the station, and the final pair hitting the building and penetrating but without causing casualties. Six terrorists were seen on the opposite bank of the river and two were possibly hit – although there was no way of confirming this as they crawled away at the end of the battle.

On 11 December, it was the turn of the garrison at Belcoo R.U.C. Station to be attacked by the same methods, this time by night. Here, Trooper D. G. Woolley, with mature tactical insight, appreciated that the enemy had chosen their position so well that fire could not be brought to bear on them from the station. Running under fire to his Ferret, he drove it out of the station, halted in full view while he scrambled up into the turret, and then brought the Browning accurately into action against the flashes from the enemy weapons 300 metres away, with the result that the terrorists stopped shooting and ran.

Firm counter-action, such as Woolley's, reminded the 1st's opponents that, in guerilla warfare, when the game ceases to be worth the candle in one area it is wise to try elsewhere. Certainly the furious defence of the R.U.C. stations in Fermanagh and Tyrone made the I.R.A. become more cautious so that, when Lieutenant-Colonel A. K. F. Walker arrived to command in February 1974, he had fewer anxieties than his predecessor – despite the fact that a 200lb. bomb devastated the main street of Omagh within four hours of his taking over! In an 18 months' tour, the troops' senses of detection were bound to be accentuated. When Corporal J. Johnston of the Assault Troop, B Squadron, noticed a fertilizer bag blowing in a field on 12 April, his suspicions led to the discovery of a large cache of explosives (often manufactured from fertilizer), ammunition and mines. Likewise, after 15–20 terrorists had fired 15 mortar bombs at the Deanery and killed a woman of the Ulster Defence Regiment on 2 May, the follow-up was relentless, and two days later, fresh information plus this heavy pressure, led to the rout of a car bomb party as it was in the act of loading-up, together with further finds of arms and ammunition. Bomb attacks continued, but so jumpy were the local I.R.A. that they sometimes abandoned their vehicles at the sight of a patrol of the 1st with the U.D.R. and R.U.C.

More damaging to Ulster was the strike by the Ulster Workers Council in May 1974 which practically brought the Province's economy to a standstill. To the Army fell the task of distributing fuel-oil, and to B Squadron 1st R.T.R. that of escorting fuel-tankers while the men of A and C took over requisitioned, major petrol stations in Fermanagh and Tyrone, and became petrol-pump attendants in what were called 'Government Authorized Filling Stations'. 'I suspect that the soldiers quite enjoyed their new found rôle,' wrote Walker '. . . which gave them a break from routine patrolling', but he went on to remark on the manner in which the strike seemed to persuade even the 'moderates' to take up entrenched positions. 'I think that most of us realised, perhaps for the first time, that even the most agreeable Ulsterman conceals his prejudices under a dangerously thin skin'.

In a way, this was exemplified by an outbreak of rioting in Carrickmore on 19 July, after a bomb had exploded without warning in a pub. For no clear reason, except the urgings of prejudice, fear and hatred, a crowd of 150 people attacked the local R.U.C. just as 3 Troop (Lieutenant S. Evans) of A Squadron was cordoning the area. Twenty of them went beserk, surrounded three policemen and began beating them, and threw stones which prevented the troop from going immediately to the policemen's aid. In desperation, one of the police fired in the air, and this shocked the mob which, fearing the presence of a sniper, dispersed; but, shortly afterwards, some of them were back helping to clear up the mess!

In the final reckoning, as it left Ulster in November after 18 months, the 1st could lay claim, among other details, to the arrest of 23 people, to having found 30 enemy weapons, 3,109 rounds of ammunition and some 6,000lb. of explosives. Thirty-three rockets and 25 mortar bombs had been fired at them, and they had been involved in innumerable bomb incidents and fire-fights. Yet, although several members of the unit had been injured, none had been killed, although some members of the attached Security Forces did pay the full penalty.

During the tour the pattern of warfare in Ulster had changed. Shortly after the 1st's arrival in 1973, Northern Ireland Assembly Elections had been held by Proportional Representation and, later that year, power sharing had been agreed in principle between the political parties. But in May 1974, Mr. Faulkner had resigned under pressure from a general strike, and the Executive was suspended by the British Government which announced, in September, that the R.U.C. and U.D.C. were to be expanded. Operations had entered a routine pattern without foreseeable end, which was ruled by monotony and, in general, not as perilous as it had been at the beginning. The security measures were having at least a stabilizing effect. The 1st noticed these things without drawing any strong conclusions. They noted, too, in August 1974, the withdrawal of their last Saladin armoured car, this type of vehicle having proved of little value in the kind of operation then in progress. They – and their families – discovered, also, with a sense of disappointment, that their next posting, instead of being all as one in a families' station, would take detached squadrons to peace-keeping duties in trouble spots of a different kind.

3rd R.T.R. Group, Armagh, September 1974–January 1975
When the 3rd (Lieutenant-Colonel G. Read) reached Ulster in an infantry Op 'Banner' rôle for the second time, the novelty of the situation had worn off. Replacing the original enthusiasm of early 1973 was a mood of grimmer determination to do a job which some infantrymen had already performed twice as many times as their R.A.C. comrades. The Regimental Group, consisting of A, C and H.Q. Squadrons, with three infantry companies and a Gunner Battery under command, was based on Armagh and responsible, within 3rd Brigade area, for the whole of Police Division K and a part of M. In consequence, for a few weeks, the 3rd shared an operational boundary with the 1st. 'The great cry seems to be that we are waiting for the autumn offensive', recorded *The Tank* notes, after they had mentioned a quiet start with only a few bombs and a host of minor incidents. November, with its rash of incendiary-device attacks in Armagh and Markethill, and the deaths of two attached A.T.O.s, Staff-Sergeant Rose and Staff-Sergeant Simpson, Royal Hussars, proved them only too right. To mortar and machine-gun attacks from across the border were added, on 9 November, an attempt to park a proxy bomb[1] in a

---

[1]Explosives loaded into a car, whose owner was coerced into driving it to the target.

car outside the Keady R.U.C. station, which was garrisoned by men of C Squadron. But the men of the 3rd refused to be hustled, and actually managed to persuade the unwilling driver to remove his vehicle to a distance of 300 metres, where it exploded harmlessly.

In the fore-knowledge of secret negotiations taking place between their leaders and those of the Protestant Church for a Christmas Cease-Fire, the I.R.A. stepped-up their attacks in December. Permanent V.C.P.s at main roads – which by this time had been strongly fortified – were their special targets. That at Aughnacloy fought off a determined attack lasting an hour, and the one at Middletown was twice fired upon, although the attackers were mightily deterred by the weight of small-arms fire which they drew. Again, the atmosphere is caught by the 3rd's writer in *The Tank*: 'The period before the ceasefire, which came into effect on 23 December, was extremely busy with the local opposition appearing to have a last fling, resulting in a host of minor incidents, which meant a great deal of rushing about by patrols. After the ceasefire came into effect we were thankful for relative peace and quiet to catch up with some sleep'.

With only minor scares, the truce out-lasted the 3rd's stay, but by the time the next unit of the Regiment arrived in Ulster in May, the war was in full swing again as if nothing had intervened.

2nd R.T.R. Group, Armagh, May–September 1975
The truce, in fact, lasted rather longer than had been expected, with the hard-core I.R.A., no doubt, making the best of the lull to recruit their strength which had wilted somewhat under the strain of operations. Random bombings and sporadic shootings and murders involving both the Protestant and Catholic communities, the R.U.C. and the U.D.R., kept 2nd R.T.R.'s (Lieutenant-Colonel K. Ecclestone) Group of Ajax, Cyclops and Huntsman on the alert. Many internees had been released as part of Government policy to remove this source of provocation, and some of these undoubtedly returned to their old clandestine pastimes. But the Security Forces were by now kept extremely well-informed of their habits, and themselves often performed more like police than soldiers. When the house belonging to a well-known family of 'baddies', was blown-up in May, the 2nd paid careful attention to all its members. Two months later, they were happy to report the spectacular arrest of the most important member of the family who was found in a house which contained ammunition; a rare slip on the part

of known dissidents, who were safe, providing they were never caught with incriminating evidence on them. Lack of I.R.A. activity in one place was usually good reason to expect trouble elsewhere, and the re-deployment of troops from one area to another was a wise reaction to this.˒By now, the more experienced soldiers had settled for their preferred tasks – a permanent V.C.P. with the greater comfort provided by solid buildings being a favourite with some, but hated by many. So a re-deployment was sometimes unwelcome and could raise misgivings. When Ajax was moved from Armagh to Aughnacloy, with a troop detached to Lisnaskea under command of 15th/19th Hussars, the complaints ranged from 'working under strangers' in what was reputed to be 'the most bombed town in Fermanagh', to fears that 'there shouldn't be much of it left and life for us was likely to be uncomfortable'. Hard-luck stories notwithstanding, Ecclestone remarks that the troops 'were not afeared that life would be uncomfortable . . . they were pleased to be on their own'.

* * * * *

The soldiers, as usual, had learnt to make the best of a bad job, while the standard of accommodation provided was very much better than it had been in 1971, when members of the 4th had made up a hangar-full of 400 men. Because social life was so circumscribed by fears that off-duty contact with the local people might lead to a killing by the I.R.A., most entertainment and sport had to take place within the confines of small, fortified cantonments. Television passed much of the time between spells of duty, sleeping and eating. The standard of cooking was considerably raised, and it was made possible for a man to take a snack at any time of the day when he fancied it. The 'Golly Shops' became important features of every garrison, these small canteens sometimes opening on a round-the-clock schedule (which N.A.A.F.I. was unable to provide, because of difficulties in recruiting staff) and usually run by Pakistani or Indian contractors, who were the direct successors of the original Middle and Far East contractors, such as Roshan Din. They, with the Intelligence system at their disposal, often knew ahead of all others which unit would arrive next in sufficient time to allow them to purchase the franchise with money that was paid into unit funds.

A special jargon, allied closely to the peculiarities of the campaign, developed and was quite unlike those which distinguished the major World Wars and the later peace-keeping operations. Men fought from within sangars, took part in 'Lurks', 'Lifts' and checked out, often through a computer, the identity of local residents and their vehicles, to find out if they were 'Black' or 'White' (wanted or otherwise). At night, they scanned through passive, night-viewing devices called Starlight Scopes. At all times, they took care to avoid booby traps and 'come on' baits, and they copied police terms such as a 'Dick' (tail) and 'Mugger' (one who recognizes faces). Members of the Intelligence Sections often worked in plain clothes, dressed like the locals, with length of hair to taste and, in their demeanour, tended to emulate the heroes of T.V. detective dramas such as Harry O, and Starsky and Hutch. Naturally, they all looked forward, initially, in each tour of duty, to their four days R. and R. (Rest and Recuperation) leave, and eventually, the happy return to Germany or the United Kingdom. In the meantime, they performed their unenviable task with an almost incredibly detached fairness to all concerned, relentlessly trying to catch the P.I.R.A. (whom they loathed) endeavouring, particularly in the final weeks of a tour, to maintain their concentration while trying hard to avoid getting on each others' nerves as stress accumulated. All manner of devices such as 'sniffers', sensors, radar and a selection of electronic machines, including those needed to counter I.R.A. electronics, were put at their service, and they relied extensively on their own radio equipment to speed-up their response to every eventuality.

A unique contribution to the war in Ulster was the invention of 'Wheelbarrow' – the now famous remote-controlled machine for dealing with car-bombs and other explosive devices. It was the brainchild of a retired R.T.R. officer, Lieutenant-Colonel J. F. Miller, who was working on the staff at M.V.E.E. when, in March 1972, that establishment was asked to see if a remotely-controlled device could be produced which would tow away car-bombs, which were used so often in Ulster and other parts of the world where terrorism was prevalent. Miller, who had modified his domestic lawn-mower so that it would cut the grass, while being controlled remotely from the comfort of a deck-chair, conceived the idea of using such a machine, fitted with a suitable hook. From a local garden shop he bought an electrically-propelled, 3-wheeled wheelbarrow – hence the name – and within a few days, a hook and tiller steering had been fitted and the device successfully tested. Without delay, the original Mark 1 was sent to Ireland and used. Meanwhile, Miller and his small staff worked continuously to improve the basic idea, first on a 4-wheel basis, with skid steering and controls operated by electrical relays, followed by a tracked version which was sufficiently agile to surmount steps and stairways. Miller also turned his attention to the accessories, first making the hook collapsible on command, for easy withdrawal, and then developing a comprehensive kit of 'optional extras' such as a scissors grab which could pick up a dustbin, a nail-gun for keeping doors open after Wheelbarrow had passed through, a car window-breaking gun and a shot-gun mounting. Closed-circuit television was added, to permit close examination of a suspected object, and to enable Wheelbarrow to be operated when out of its controller's sight. In recognition of his services to Explosive Ordnance Disposal (E.O.D..) Miller, in March 1977, was made an Honorary Ammunition Technical Officer (A.T.O.) by the Director of Land Service Ammunition; a signal honour from a distinguished branch of the Royal Army Ordnance Corps.

In the final analysis, however, it was not the machines but the men's training and common-sense which was at the root of survival. Through close contact with the R.U.C. and the U.D.R., they learned the language of the locals and produced a few Appointment Titles for special use in Ulster; such as Rucksack for the R.U.C., 'Neptune' for a water-cannon, 'Green Finch' for a female member of the U.D.R., 'Wagtail' for a search dog, Brimstone for a 'padre' and Brownie for a 'photographer'. At times, they were almost as hard to comprehend as the Ulster people. Their armoured skills suffered, but to help correct the balance, they learned what it was to be under fire, the value of training junior leaders and the vital importance of Intelligence.

In the back of everybody's mind lived the thought that, when an Op. 'Banner' tour was over, the first essential, after leave, was to restore the unit's efficiency as an Armoured Regiment. A four-month tour in Ulster diverted a tank unit from its primary task for seven months, all told, and took it into a totally different environment. Although many would enjoy and profit from the experience of Ulster, in the meantime, the Rear Party had a hard task maintaining expensive and valuable equipment at peak. When soldiers, who had learned to be good infantry and police, came back to the Tank Park, they had to perform psychological acrobatics of readjustment to re-acquire the basic skills they had temporarily put aside. Undeniably, the efficiency of B.A.O.R. Armoured Regiments went into decline the moment Op. 'Banner' was introduced, and more than one C.O. made it his firm resolve that it should not be allowed to reduce armoured expertize. With shrewd insight, those who composed the notes for *The Tank* began to lay quite as much emphasis on the activities of the Rear Parties in B.A.O.R. as on the men in Ulster. For it was not simply a case of maintaining the equipment with which Technical Quartermasters, R.E.M.E. and the stay-behind crews concerned themselves, or the task of keeping the families informed of the welfare of their men who were away. It was an essential part of the services rendered by Unit Families Officers, Welfare Officers, clerks and all the other administrators, that their work was carried out with such efficiency and sympathy, reacting instantly and sensitively to any family crisis which arose, that the minds of their menfolk at the 'front' were kept at ease. It could be claimed that few civilian employers took the same amount of trouble over their men.

Nobody could afford to dismiss the thought that to neglect training for Op. 'Banner' might jeopardize lives, let alone forsaking the crucial aim of the operation which was intended to create conditions for peace. No longer, however, was the I.R.A.'s threat in Ulster one that could lead to their victory. This the troops knew, and knew too that they could lay claim to a large share of the credit. At the end of 1975, the peace-keeping operation had entered a phase in which both sides waited for the other to call a halt. In these circumstances, the struggle, so far as tank soldiers were concerned, became a menacing inconvenience which tested their patience, but no longer a severe threat or a profound challenge.

CHAPTER XIII

Carver's Army
1971-1975

The British Army of which General Sir Michael Carver became Chief of the General Staff in 1971, was very different in size, aspect and outlook from the one that had come under Field Marshal Lord Montgomery's jurisdiction in 1946. It was smaller by considerably more than half, and all-Regular instead of being mainly conscript. As a result, it was much more like a compact, well-run family than a gathering of passers-by, and infinitely more professional in its overall performance. There was hardly an item of major equipment left in service that had been in use in 1946, and the replacements – notably the Armoured Fighting Vehicles – were strikingly more powerful if, in some cases, somewhat less reliable. But if the tank gun had, to some extent, been challenged by the A.T.G.W., the communication equipment made far more reliable and adaptable, and a plethora of original devices been acquired to improve command and control and to enhance combat capability, the men who manned the machines remained, essentially, as intelligent as their forebears and, on average, were better educated. True, the R.T.R. soldiers looked very different. The shapeless battledress had long since gone, to be replaced by new forms of combat clothing, and by the return of black overalls which, temporarily, had fallen out of use after 1939. And the 4th, with its Scottish recruiting connection, had obtained permission in 1972 to adopt the tartan of Clan Rose of Kilravock, with its dark blue hue, and to dress its embryo (and unofficial) pipe band in kilts made of this material – the band giving its first public performance on Cambrai Day of that year. Indeed, just about the only piece of external wear which remained the same as in 1946 was the black beret, though the hair beneath it was sometimes worn a little longer!

An Old Comrade from Montgomery's Army might easily have gained the superficial impression that Carver's men were a trifle careless in their appearance and bearing – and, indeed, it was true that less time was spent on formal drill, and hardly any at all on spit and polish, since nearly every item of personal kit, which used to need cleaning, was now made of materials which stayed bright. But closer examination would reveal that the men of the 1970s exhibited just as strict a sense of discipline as that of their predecessors. The difference was a matter of emphasis based on less visible forms of display – and of more attention to the maintenance and operation of their equipment at peak performance, through the employment of precisely actuated drills applied to the machines of the day, instead of preserving obsolete procedures from past decades. Not that Carver's Army had abandoned the trappings of tradition. They could dress and drill quite as smartly as their forebears. Simply, they spent more time on other forms of essential work in maintaining a lot of highly expensive equipment which could not be left for long without attention. Their standards were those of the pre-1939 R.T.C.

Yet it is arguable whether or not the Regulars of Carver's army were more dedicated than those of Montgomery's, any comparison needing to be related to the changed circumstances and attitudes governing the respective times in which they lived. If, for example, there was less likely to be damage to discipline when, in 1946, a man was separated from his family for more than 18 months, than would have been the case in 1972, this was largely due to the continuation of habits which had been instilled by wartime conditions of service and the fact that, prior to 1946, a lower percentage of officers and men were married. As the disciplines of wartime relaxed, and civil life took on a more congenial aspect, so too did the application of discipline within the Services have to change, and particularly when it became essential to compete with civil employers for manpower. The infinitely more relaxed code of behaviour in the Welfare State, which accompanied the undermining of the old authoritarianism, and presaged the era of permissiveness, also modified the relationship between officers and men within the Army. In few regiments was this more noticeable than those of the R.A.C., wherein the recruitment of many intelligent and dexterous individuals, of marked opinions and convictions, made it ridiculous to treat them as if they were nonentities. To obtain strict compliance with orders, a balance had to be struck between the out-moded tendency to rigidity of obedience and the modern style of getting a job done, by persuasion – in due course. Leadership was at a premium, command more difficult to apply! At their best, they could be found within the R.T.R. where the criterion of performance was excellence and where the rejection of many out-moded practices, which seemed to distract the soldier from his job, was the norm. This was the same standard J. D. Lunt had extolled in 1957. At the same time, far more careful consideration had to be given to the welfare of families. For one thing, considerable forethought and compassion had to be exercised when postings were contemplated, and, for another, it would be deemed proper to amend the system of payments in 1970 with a new Pay Code, the basic concept of which was to pay the soldier a salary, taxed in the normal way, from which deductions would be made for food, accommodation, clothing (except uniform) and other items, as for civilians.

The R.T.R. of Carver's army was strong in leadership from top to bottom. It was a measure of that strength that, in the footsteps of Sir John Crocker (its first member to reach the Army Council as Adjutant General) and Sir Harold Pyman, as D.C.I.G.S. in the 1950s, it produced officers in the next two decades who, between them, filled, at one time or another, nearly all the vital posts the Army had to offer. While making allowances for its proportionately larger size, few regiments at the time could lay claim to bringing forward so many men of the calibre of Sir Alan Jolly (Quartermaster General, 1966–1969), Sir Richard Ward (Chief of Personnel and Logistics, 1974–1976), and Sir Allan Taylor (Commandant of the Staff College, 1970–1972), of whom Jolly and Ward, at some time, held the equivalent appointment of Army Commander; or of P. R. C. Hobart (Director of Military Operations, 1966–1968), and R. L. C. Dixon (Director of Land Air Warfare, 1974–1977). The one who rose highest was Carver who, since giving up as D.A.S.D. in 1966, had advanced progressively through the appointments of Commander, Far East Land Forces, C.-in-C. Far East, G.O.C.-in-C. Southern Command (1969–1971) (as well as Representative Colonel Commandant, R.T.R.), to that of Chief of the General Staff before he became Chief of the Defence Staff, when he was promoted to the rank of Field Marshal. Thus he became the first member of the Regiment to hold either of the two latter appointments, and the first of those commissioned initially into the R.T.R. to reach that rank.

The R.T.R. profited, too, from its closer association with the Cavalry in a Royal Armoured Corps which had tightened its organization in the early 1970s. There is the ring of truth in a statement by J. S. F. Murray (15th/19th Hussars) when he writes, 'I believe that, as a Corps, the RAC benefits enormously from the mixing of the Cavaliers and the modern Roundheads; we both do the same job but from a different point of view; we both have much to learn from each other.' Together with the increased willingness of R.T.R. officers to serve in Cavalry

units, came the necessary cross-fertilization of ideas and outlook which Murray implied, and a better utilization of talents
than had been the case when the two sides tended to stand
apart.

Sharing a common task in Ulster contributed to the
cementing of the R.A.C. besides testing the steadfastness of
the Regiment for whom active service was harder to come by
than at any other time in its existence. Almost every day, men
of all ranks were demonstrating those qualities which combined to keep high the reputation the R.T.R. had earned in
nearly sixty years of existence, for there were but few months
at any one time when one sub-unit or another (let alone
individuals) were not engaged in that dolorous campaign. But
in other places of stress, officers and men of the R.T.R. were
just as heavily involved.

No sooner had 1st R.T.R. left Ulster in November 1974
and moved to Tidworth, than it was dispatching B Squadron
(Major A. S. J. Blacker), unaccompanied by families, to
Cyprus as part of the British garrison, and C Squadron (Major
A. R. Jones), with its families, to Hong Kong. All except
B Squadron took over the new C.V.R. (T.) Scorpion light
tanks, for B Squadron's task was not the sort which admitted
tanks. In the peace-keeping rôle, the wheeled Ferrets and
Saladins alone were appropriate, but now the task was more
delicate than that which Ajax of the 2nd R.T.R. had tackled
in 1965 in the U.N.F.I.C.Y.P. rôle. For the situation had
deteriorated in 1974, when the Turkish Army had invaded
Cyprus in order to protect the Turkish minority community
from what was seen, by the Turks, as a serious threat by the
Greeks to assume complete control over the island. Blacker's
task was to maintain patrols along the boundary of the
Eastern Sovereign Base Area (E.S.B.A.) where, by treaty, the
British forces lived, and keep an eye on the Turks in the hope
of circumventing incidents should they accidentally, or as a
'try-on', happen to enter territory belonging to the (Greek)
Republic of Cyprus. In one place they would find themselves
keeping watch over a deserted village that was once Greek
and now stood within the Turkish lines. In another, at
Akrotiri, within the Republic, there was always the danger
that the indigenous Turkish population would be attacked by
the Greeks. Indeed, for one period of crisis, they were placed
for 24 hours under U.N. control.

In the councils of statesmen, interminable negotiations
endeavoured to defuse a situation which always looked liable
to explode, and in March, at a moment of crisis, the elements

of the 1st, less Rear Party which had stayed at Tidworth, were flown out under the C.O., Lieutenant-Colonel A. K. F. Walker, to strengthen the U.N. forces. It would be good-bye to Scorpions, for the time being, and back to Saladins, Saracens and Ferrets.

B Squadron went home in May to re-equip with the brand-new C.V.R.(W.) Fox armoured car, leaving Walker in command of a Group consisting of A Squadron (Major R. G. Oliver), two companies from the 1st Battalion Duke of Wellington's Regiment and 20 Australian civil policemen, who were invaluable in establishing liaison with the local Cyprus police. For nearly six months, the troops lived in isolated observation posts, lodged in villages where there was a potential for trouble. Some communities they liked and some they loathed, but to none could they be indifferent, as they came to realize after the International Conference at Vienna had paved the way for a massed transfer of Turks from the Greek sectors. Operation 'Mayflower' took place from 9 August to 7 September, and laid heavy demands upon the men of the 1st in that, with the full glare of the world's Press upon them, they were charged with removing some 9,000 Turks a distance of 100 miles from 66 scattered rural localities throughout the southern part of the island. Their notes in *The Tank*, sometimes frivolous, perhaps to disguise their inner feelings, were misleading, but somebody from Oliver's squadron went to the heart of the matter with a flat expression of compassion which represented the feelings of them all as they tackled a human problem with military precision:

'A way of life which has existed for over 400 years has now been destroyed. . . . We have witnessed and assisted in their departure. Each troop has escorted the 120 vehicle convoys on the 100-mile journey to Nicosia. Each soldier has witnessed the drama of a community being uprooted. They have helped load the lorries with the belongings allowed to be taken, numerous bags of clothes . . . the contents of a kitchen, the beds, the toys, sewing machines and the treasured religious pictures and icons. The Turkish community seems to expect our assistance and work, and little thanks is given to the sweating soldier. Maybe they are bound up in emotion of the moment, for on the whole they are generous and friendly. . . . The overall impression when we leave will be of generosity from both communities . . . and the Greek Cypriot community will be sorry to see us go. . . . In spite of our inherent rôle to protect the

Turkish minority . . . they welcomed our presence and our patrols day and night at their check points. Cypol [Cyprus Police] too, have given us every support in our operations, which were often blatant checks on the very work they were doing.'

Upheavals such as these were the inevitable and natural products of the British withdrawal from Empire. As their rule – harsh and self-interested though it sometimes might have been – came to an end, the traditional racial jealousies and enmities they had often managed to contain, came to the surface again in expressions of bigotry and outbreaks of violence. As members of the U.N. forces, the Army could but act as witnesses of the tragedy. It was some consolation when a journalist could report that he was 'staggered' by the 1st's efficiency.

In other countries where British influence had recently been dominant, R.T.R. officers and men still played an active part bushwhacking and, at the same time, helping to delay the onset of malign influences against friendly powers – particularly in the friendly, oil-rich Arab States of the Persian Gulf. Sergeant G. Perkin found this out for himself within a few days of joining the forces of the Sultan of Oman in September 1975. Sent out in command of a Saladin, and hearing firing, he moved towards the sound of the guns and was at once involved in a fire-fight without having sufficient knowledge of Arabic to help him give clear fire-orders to his crew. To make matters worse, one of his episcopes was hit and glass flew into his face, but this did not deter him. He continued to advance until he made contact with some infantry of his own side who were pinned down and had suffered a number of casualties. These he loaded onto the back of his armoured car and drove them to safety.

That same year, Major E. A. N. Winship, as the R.A.C.'s sole representative, went to Nepal with the British Army/Nepalese Army Nuptse Expedition, although with the initial intention of climbing Everest. Unfortunately the expedition failed to reach the summit of Nuptse and, in the course of the climb, four members were lost in two separate accidents as the weather deteriorated. But Winship's account, thoroughly modest in its composition, speaks volumes for the pluck and endurance of those who survived and for his own performance. This represented a first-class example of strenuous Adventure Training which, despite Ulster, the Regiment needed. Likewise, Major C. J. Davey began the pursuit of free-ballooning in 1972, an activity which, in 1978, so nearly made him the first man to cross the Atlantic by balloon, in an epic voyage which failed by just 110 miles.

Less testing, but much more directly related to the basic task of armoured warfare, were the regular visits undertaken to the Suffield Training Area in Canada, which had its derivation in the original Hale Force expedition in 1964. 4th R.T.R. Battle Group (Lieutenant-Colonel L. A. W. New) went there first in June 1972, and returned, to quote themselves, 'filled with a tremendous sense of realism and of battle innoculation, particularly during the daring night firing battle'. As one of their soldiers said, 'Suffield, basically, is bloody good news' and these were the sentiments of B Squadron 1st R.T.R. also, when they went there as part of 1st Queen's Lancashire Regiment Battle Group in September. Next to go, in April 1973, was a Battle Group from 2nd R.T.R. (Lieutenant-Colonel M. J. Evans), consisting of the Command and Reconnaissance Troops, Cyclops, a company from the Queen's Own Highlanders plus Gunners and Sappers. In that same year, too, Cyclops (Major M. J. Rose) had the most unusual experience of being Trials Squadron in Germany to help make a tactical evaluation of the Swedish S. turretless tank, leading towards a decision as to what design of tank should be adopted after Chieftain. Completely equipped with this unique vehicle, Cyclops took part in prolonged and rigorous field tests – and, incidentally, was to spend in aggregate about three-quarters of 1973 away from base and mainly in the field.

It would be the turn of Badger (Major M. G. Tweed) to form another infantry-led Battle Group, in the autumn of 1974, only to engage in a hard tussle with the recalcitrant Chieftain tanks they had drawn from the pool at the end of a tough training season, on prairie which was once likened to 'desert with grass'. The value of this training lay, not only in the fact that it was a change from Soltau, and took place across ranges where 30-mile battle runs against many hard targets could be held, but also in that it served the important purpose of making it possible to create realistic tactical situations which, in the words of a trooper in Badger, were 'bloody dangerous'. A squadron returning from Suffield felt that it had been tested in all departments. When the 3rd (Lieutenant-Colonel G. Read) went in May 1975, they too discovered the difficulties of navigating across featureless terrain which, for much of the time, was waterlogged. But with their 120mm guns, they scored more hits than their predecessors (87.32 per cent in B Squadron) and this improved their confidence. A notion of what this vast training area offered to the troops can be judged by the 3rd's description of the final battle run:

'This was the one everybody looked forward to. It began with a dry night attack through a minefield gap; we then moved through the gap at dawn – the start line having been secured by the infantry. The first day's battle ended with an attack on three hills, each about 1 km apart, and finished by consolidating our position just south of the OK Corral. The final day began with a first light move to an FUP where the BG [Battle Group] attacked a monstrous hill – known as Watching Hill – in fact most of the squadron were the fire base, but were unable to fire for safety reasons. By midday the final objective had been taken and we lined up ready for the march back to Camp Crowfoot.'

Shafts of enthusiasm break through as, despite all the difficulties, each squadron in the mixed battle groups found itself able to motor for miles without becoming over-concerned about wandering outside the training area, or of inflicting damage, with political (quite apart from physical) consequences, upon a German farmer's fields. For once, the men of the R.T.R., and those who trained alongside them, could immerse themselves in the rich throbbing sound, smell and sight of tracked armoured vehicles manoeuvring with verve, while uninhibitedly firing their guns. So it was, too, for the 4th (Lieutenant-Colonel D. Sands) when (less A Squadron) it trained at Suffield in the autumn of 1975. No sooner had they got back to Germany than they were faced with the further task of taking part in a fully-instrumented scientific trial for D.O.A.E.

Exercise 'Chinese Eye III' was primarily intended to help evaluate the tactical effectiveness of the Infantry's proposed new A.T.G.W., Milan. For this purpose, each of the 4th's tanks was equipped with Simfire as well as Navaid (the device by which a vehicle's exact position was constantly known) and a tape-recorder. But the opportunity was also taken to experiment with organization. B Squadron, with ten tanks, was made to provide the nucleus for a Blue Combat Team, while the remainder were re-shuffled into a Medium Tank Battalion of 31 tanks, with three companies of ten tanks each, such as would be the basis of the future shape of armoured units in B.A.O.R. described below. In other words, no sooner had the 4th R.T.R. returned from Canada in October, than it was pitched into another important exercise in November, and once that was over it had to complete the full gamut of annual inspections prior to handing in its tanks before Christmas, and commence training for Ulster. There is much to be learnt from an extract from B Squadron's notes in *The Tank* of January 1976 – which, for all the overloaded suggestion of repetition, was not a tale of boredom! After describing the intensity of the exercises they hinted at the approach of Christmas, '. . . in a whirl of P.R.E. [Periodic R.E.M.E. Examination], Cambrai, leaf sweeping, sponsoring the Wives' Club, leaf sweeping, Op. 'Banner' training, thinking of leave (and leaves) and more leaf sweeping. By the time you read these notes we shall have reorganised as a Rifle Squadron and be well into our infantry training for Northern Ireland.'

This was the pace at which all four units of the R.T.R. lived in 1975. The prospects of repeated visits to Ulster loomed perpetually ahead, and upon this disruption was heaped the impending upheaval promised by what was heralded as 'Restructuring' and known later as Operation 'Wide Horizon'. Once again, a national financial crisis, coming in the aftermath of the. Arab-Israeli conflict in October 1973, with its attendant sharp rise in oil prices and world-inflation, accelerated change. At the same time, a build-up of Soviet armoured power in Europe made it all the more important to maintain strong forces in B.A.O.R. as part of N.A.T.O. As much as ever was it essential for the armoured regiments to carry out their vital rôle, but now they had to operate more equipment with roughly the same number of men – an apparently overstretched condition which led to expressions of concern, but which may only have amounted to Carver's feelings that '. . . when the Army is fully stretched it complains about over-stretch, and when it is not, if complains of boredom'. An armoured regiment, for example, though divesting itself of its Reconnaissance Troop to the Divisional Reconnaissance Regiment, and its six FV 438 A.T.G.W. launchers to the Royal Artillery, would increase its strength from 47 to 66 Chieftains. At the same time, the three existing standing divisions, with their incorporated brigades, would be disbanded and replaced, eventually, by four Armoured Divisions, each capable of forming five Battle Groups comprising variations, as required, from the eight squadrons and twelve mechanized infantry battalions within the division. Brigades would be abolished and in their place would stand two Task Force H.Q.s (remarkably like the H.Q. of a brigade), whose job it would be to coordinate and command the Battle Groups under the control of the divisional commander. Crucial to this reorganization was the provision of an improved anti-tank capability for the infantry, by the addition to its establishment of the Milan A.T.G.W. and, above all, the introduction of the much more versatile and effective transistorized Clansman communications system, without which the flexibility of the Battle Groups would be impaired. In 1976, the 2nd Armoured Division (Major-General F. E. Kitson, late Rifle Brigade) – the first wholly armoured and tracked British division – would carry out trials with the new organization. Units of the R.T.R. would be deeply involved in what amounted to yet another step forward from the ground-work laid by R. E. Ward in Exercise 'Eternal Triangle' ten years previously (see Chapter XI). No doubt Fuller, Lindsay, Broad, Hobart and all the other great tank pioneers would have applauded. Ostensibly, it enables this history to end on a new and encouraging note. But nothing stands still.

REGIMENT	1945 (May-Dec)	1946	1947	1948	1949
1 R.T.R.			——————— B.A.O.R. ———————		
2 R.T.R.	——— Italy/Austria ———		B.A.O.R.	B.A.O.R. (Jan-Apr) U.K.	
3 R.T.R.	——————— B.A.O.R. ———————			U.K.	U.K. (Jar Hong Ko
4 R.T.R.	B.A.O.R.	Italy	Italy/Austria (Jan-Jun) Egypt	(Palestine (May-Jul))	(1 Sqn Ae
5 R.T.R.			——————— B.A.O.R. ———		
6 R.T.R.	——— Italy/Austria ———		Italy/Austria (Jan-Jul) Egypt		———
7 R.T.R.	B.A.O.R.	B.A.O.R. (Jan-Sep) U.K. (Sep-Dec)	India (Jan-Oct) U.K.		———
8 R.T.R.	Italy/Austria	Austria (Jan-May) Egypt (Palestine (Jun-Sep))	Egypt (Jan-Aug) U.K.		——— U.K.
9 R.T.R.	B.A.O.R.				
11 R.T.R.	B.A.O.R.	Disbanded			
12 R.T.R.	Italy/Austria				
BERLIN SQUADRON R.T.R.					
40 R.T.R. (T.A.)	Greece	Greece (Jan-May) U.K.			
41 R.T.R. (T.A.)			Re-formed from May U.K.		
42 R.T.R. (T.A.)			Re-formed from May U.K.		
43 R.T.R. (T.A.) 1/43 2/43	U.K. (May-Aug) India	India	Re-formed from May U.K. India (Jan-Oct); U.K.		
44 R.T.R. (T.A.)	——— B.A.O.R. ——— Disbanded		Re-formed from May U.K.		
45 R.T.R. (T.A.)			Re-formed from May U.K.		
46 R.T.R. (T.A.)	Greece	Greece (Jan-May) U.K.	Disbanded		
48 R.T.R. (T.A.)	Italy/Austria	Disbanded			
50 R.T.R. (T.A.)	Greece	Greece (Jan-May) U.K.	Disbanded		
51 R.T.R. (T.A.)	Italy/Austria	Disbanded			

1950	1951	1952	1953	1954	1955
		B.A.O.R. (Jan-Sep) U.K. (Oct-Nov) Korea	Korea	Egypt	Egypt (Jan-Aug) U.K. (1 Sqn Egypt)
U.K. ————		U.K. (Jan-Feb) B.A.O.R.	———— B.A.O.R. ————		
—— Hong Kong (1 Sqn Malaya) ——		Hong Kong (Jan-Mar) (1 Sqn Malaya (Jan-Feb)) U.K. (Apr-Sep) B.A.O.R.	———— B.A.O.R. ————		
Egypt ————			Egypt (Jan) U.K.	U.K. (Jan-Aug) B.A.O.R.	B.A.O.R.
—			B.A.O.R. (Jun-Aug) U.K. (Aug-Nov) Korea	Korea	Cyrenaica
—		———— B.A.O.R. ————			
rea (Nov-Dec))	(1 Sqn Korea (Jan-Oct))	U.K. (Jan-Feb) Hong Kong	Hong Kong	Hong Kong (Jan-Oct) U.K.	U.K.
	U.K. (Jan-Sep) B.A.O.R.	———— B.A.O.R. ————			

	Formed	B.A.O.R.			
———— U.K. ————					
———— U.K. ————					
———— U.K. ————					
———— U.K. ————					
———— U.K. ————					
———— U.K. ————					

APPENDIX 1
R.T.R. Organization and Locations

REGIMENT	1956	1957	1958	1959	1960
1 R.T.R.	U.K. (Jan-Nov) (1 Sqn Eqypt (Jan-Mar)) Malta	U.K. (Jan-May) Hong Kong	———— Hong Kong ————		Hong Kong (Jan) B.A.O.R.
2 R.T.R.	———— B.A.O.R. ————			B.A.O.R. (Jan-Jul) U.K. (Aug-Sep) Cyrenaica	—— Cyr
3 R.T.R.			———— B.A.O.R. ————		
4 R.T.R.			———— B.A.O.R. ————		
5 R.T.R.	Cyrenaica	Cyrenaica (Jan-Mar) U.K.	U.K.	U.K. (Jan-Nov) B.A.O.R.	
6 R.T.R.	B.A.O.R. (Jan-Feb) U.K. (Feb-Sep) Malta/Suez	U.K. (Jan-Mar) Cyrenaica (1 Sqn Cyprus (Jul-Dec))	Cyrenaica (1 Sqn Cyprus)	Cyrenaica (Jan-Aug) U.K. (Sep) B.A.O.R. (Oct)	Amalgamated 3 R.T.R.
7 R.T.R.	U.K.	U.K. (Jan-Sep) B.A.O.R.	B.A.O.R.	B.A.O.R. (Jan-Apr)	Amalgamated 4 R.T.R.
8 R.T.R.	—	———— B.A.O.R. ————			B.A.O.R. (Jan
BERLIN SQUADRON R.T.R.	B.A.O.R.	Disbanded			
40 R.T.R. (T.A.)	U.K.	} Amalgamated to form 40/41 R.T.R. (T.A.)			——
41 R.T.R. (T.A.)	U.K.				
42 R.T.R. (T.A.)	U.K.	} Disbanded			
43 R.T.R. (T.A.)	U.K.				
44 R.T.R. (T.A.)	U.K.	Amalgamated to form N.S.Y./44 R.T.R. (T.A.)			——
45 R.T.R. (T.A.)	U.K.	Disbanded			

1961	1962	1963	1964	1965	1966
——— B.A.O.R. ———				B.A.O.R. (Jan-Nov) Persian Gulf (1 Sqn Hong Kong)	Persian Gulf (1 Sqn Hong Kong)
	Cyrenaica (Jan-Sep) Ulster (1 Sqn U.K. (Oct-Dec))	Ulster (1 Sqn U.K.)	Ulster (1 Sqn U.K.) (1 Sqn Cyprus (Nov-Dec))	U.K. (Jan-Nov) (1 Sqn Cyprus (Jan-May)) B.A.O.R.	B.A.O.R.
	B.A.O.R. (Jan-Aug) U.K.	U.K.	U.K. (Jan-Feb) B.A.O.R.	——— B.A.O.R. ———	
		B.A.O.R. (Jan-Apr) U.K. (Apr-Sep) Persian Gulf	Persian Gulf (Jan-Aug) Malaysia	Malaysia	Malaysia (Jan-Jun) B.A.O.R.
——— B.A.O.R. ———				B.A.O.R. (Jan-Feb) U.K.	U.K. 1 Sqn Malaysia (Feb-Sep)

mated with 5 R.T.R.

| | Re-formed | B.A.O.R. (Mar-Dec) | B.A.O.R. | B.A.O.R. (Jan-Nov) Disbanded | |

——— U.K. ———

K. ———————   Disbanded

Note: "U.K." does not include Ulster, which is shown separately.

APPENDICES

REGIMENT	1967	1968	1969	1970
1 R.T.R.	———— U.K. ————			———— B.A
2 R.T.R.	———————— B.A.O.R. ————————			B.A.O.R. (Jan U.K.
3 R.T.R.	B.A.O.R.	B.A.O.R. (Jan) U.K. (1 Sqn Cyprus) (1 Sqn Sharjah)	U.K. (Jan-Nov) B.A.O.R. (1 Sqn Cyprus) (1 Sqn Sharjah)	
4 R.T.R.	———————— B.A.O.R. ————————			
5 R.T.R.	U.K. 1 Sqn Aden/Persian Gulf (Apr-Jul)	B.A.O.R.	B.A.O.R. (Jan-Nov)	Disbanded
40/41 R.T.R. (T.A.)	U.K.	Disbanded		

268

1971	1972	1973	1974	1975
—	(2 Sqns Ulster (Jan-May))	B.A.O.R. (Jan-Apr) Ulster	Ulster (Jan-Nov) U.K. (1 Sqn Cyprus) (1 Sqn Hong Kong)	U.K. (1 Sqn Cyprus) (1 Sqn Hong Kong)
U.K.	U.K. (Jan-Aug) B.A.O.R.	(1 Sqn Ulster (Sep-Dec))	——— B.A.O.R. ——— (1 Sqn Ulster (Jan)) (1 Sqn Ulster (Jan-May))	(1 Sqn Ulster (May-Sep))
——— B.A.O.R. ———		(1 Sqn Ulster (Jan-May))	(1 Sqn Ulster (Sep-Dec))	(1 Sqn Ulster (Jan))
Ulster (Jul-Dec))		——— U.K. ——— (1 Sqn B.A.O.R.)	(1 Sqn B.A.O.R.)	B.A.O.R.

Note: "U.K." does not include Ulster, which is shown separately.

APPENDIX 2

British Tracked A.F.V.s
in service with the R.T.R.,
1945-1975

Type	Date in service	Weight* (tons)	Dimensions**	Crew	Armament
Cromwell VII	1944	28	H: 8' 2" W: 10' 0" L: 20' 10"	5	1 x 75mm. 2 x 7.92mm.
Churchill VII	1944	40	H: 9' 0" W: 11' 4" L: 24' 5"	5	1 x 75mm. 2 x 7.92mm.
Comet I	1944	32.5	H: 8' 9½" W: 10' 0" L: 25' 1½"	5	1 x 77mm. 2 x 7.92mm.
Centurion 2	1946	48	H: 9' 8" W: 11' 0" L: 29' 11"	4	1 x 17pdr. 1 x 7.92mm.
Centurion 3	1949	49.25	H: 9' 8" W: 11' 1" L: 32' 3"	4	1 x 20pdr. 1 x 7.92mm.
Charioteer	1952	28.5	H: 8' 6" W: 10' 1" L: 28' 7"	4	1 x 20pdr. 1 x .30in.
Conqueror	1954	65	H: 10' 4½" W: 13' 1" L: 39' 0"	4	1 x 120mm. 2 x .30in.
Centurion 7/2	1962	50	H: 9' 11" W: 11' 1½" L: 32' 4"	4	1 x 105mm. 2 x .30in.
FV 438	1967	8	H: 8' 10½" W: 9' 9" L: 16' 9"	3	Swingfire G.W 1 x 7.62mm.
Chieftain 2	1967	51.6	H: 9' 3" W: 11' 6" L: 35' 4"	4	1 x 120mm. 1 x .50in. 2 x 7.62mm.
Scorpion	1972	7.8	H: 6' 10½" W: 7' 2" L: 14' 4½"	3	1 x 76mm. 1 x 7.62mm.

*Fully laden. **Overall; length includes gun. ***Max. speed on road.

Ammunition (no. rounds)	Engine	BHP	Speed*** (max.)	Armour (max.–min.)	Last in service
64 4,950	Meteor III	600	32mph.	101–10mm.	1953
84 6,525	Bedford	350	12.5mph.	152–25mm.	1951****
61 5,175	Meteor III	600	29mph.	101–14mm.	1959
73 3,375	Meteor IV	600	21.5mph.	152–17mm.	1952
65 3,600	Meteor IVB	650	21.5mph.	152–17mm.	1956
25 3,375	Meteor III	600	32mph.	64–10mm.	1956
35 7,500	RR M120	810	21.3mph.	200–20mm.	1966
63 4,500	Meteor IVB	650	21.5mph.	152–17mm.	1965
14 2,200	RR K60	240	32mph.	12–6mm.	
53 600 6000	Leyland L60	650	25mph.	–	
40 3,000	Jaguar	195	50mph.	–	

****Date is for last active service (Korea).

APPENDIX 3

British Wheeled A.F.V.s in service with the R.T.R., 1945-1975

Type	Date in service	Weight* (tons)	Dimensions**	Crew	Armament
Daimler Scout Car	1939	3.1	H: 4' 11" W: 5' 7½" L: 10' 5"	2	1 x .303in.
G.M.C. Fox	1942	7.4	H: 8' 1" W: 7' 5½" L: 14' 8½"	4	1 x .50in. 1 x .30in.
Daimler Ferret/2	1952	4	H: 6' 2" W: 6' 3" L: 12' 7"	2	1 x .30in.
Alvis Saracen	1952	8	H: 8' 1" W: 8' 3" L: 16' 6"	12	1 x .30in.
Alvis Saladin	1958	11.1	H: 7' 10" W: 8' 5" L: 17' 3½"	3	1 x 76mm. 1 x .30in.
Humber Hornet	1963	6	H: 7' 8" W: 7' 3½" L: 16' 7"	3	Malkara 1 x 7.62mm.
Ferret 2/6	1964	4.2	H: 6' 9" W: 6' 3" L: 12' 7"	2	Vigilant 1 x .30in.
Daimler Fox	1973	3	H: 6' 10" W: 7' 0" L: 16' 9"	3	1 x 30mm. 1 x 7.62mm.
FV 712	1970	5	H: 6' 8" W: 7' 0" L: 13' 0"	2	Swingfire 1 x 7.62mm.

*Fully laden. **Overall.

Ammunition (no. rounds)	Engine	BHP	Speed (max.)	Armour (max.–min.)	Last in service
750	Daimler	70	59mph.	30–3mm.	1960
	GM	104	44mph.	15mm.	1947
2,500	RR B60	120	58mph.	16–6mm.	
3,000	RR B80	160	45mph.	16–8mm.	
43 2,750	RR B80	160	45.5mph.	16–8mm.	
4	RR B60	120	50mph.	13–5mm.	1970
4 3,000	RR B60	120	58mph.	16–6mm.	
96 2,600	Jaguar	195	65mph.	Aluminium	
6 3,000	RR B60	120	40mph.	16–6mm.	

Specialized Armour used by R.T.R. units, 1945-1975

L.V.T.
American-built, unarmoured, inherent amphibian propelled in water by its tracks at a speed of 7mph. and on land at 25mph. Armament: 1 x .30in. machine gun. Weight 4 tons.

C.D.L.
A tank-borne searchlight, mounted mostly in the American-manufactured Grant tank, which retained its 75mm. sponson-mounted gun.

Crab Flail
American Sherman tank, retaining its full armament of 1 x 75mm. gun and 1 x .30in. MG and fitted with a rotary flail actuated by the tank engine to detonate mines. Speed when flailing, 2 mph.

Crocodile
Churchill VII with a flame-gun fitted in place of the hull MG. 400 gallons of flame fuel carried in a two-wheeled trailer and delivered under pressure to a range of 120 yards.

D.D.
Modified Sherman gun-tank fitted with a collapsible screen to help it swim. Propelled in water by two propellers driven by the main engine.

Bridgelayers
Various types, carried or conveyed on Churchill or Centurion hulls.

R.T.R. Honours and Awards, 1945-1975

KNIGHT GRAND CROSS OF THE ORDER OF THE BATH (G.C.B.)
Carver, General Sir Michael	1970
Jolly, General Sir Alan	1968

KNIGHT COMMANDER OF THE ORDER OF THE BATH (K.C.B.)
Carver, Major-General Sir Michael	1966
Crocker, General Sir John	1947
Jolly, Lieutenant-General Sir Alan	1964
Pyman, Lieutenant-General Sir Harold	1958
Ward, Lieutenant-General Sir Richard	1971

COMPANION OF THE ORDER OF THE BATH (C.B.)
Cooper, Major-General K. C.	1955
Duncan, Major-General N. W.	1951
Foote, Major-General .H. R. B.	1952
French, Major-General J.	1960
Hobart, Major-General P. R. C.	1970
Holden, Major-General J. R.	1965
Hopkinson, Major-General G. C.	1960
Hutton, Major-General W. M.	1964
Lascelles, Major-General H. A.	1967
Leakey, Major-General A. R.	1967
Lucas, Brigadier G.	1957
Ward, Major-General R. E.	1969

KNIGHT COMMANDER OF THE ORDER OF ST MICHAEL AND ST GEORGE (K.C.M.G.)
Lewis, Major-General Sir Richard	1952

KNIGHT COMMANDER OF THE ORDER OF THE BRITISH EMPIRE (K.B.E.)
Scoones, Major-General Sir Reginald	1955
Taylor, Lieutenant-General Sir Allan	1972

COMMANDER OF THE .ORDER OF THE BRITISH EMPIRE (C.B.E.)
Bright, Brigadier R. H.	1965
Brown, Brigadier A. W.	1955
FitzPatrick, Brigadier J. A.	1964
Holden, Brigadier J. R.	1960
Hutton, Brigadier W. M.	1960
Jolly, Brigadier A.	1955
Lascelles, Brigadier H. A.	1962
O'Flynn, Brigadier D. J.	1960
Sleeman, Brigadier J. C. de F.	1960

APPENDICES

COMPANION OF THE DISTINGUISHED SERVICE ORDER (D.S.O.)
Lawson, Major R. G.	1962

OFFICER OF THE ORDER OF THE BRITISH EMPIRE (O.B.E.)
Anstey, Lieutenant-Colonel E. W.	1964
Attwood, Major C. H. M.	1953
Blott, Lieutenant-Colonel R. V.	1965
Coombes, Lieutenant-Colonel F. W.	1968
Cooper, Lieutenant-Colonel A.	1955
Dixon, Colonel J. G. R.	1974
Gibbòn, Lieutenant-Colonel T. H.	1957
Gingell, Lieutenant-Colonel L. W. A.	1966
Glazebrook, Lieutenant-Colonel D.	1973
Gray, Lieutenant-Colonel I. S.	1955
Hind, Lieutenant-Colonel J. G.	1975
Holden, Lieutenant-Colonel R. E.	1953
Hopkinson, Lieutenant-Colonel G. C.	1953
Hordern, Lieutenant-Colonel P. H.	1959
Ironside, Major H. C. W.	1955
Jago, Major W. G.	1947
Kynaston, Lieutenant-Colonel E. G. A.	1956
Laurence-Smith, Lieutenant-Colonel J.	1966
Lawson, Lieutenant-Colonel R. G.	1968
Mackenzie, Lieutenant-Colonel F. S. R.	1953
Maxwell, Lieutenant-Colonel J. P.	1974
Mennell, Colonel J. S.	1962
Monteath, Lieutenant-Colonel A. D.	1967
Moss, Lieutenant-Colonel R. R.	1964
Robinson, Lieutenant-Colonel W. E.	1963
Ryle, Lieutenant-Colonel I. N.	1961
Simpkin, Lieutenant-Colonel R. E.	1964
Squirrell, Lieutenant-Colonel D. S.	1965
Vaux, Lieutenant-Colonel P. A. L.	1956
Vickers, Lieutenant-Colonel R. M. H.	1970
Ward, Major H. D.	1953
Wilde, Lieutenant-Coloncl E. A. D.	1966
Witheridge, Lieutenant-Colonel G.	1953
Wood, Lieutenant-Colonel S. P.	1957

MEMBER OF THE ORDER OF THE BRITISH EMPIRE (M.B.E.)
Alley, Major H. V.	1953
Ambidge, Captain D. W. A.	1953
Armit, Warrant Officer I W. R.	1956
Austin, Warrant Officer II W.	1955
Baker, Major I. H.	1965
Basey, Major J. G.	1968
Bastick, Major J. D.	1969
Blad, Major A. J.	1968
Bligh, Major C. H.	1968
Canning, Major O. F. C.	1952
Chapman, Brigadier O. E.	1951
Cooper, Major (Quartermaster) G. R.	1960
Craig, Major T. S.	1957
Davies, Major E. V.	1966
Dey, Major P. E.	1961
Dickinson, Major E. M.	1960

Dodd, Lieutenant F. J.	1953
Duncan, Captain H. D. C.	1974
Emerson, Captain R. R.	1971
Fraser, Warrant Officer I A. H.	1953
Gingell, Major L. W. A.	1959
Glarvey, Lieutenant D. J.	1966
Grantham, Captain G. A. S.	1953
Gregson, Major P. F.	1972
Hotblack, Major W. J.	1960
Jerram, Captain R. M.	1961
Kendell, Warrant Officer I T.	1961
Kimberley, Captain D. R.	1975
Knott, Warrant Officer II H.	1961
Leach, Captain H. R.	1962
Lester, Warrant Officer I O. A.	1957
McLeod, Captain A.	1955
Mallam, Major D. F.	1972
Marshall, Major J.	1969
Mosley, Major J. F.	1952
Osborne, Warrant Officer II F. G. A.	1959
Pasker, Warrant Officer I W.	1952
Phillips, Major F. C.	1961
Powell, Lieutenant-Colonel R. H. A.	1959
Roberts, Warrant Officer II E. P.	1955
Robinson, Major A. W.	1953
Rogers, Major (Quartermaster) C. J.	1964
Seymour, Captain M.	1975
Shackleton, Captain R. J.	1957
Slater, Warrant Officer II D. H.	1974
Starr, Major H. C.	1970
Sutherland, Major J. S.	1961
Taylor, Captain J.	1952
Tocock, Major P. H.	1969
Vickers, Major R. M. H.	1965
Wallace, Captain R.	1973
Watkins, Major H. B. C.	1955
Wattenbach, Major J. R. D.	1963
Weeks, Major A. L. P.	1972
White, Warrant Officer II C. J. J.	1965
Wright, Major H. J. I.	1953
Yorke, Captain A. T.	1971

MILITARY CROSS (M.C.)

Mathieson, Major A. A.	1965
Muir, Lieutenant N. B.	1973
Windeler, Captain D. A.	1948

DISTINGUISHED FLYING CROSS (D.F.C.)

Crouch, Major D. C.	1966

AIR FORCE CROSS (A.F.C.)

Mallock, Captain G. R.	1971

THE QUEEN'S GALLANTRY MEDAL (Q.G.M.)

Richart, Corporal P. V.	1975
Simpkin, Sergeant P. H.	1975

MILITARY MEDAL (M.M.)
Brundish, Sergeant J.	1953
McFarlane, Sergeant N.	1953
Robinson, Warrant Officer I J.	1947
Rustage, Staff-Sergeant W.	1959
Silverson, Staff-Sergeant T. E. F.	1965
Wallace, Sergeant A.	1953

BRITISH EMPIRE MEDAL (B.E.M.)
Ashworth, Sergeant K. K. J.	1954
Broughton, Staff-Sergeant T. E	1965
Cobb, Sergeant H. B.	1952
Cornish, Sergeant A. A.	1964
Dawson, Staff-Sergeant D.	1972
Dennis, Sergeant L. D.	1957
Divall, Trooper J. D.	1947
Donovan, Sergeant D. P.	1957
Emerson, Sergeant R. R.	1956
Evans, Sergeant G. A.	1959
Foster, Staff Quartermaster-Sergeant J. E.	1962
Fraser, Warrant Officer II J.	1956
Hammond, Corporal V. C. E.	1956
Hayes, Staff-Sergeant A. H.	1948
Lines, Sergeant M.	1967
Lucas, Trooper G.	1956
Newton, Sergeant M.	1974
Pitt, Staff-Sergeant J.	1956
Storks, Warrant Officer II C. F.	1955
Simcock, Staff-Sergeant A. R. N.	1964
Tosdevine, Warrant Officer II W. G.	1955
Weaver, Staff-Sergeant H. S.	1961
Williams, Staff-Sergeant P.	1971
Woolley, Trooper D. J.	1974

MENTIONED IN DISPATCHES (M.I.D.)
Aldridge, Major J. D.	1949
Allen, Major W. A.	1974
Bentley, Sergeant R. L.	1972
Berry, Captain P. S.	1957
Carver, Colonel R. M. P.	1955
Corkery, Major H. T. R. G.	1959
Cowling, Corporal J.	1953
Crassweller, Sergeant D. W.	1975
Cummings, Corporal D. A.	1974
Farmer, Lieutenant M. G.	1953
Fisher, Sergeant J. W. H.	1957
Garnett, Major J.	1951
Glazebrook, Captain D.	1961
Griffiths, Corporal J.	1953
Hall, Lieutenant T. E.	1974
Jarvis, Captain P. N.	1967
Johnson, Corporal J.	1972
Lewis, Major D. L.	1974
McAfee, Captain R. W. M.	1974
Mallam, Captain D. F.	1967
Ockenden, Lieutenant-Colonel R. V.	1974

Offord, Major E. F.	1949
Pearce, Captain H. L.	1949
Rawlins, Captain J. G.	1965
Roberts, Sergeant A. A.	1957
Smith, Major L. G. G.	1967
Sullivan, Major W. D. P.	1953
Sutton, Major S. P. M.	1950
Uloth, Lieutenant A. C.	1953
Walker, Lieutenant-Colonel A. K. F.	1974
Ward, Major R. E.	1953
Welch, Captain T. S. M.	1953
Wood, Lieutenant-Colonel S. P.	1950

QUEEN'S COMMENDATION
Goble, Major C. P. J.	1968

COMMANDER-IN-CHIEF'S COMMENDATION
Bourne, Sergeant T.	1965
Clitheroe, Lance-Corporal	1966
Corbin, Sergeant P. S.	1965
Wilding, Corporal G. K.	1975

COMMANDER-IN-CHIEF'S CERTIFICATE
Kelly, Lance-Corporal P.	1953

MERITORIOUS SERVICE MEDAL (M.S.M.)
Angliss, Staff-Sergeant F.	1954
Burton, Warrant Office I A. E.	1954
Byrne, Sergeant W. E.	1961
Churchman, Major (Quartermaster) F. C.	1955
Clayton, Warrant Officer II A.	1967
Coughlan, Sergeant J. D.	1967
Donovan, Warrant Officer II C. S.	1956
Firmstone, Warrant Officer II W.	1954
Fox, Warrant Officer II E. A. P.	1956
Fraser, Warrant Officer I A. H.	1957
Hornsby, Warrant Officer I J.	1972
Hyland, Warrant Officer II J.	1954
Jackson, Sergeant B.	1962
Knight, Warrant Officer II F.	1955
Lawrence, Warrant Officer II R. P.	1956
Lempriere, Warrant Officer I E. R.	1954
Lester, Warrant Officer I O. A.	1956
Lloyd, Warrant Officer II J. W.	1954
Lowndes, Sergeant W. E.	1954
Mellor, Sergeant A. J.	1963
Phillpotts, Warrant Officer II W. E.	1956
Probert, Warrant Officer C.	1963
Wall, Warrant Officer I E.	1956

KNIGHT COMMANDER OF THE ORDER OF ST SYLVESTER
Lawson, Major R. G.	1964

SULTAN OF OMAN'S DISTINGUISHED SERVICE MEDAL
Glazebrook, Lieutenant-Colonel D.	1973
Perkin, Sergeant G. R.	1975

SULTAN OF OMAN'S BRAVERY MEDAL
Shillinglaw, Major D. C.   1970

SULTAN OF OMAN'S COMMENDATION
Duncan, Captain H. D. C.   1973
Gregg, Lieutenant T. D.   1973

APPENDIX 6

Colonels Commandant of the R.T.R., 1945-1975

Name	Colonel Commandant	Representative Colonel Commandant
Major-General G. M. LINDSAY, C.B., C.M.G., D.S.O.	1938-1947	1940-1943
Lieutenant-General Sir Charles F. N. BROAD, K.C.B., D.S.O.	1939-1948	1944-1947
Field Marshal The Viscount MONTGOMERY, K.G., G.C.B., D.S.O., D.L.	1945-1957	
Major-General Sir Percy C. S. HOBART, K.B.E., C.B., D.S.O., M.C.	1947-1951	1948-1951
General Sir John T. CROCKER, G.C.B., K.B.E., D.S.O., M.C.	1949-1961	
Major-General N. W. DUNCAN, C.B., C.B.E., D.S.O., D.L.	1952-1959	1952-1957
Major-General H. R. B. FOOTE, V.C., C.B., D.S.O.	1957-1964	1958-1961
Lieutenant-General Sir Harold E. PYMAN, K.C.B., C.B.E., D.S.O.	1959-1965	
Major-General H. M. LIARDET, C.B., C.B.E., D.S.O., D.L.	1961-1967	1962-1967
General Sir Alan JOLLY, K.C.B., C.B.E., D.S.O.	1964-1969	1968-1969
Major-General J. R. HOLDEN, C.B., C.B.E., D.S.O.	1965-1968	
Field Marshal Sir Michael CARVER, G.C.B., C.B.E., D.S.O., M.C., A.D.C.	1968-1973	1970-1971
Major-General P. R. C. HOBART, D.S.O., O.B.E., M.C.	1969-1978	1971-1974
General Sir Richard E. WARD G.C.B., D.S.O., M.C.	1970-1975	1974-1975
Lieutenant-General Sir Allan McN. Taylor, K.B.E., M.C.	1973	

R.T.R. Dress, 1945-1975

No. 1 Dress
This uniform succeeded the pre-war Blue Patrols and was designed to be the parade dress of the Army. It was succeeded by No. 2 Dress in 1960 and thereafter was reserved for a parade dress for cadets at Sandhurst and for other specified categories. It continues to be worn by officers and warrant officers of the Regiment on special occasions.

No. 2 Dress
A khaki uniform of Service Dress pattern, introduced in succession to No. 1 Dress as a parade dress and 'walking-out' uniform in place of Battle-Dress. Initially, and to relieve the drabness of this uniform, R.T.R. soldiers on parade wore a black web belt; but this stained the jacket, and a black plastic belt, bearing the R.T.R. crest on the chrome buckle, was introduced in 1964. The officers' uniform, which had traditionally been of the infantry pattern, was changed in style in 1960 to conform to that adopted by the Royal Armoured Corps.

Mess Kit
The demise of No. 1 Dress with the introduction of No. 2 Dress indicated the need of a smart uniform for formal evening occasions. Officers had always had their Mess Kit – a jacket of dark blue barathea with watered silk facings, and a scarlet waistcoat worn with a stiff shirt and collar – but nothing similar had been authorized for warrant officers and sergeants. This was rectified in 1961 and a pattern similar to that of officers', but of cheaper material, was selected. It was designed to be worn with a soft shirt.

With changing fashions in civilian life, it was felt that the pattern of the officers' Mess Kit was out of date, and, in addition, it had become increasingly difficult in the 1960s to find laundries able to starch shirts and collars. This coincided with the opinion that the Regiment should come into line with the rest of the Royal Armoured Corps. Thus, in 1970, a new pattern of Mess Kit was approved for officers. This is of 1902 cavalry pattern, of black superfine cloth with stand collar and a scarlet vest. Both the jacket and the vest carry an amount of gold lace.

In 1971, the custom of wearing Mess Kit was extended to corporals, with the warrant officers' and sergeants' pattern being adopted.

Coveralls
Black coveralls are worn by all ranks. This custom was introduced at the Royal Review in 1935, lapsed during the Second World War and was reintroduced in the 1950s. The custom is now officially recognized, and black coveralls may be worn only by members of the Regiment.

APPENDICES

Lanyards

With the introduction of No. 2 Dress in place of Battle-Dress, the practice of wearing regimental shoulder flashes lapsed. With the majority of regiments wearing the black lanyard, the First being the exception with their red one, the requirement was recognized for distinctive regimental lanyards. These were approved in 1960, with each regiment adopting the colour of its shoulder flash.

Combat Uniform

The Korean War, 1950–53, highlighted the need for a loose fitting combat uniform for wear in the field, to replace Battle-Dress, and similar to that already adopted by U.S. forces.

The uniform has with it ancillary items of clothing including a thick sweater, 'Long Johns', and short puttees. In very cold weather a Parka is worn.

During 1970, the green combat uniform was superseded by a camouflaged pattern.

Barrack Dress

As neither Combat Uniform nor No. 2 Dress was satisfactory for day to day wear in barracks, the custom grew of wearing the thick Combat Uniform sweater with old Battle-Dress trousers, and later, with No. 2 Dress trousers together with a Stable Belt in R.T.R. colours. From this stemmed the introduction of coloured sweaters, virtually throughout the Army, with the R.T.R. adopting black. So popular has this form of uniform been, that green 'barrack dress' trousers later became an official issue to save the wear and tear on No. 2 Dress.

Bibliography

The following books were consulted during the preparation of this history.

Beaufre, A. *The Suez Expedition, 1956*. Faber and Faber, London, 1969; Praeger, New York, 1970

Begin, M. *The Revolt*. W. H. Allen, London, 1952, rev. ed. 1979; Nash, New York, 1971

Blaxland, G. *The Regiments Depart*. Kimber, London, 1971

Hodson, H. V. *The Great Divide*. Hutchinson, London, 1968

Lawson, R. G. *Strange Soldiering*. Hodder and Stoughton, London, 1963
Strictly Personal. Ministry of Defence, London, 1972

Lewin, R. *Slim: The Standardbearer*. Leo Cooper, London, 1976; Shoe String Press, Hamden, 1976

Montgomery, B. L. *Memoirs*. Collins, London, 1958; World Publishing, New York, 1958

Shepherd, C. A. *Arabian Adventure*. Collins, London, 1961

Skentelberg, R. *Arrows to Atom Bombs*. HMSO, London, 1975

Wilson, R. D. *Cordon and Search*. Gale and Polden, 1949; British Book Centre, New York, 1952

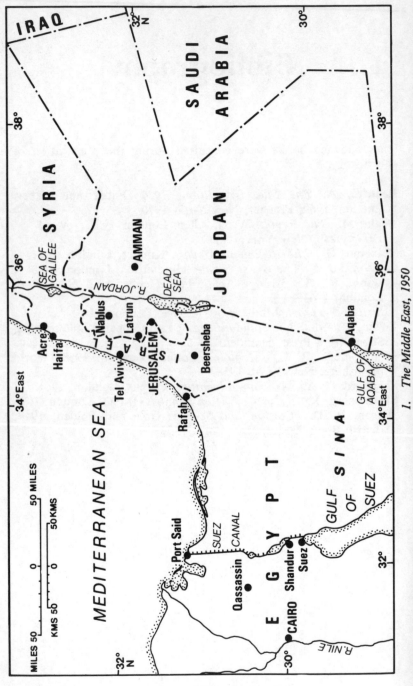

1. *The Middle East, 1950*

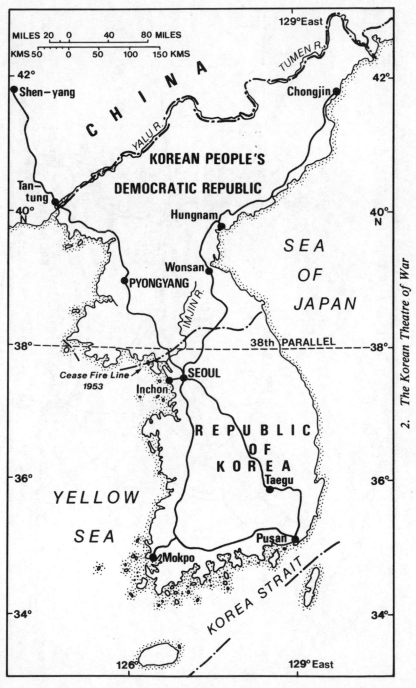

2. The Korean Theatre of War

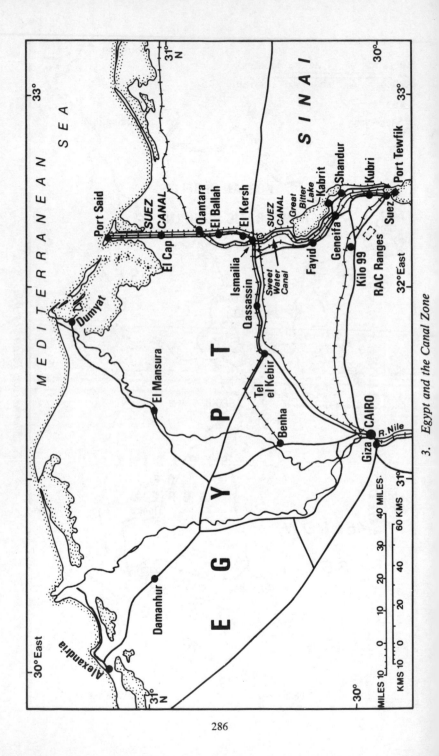

3. *Egypt and the Canal Zone*

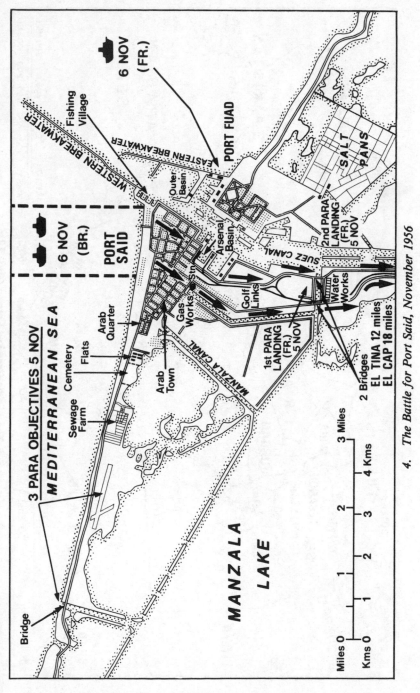

4. *The Battle for Port Said, November 1956*

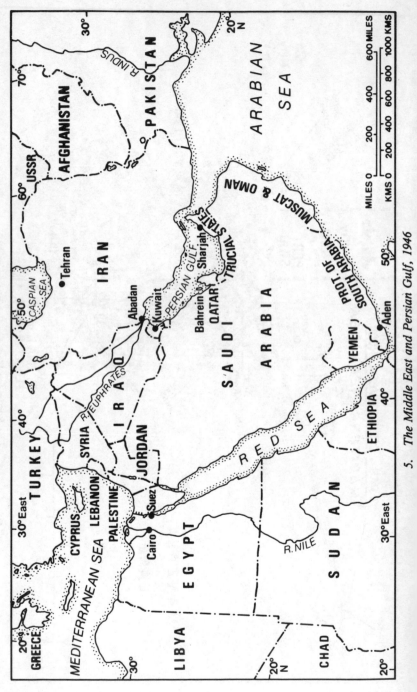

5. *The Middle East and Persian Gulf, 1946*

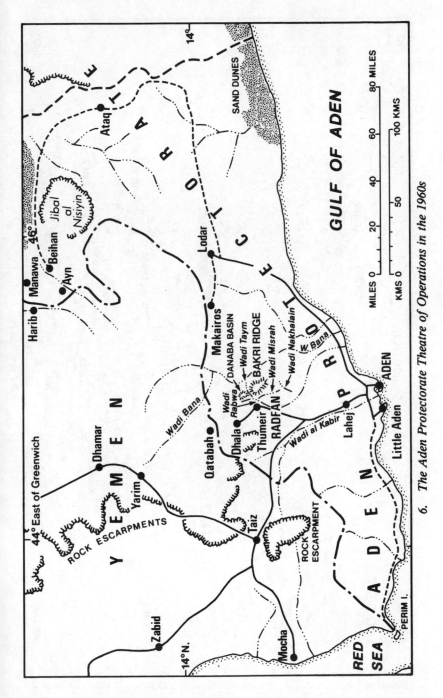

6. *The Aden Protectorate Theatre of Operations in the 1960s*

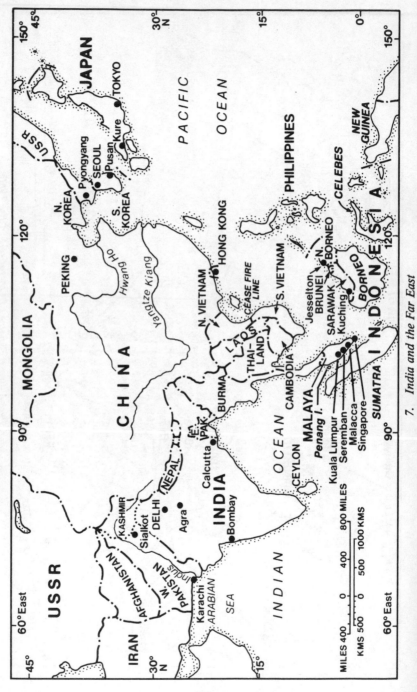

7. *India and the Far East*

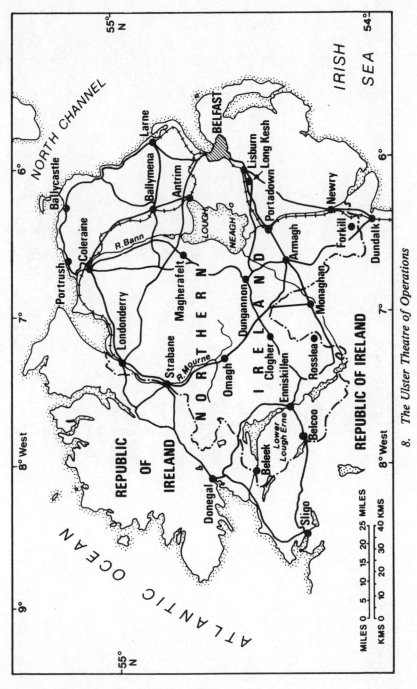

8. *The Ulster Theatre of Operations*

Index

GENERAL INDEX

R.T.R. UNIT INDEX